ENCYCLOPEDIA

OF

SCHOOL LETTERS

P. Susan Mamchak

and

Steven R. Mamchak

Parker Publishing Company, Inc.

West Nyack, New York

Library of Congress Cataloging in Publication Data

Mamchak, P Susan
Encyclopedia of school letters.

1. Schools--Records and correspondence--Forms.
2. Form letters. I. Mamchak, Steven R., joint author.
II. Title.
LB2845.7.M35 651.7'4 79-17063
ISBN 0-13-276352-4

Printed in the United States of America

DEDICATION

to

. . .Everett C. Curry. . .
an outstanding example
of a dynamic and
dedicated administrator

ACKNOWLEDGMENTS

It is our pleasure to acknowledge the assistance of many fine educators who aided us in the preparation of this book. These outstanding teachers and administrators represent, in our opinion, the highest ideals of the profession.

Special thanks are due to Frederick Ball, Allan Bartholemew, Kathleen Brazas, James Callum, Barbara Dean, Vito D'Eufamia, Elaine Douglas, Fred Gernsbeck, Rosemary Knawa, Don Kurz, Maureen Mulholland, John and Peggy Najar, Joseph Percipunko, Bernhard Schneider, Daniel Sorkowitz and Victoria Taylor.

How This Book Will Aid the Professional Educator

As an Administrator, you begin your day five minutes before you are ready for it and finish it an hour after you thought it had ended. There are just *so many duties,* not the least of which is that you are faced each day with tasks which call upon your skills in the art of written communication. There are letters and memos to parents, other administrators and faculty members; in-house communications and bulletins; policy statements and public-relations work—the list seems endless and the paperwork never ending.

Yet, as one speaker at a recent convention of the American Association of School Administrators put it, "Somehow, we have to learn how to manage our paperwork. Otherwise, our paperwork will end up managing us."

Very few Administrators would disagree with that statement. Indeed, we all realize that every minute spent doing sequestered, laborious, time-consuming paperwork is a minute *not* spent as a visible, involved instructional leader, which is, after all, the Administrator's number one professional commitment.

How often, therefore, have Administrators longed for a single source to which they might turn to find the precise message they wished to convey; to find powerful, effective and tested models of the particular letter, memo or bulletin they required; to find models of forms that will fill a need effectively and with dispatch: in short, to save invaluable time and efficiently manage their paperwork through the sharing of model forms of communication which have worked for other educators in similar situations?

This is precisely why this book was written.

Here, in one volume, listed alphabetically, is a compilation of hundreds of topics relevant to School Administration and the wide world of Education. Under each subject listing you will find tested, reliable models of letters, memoranda, forms and bulletins—models which *you* can use in drafting *your* written communications.

Do you need to write a letter on the suspension of a student; compose a memo to parents on a troublesome problem; write a message for the student handbook that is clear, concise and effective; compose a letter of recommendation for a faculty member or student; send condolences on the death of a colleague; create an effective form for disciplinary referral or teacher observation; set down policy that is clear enough to answer every question? This book contains actual models of all of these and many, many more–models which you can quickly, easily adapt by the change of a name or date to your particular situation, saving you hours of valuable time. . . while serving your needs precisely and effectively.

Here you will find models or written communications on the widest possible spectrum of Educational topics; effective models of letters, bulletins, memos and forms relating not only to those topics which have been and continue to be in the mainstream of American Education; topics like *Attendance, Behavior, Curriculum, Discipline, Report Cards* and *Schedules,* but also on those topics which relate to Education now, today–subjects such as *Alternate School Program, Child Study Team, Mainstreaming, Psychological Services, PSAT/SAT Scores, Rights and Responsibilities, Special Education* and many, many more.

From an Administrator's introduction to a staff handbook to the Principal's message in the yearbook; from a form for teacher observation (three models from which to choose) to a notice to parents of their child's academic difficulties; from a memo on procedures for closing school due to inclement weather to a statement of philosophy for a school or school district–it's all here, waiting to be used as is or easily adapted to *your* particular set of circumstances; waiting to serve your needs and free your valuable time.

This is a *practical* book of model written communications designed specifically to meet your needs–the needs of the active, involved Administrator; a daily reference book you will use to aid you in drafting those letters and memos which are such a vital part of your day; a book you will use to find just the right form or bulletin to fill your needs on a myriad of Educational topics and situations; a book which will save you hours of laborious, time-consuming work; a book which will *free your time* and allow you to function as a vital, dynamic Administrator.

This is not a book which you will find gathering dust on a bookshelf. Rather, it is a volume which will occupy a featured position on your desk among those items which you use, use day in and day out, use now–and throughout the entire school year.

P. Susan Mamchak
Steven R. Mamchak

CONTENTS

CONTENTS

A

ABSENCE (See Also: ATTENDANCE; CUTTING; DISMISSAL PROCEDURES; PASSES; SIGN-IN SHEETS; TARDINESS)

. . .Absentee Breakdown Form

Date: ______________________________

GRADE	TOTAL NUMBER OF STUDENTS ABSENT boys	girls	RUNNING TOTAL
K			
1			
2			
3			
4			
5			
6			
7			
8			
9			
10			
11			
12			
Total			

. . .Absentee Form

(A) for a student

FORM FOR STUDENT ABSENCE

Name: ______________________________ Grade: __________

Home Room: ______________ Date: ______________________

ABSENCE

This is to state that I was absent from school on (Give Date(s)): ____________________

____

because (State Reason): ____

____

I hereby state that the above is the true reason for my absence.

Signature of Student: ____________________________

Signature of Parent: ____________________________

(B) for a teacher

Date: ____________________________

REASON FOR ABSENCE FROM DUTY

Name of Employee: ____

Grade and/or Subject: ____

I hereby certify that my absence from duty on

____________________________ was caused by ____________________________

____

____

Number of Days Absent: ____

Substitute(s): ____

Signature of
School Employee: ____________________________

This form is to be filled out and returned to the principal's office after each absence.

. . .Absentee Report

(A) monthly absentee report

ABSENTEE REPORT

for the month of

________________________, 19 ____________

School: ____

Date	1	2	3	4	5	6	7	8	9	10	11	12	Running Total
1													
2													
3													
4													
5													
6													
7													
8													
9													
10													
11													
12													
13													
14													
15													
16													
17													
18													
19													
20													
21													
22													
23													
24													
25													
26													
27													
28													
29													
30													
31													
Total													

(B) yearly absentee report

REPORT ON ABSENTEES

School: ______________________________

For the School Year: ______________________

Month	K	1	2	3	4	5	6	7	8	9	10	11	12	Total	Running Total
Sept.															
Oct.															
Nov.															
Dec.															
Jan.															
Feb.															
Mar.															
Apr.															
May															
June															
Yearly Total															

(Column heading over K–12: Number of Absences in Grade)

Signature: ______________________________

Title: ______________________________

. . .Request for Leave of Absence

REQUEST FOR LEAVE OF ABSENCE

Name: ______________________________ Date: ______________

Position: ______________ Grade and/or subject: ______________

School: ______________________________

Number of Years in System: ______________________________

Date First Employed in System: ______________________________

LEAVE OF ABSENCE REQUESTED: From: ____________ To: ____________

Purpose of Leave (If for advance study, give name of institution and degree sought.):

____

____

____

I understand that this leave will be ( ) at half salary ( ) without salary (Please see Board of Education Policy Statement on Leave of Absence.)

Any other factors the Board should know in making their decision: ____________

____

____

Signature: ______________________________________

. . .Request to Be Absent from Duty (Two Forms)

(A) first form

REQUEST FOR PERSONAL, PROFESSIONAL DAY

Name: ______________________________________ Date: ____________

Date(s) Requested: ____

____

Reason for Request: ____

____

____

For Professional Days, please attach institute brochure or other descriptive literature. Incomplete request forms will not be considered.

- -

Your request has been (   ) approved (   ) not approved.

______________________________________, Principal

(B) second form

______________, 19 __________

School: ____________________

I desire to be excused from my school duties on:

Date(s): ________________________ A.M. -- P.M. -- ALL DAY

________________________ A.M. -- P.M. -- ALL DAY

Reason: ____

____

I understand that expenses will be borne by: (   ) Teacher

(   ) Board of Education

ACCEPTANCE

A substitute teacher ( ) will ( ) will not be needed.

Signature: ______________________________

Grade or Subject: ______________________________

Principal's Signature: ______________________________

______________________________, 19 ________

M______________________________

______________________________ School

Your request to be absent from your duties, as stated above, ( ) has ( ) has not been approved. A deduction ( ) will ( ) will not be made from your salary.

Explanation: ______________________________

____

Your absence will be charged as indicated below:

( ) Professional ( ) Emergency ( ) Funeral ( ) Marriage
( ) Personal ( ) Vacation ( ) Court ( ) Other

Approved by: ______________________________

ACCEPTANCE

(See Also: ACHIEVEMENT; APPLICATION; BIDS; DEGREES; IDEAS; NEGOTIATIONS; RESIGNATION; STUDENT TEACHER; VENDORS)

. . .By a Candidate of a Position

Dear Dr. Smith,

Enclosed you will find the contract form which I am delighted to accept and return to you for your records.

I wish to express my gratitude for your faith in offering me the position of principal of Rock Township High School. I accept with thanks and with a deep commitment to do as good a job as possible in order to justify the trust you have placed in me.

I look forward to working with you and to assuming my new responsibilities.

Yours sincerely,

. . .Of a Candidate for a Position

Dear Mr. Benson:

It gives me great pleasure to inform you that at the June 26, 19XX meeting of the Rock Township Board of Education your candidacy for the position of principal of Rock Township High School was unanimously approved.

Your credentials, your references, and your erudite handling of questions during your interview were most impressive. That, combined with what we discerned as a dedication to the highest ideals and purposes of public education, made your candidacy all the more attractive. We are confident that we have selected the best person for the position.

I am enclosing a contract which we would like you to sign and return to us at your earliest convenience. I would also appreciate your calling for an appointment in order that we may discuss your new duties in greater detail.

Sincerely,

. . .Of an Idea

Dear Kenny,

I sometimes think that I am the most fortunate of people to have ingenious and creative people like you in the school.

The idea you were kind enough to share with me at our last faculty meeting is an outstanding one, reflective of the concern for the welfare of our school and its students which I have come to expect from you. Your idea will, when implemented, solve an overcrowding problem that could have become very serious.

I'd like you to set up an appointment with me so we can move ahead on your idea.

Again, let me thank you for your most valuable contribution.

Sincerely,

. . .Of Reports

MEMO

To: ALL MEMBERS OF THE DISCIPLINE COMMITTEE
From: J. BENSON, PRINCIPAL
Re: ACCEPTANCE OF DISCIPLINE REPORT

I am in possession of the report of the Discipline Committee on the state of discipline in our school and suggestions for improvement.

I am happy to accept this report, for it is obviously indicative of a good deal of hard work and a deep concern for the good of our school. A precursory reading has indicated that you have isolated and identified several areas where improvement is needed and have given positive suggestions as to how to bring about constructive change. The report bespeaks professionalism of the highest rank.

As soon as I have had time to give your report the in-depth attention it deserves, I shall get back to you. in the meantime, I accept your report with gratitude and thanks for a job well done.

ACCOUNTABILITY

(See Also: ACHIEVEMENT; ASP; COMPLAINTS; CURRICULUM; EVALUATION; GRADES; IN-SERVICE; INSTRUCTION; LEARNING DISABILITIES; MAINSTREAMING; MINORITIES; MONTHLY REPORTS; OBSERVATION; PERCENTAGE OF PROMOTION SHEETS; PHILOSOPHY; QUALITY; RIGHTS AND RESPONSIBILITIES; SPECIAL EDUCATION; UNIT COORDINATION; YEAR-END REPORT)

. . .Form for

Name: ________________________________ Date: ____________

Subject Area: ______________________________________

Test Used: ____

Standardized Norm of Test: ____________________________

NAME	SEPTEMBER SCORE	JUNE SCORE	DIFFERENTIAL + or –
Class Median			

Special Problems:

Signature: ____________________

. . .Policy Statement on

In a democratic society, each person is ultimately responsible for his or her actions and accountable for those actions to the body of society. In a like manner, we in education are responsible for the education of all students and must stand accountable for that education.

Common sense, however, dictates that many variables, not the least of which is the degree of motivation of the individual student, influence the outcomes of education.

We feel, therefore. that we must be accountable for doing all within our power to see that every student has every opportunity the school provides for his education. That, combined with individual motivation and cooperation from the student and the home, should, we hope, provide the maximum in education for all concerned.

ACHIEVEMENT

(See Also: ACCEPTANCE; ACCOUNTABILITY; CITIZENSHIP; CONGRATULATIONS; DEGREES; GIFTED STUDENTS; NATIONAL HONOR SOCIETY; QUALITY; THANKS)

. . .Certificates of Achievement (Two Forms)

(A) first form

ROCK TOWNSHIP HIGH SCHOOL

____

is awarded this

Certificate of Achievement

for

____

____

. . .PRESENTED THIS ______ DAY OF _____________________ , 19____

____

____

(B) second form

Date: ____________

To Whom It May Concern:
This is to certify that ____
a student at Rock Township High School, has indicated a high degree of achievement in that ____

____

In testimony thereof, this certificate is gratefully presented.

Signed: ____________________________________

. . .Letter Acknowledging Achievement

Dear Laura,

How proud and happy we all were to hear that you were selected for All-State Chorus. This is an achievement of which any student might be justifiably proud, and the fact that you achieved this distinction while still in your freshman year makes it all the more wonderful.

I certainly hope that you will continue your study of voice, and that it will lead to even greater achievements in the future.

With heartiest congratulations,
J. Benson, Principal

ADDRESS (See Also: ATTENDANCE; EMERGENCY; PERMANENT RECORDS; STUDENT INFORMATION; ZONING)

. . .Change of Address Form for a Student

CHANGE OF ADDRESS FORM

Name: ______________________________ Date: __________

School: ______________________________ Grade: __________

Name of Parent or Guardian: ______________________________

Old Address: ______________________________

Assigned Bus Stop, if any: ______________________________

New Address: ______________________________

Telephone Number: ____________________ Transportation: Yes__ No __

This form is to be filled out and presented to the Guidance Office upon student's change of address within the township.

. . .Change of Address Form for a Teacher

CHANGE OF ADDRESS FORM

Name: Date: __________

School: Grade or Subject: __________

This is to inform you that my address has changed as indicated below:

Old Address: ______________________________

______________________________ Zip __________

Telephone Number: ______________________________

New Address: ______________________________

______________________________ Zip __________

Telephone Number: ______________________________

My telephone number is (   ) listed (   ) unlisted.

ADULT EDUCATION

(See Also: ALUMNI; BACK-TO-SCHOOL NIGHT; CAREER; OPEN HOUSE; TEACHER AIDE; VOLUNTEERS)

. . .Advertisement in Local Paper

> –IT IS NEVER TOO LATE–
>
> . . .to learn. . .to grow
> . . .to expand. . .to experience. . .to develop
> . . .to laugh. . .to enjoy
>
> The
>
> ROCK TOWNSHIP BOARD OF EDUCATION
>
> announces
>
> ADULT EVENING CLASSES
>
> beginning Monday, October 3, 19XX
>
> . . .watch for Adult Education Bulletin
> in the mail soon or call
>
> The Rock Township Board of Education
> 123-4567

. . .Introduction to Adult Education Bulletin

Enclosed in this brochure is a selection of courses prepared especially for you, the adult citizen of Rock Township. Whether you need courses for high school equivalency, to learn a new skill, to practice or perfect a skill you already have, to shape up physically or to sharpen your wits, you will find something within these pages to fill those needs.

We invite you to browse at your leisure, read the course descriptions and decide which course or courses are for you. We hope you will want to take advantage of these offerings, just as we hope to see you on the first night of class.

Here's to happy learning for everyone!

. . .Letter to the Community

Residents and non-residents who wish to pursue courses of study in the evening can do so by enrolling in the Community Evening School, a non-profit, self-supporting educational program sponsored by the Board of Education. Semesters in the evening school are ten weeks in duration with classes usually conducted at the high school.

The evening school offers a wide variety of educational and enrichment programs under such headings as: commercial and distributive education, civic and public affairs, home-making and family education, English and literature, foreign languages, health, safety and physical education, music, arts and crafts and driver education. A program to obtain a high school equivalency diploma is also offered.

Brochures announcing courses for each semester are mailed to every homeowner in the township twice a year.

. . .Progress Report

(A) for the program

ADULT EDUCATION YEARLY EVALUATION

School Year: ______________________________

Number of Courses Offered: ______________ Number of Teachers: __________

Number of Registered Students: ______________________

Number of Students in High School Equivalency Program: ______________

Number of Students in ESL Program: ______________________

Number of Courses Run at Capacity: ______________________

Any Written Comments from Students: ( ) Yes ( ) No
(If 'Yes,' please attach.)

Personal Comments: ______________________________

____

Date: ____________ Signature of Program Director: ______________________

(B) for the student

ADULT EDUCATION PROGRESS REPORT

Name of Student: ____________________

Title of Course: ____________________

Final Grade or Evaluation: ____________________

Teacher Comment: ____________________

____

____________________ **, Teacher**

ALUMNI (See Also: ADULT EDUCATION; BACK-TO-SCHOOL NIGHT; CAREER; OPEN HOUSE)

. . .Administrator's Message to

TO ALL ALUMNI

Welcome back! This time you travel the halls of Rock Township High School as an observer rather than a participant. You will find no one who is going to tell you to stop chewing gum or send you to the office for smoking in the lavatory. What you will find, however, are memories around every corner.

You met your girlfriend by the water fountain; you joined the rest of the girls around that locker; there's the table where you ate lunch with the rest of the gang! They are all here; these memories of the time when this was your school.

Yet in a very real sense, this still is *your* school. You have become a part of it as it has become a part of you that can never be erased.

Yes, welcome back. This will always be your school!

. . .Introduction to Alumni Bulletin

INTRODUCTION

Surely there must have come the moment, as it comes to all of us, when you turned your mind toward the days of your youth. It was inevitable in such a reverie that you returned to the school which played such a major part in your life at that time. Indeed, it is inevitable that you and your school are intrinsically a part of each other. We can only hope that the association was happy and beneficial, and that you are eager to learn more about your school and your fellow classmates.

This Alumni Bulletin is specially prepared for you, the alumnus of Rock Township High School. Hopefully, you will find within its pages the news of your friends and what is happening to them, developments in and around the high school, and upcoming events and activities which you may wish to attend.

Here's hoping that the memories this Bulletin engenders will be happy ones, and that we will have the pleasure of seeing you very soon at one of our Alumni functions.

J. Benson, Principal

APPLICATION

(See Also: ACCEPTANCE; BIDS; DEGREES; HONOR ROLL; SUMMER SCHOOL; TUTORS)

. . .Acknowledgment of Receipt

Dear ______________________________ ,

This is to inform you that we are in possession of your application for the position of ______________________________ , dated ______________ ______________ . We shall send you further notification upon review.

ROCK TOWNSHIP BOARD OF EDUCATION

. . .Forms of Application

(A) for a teacher

Name: ______________________________

Position Desired: ______________________ Date: ____________

Address (Permanent): ______________________ Phone: ____________

______________________________ Zip: ____________

Address (Temporary): ______________________ Phone: ____________

______________________________ Zip: ____________

Social Security Number: ____________ Date of Birth: ____________

APPLICATION

Are you now in sound health: ______________________ Weight: ____________

Have you any physical defects: ______________________ Height: ____________

If you have a physical defect, please explain on the back of this sheet.

Date of last Tine Test or chest x-ray: ______________________________

Will you comply with local and state regulations regarding health examinations: ______________ Fluent language of applicant: ______________________

Name of person to be notified in emergency: ______________________________

Address: ______________________________________ Phone: ____________

EDUCATION:

Type	Name & Location	From	To	Major	Minor	Degree/credit	Date of
High School							

Title of Certificate you hold: ______________________________________

EXPERIENCE:

Name	Location	Position	Years	From	To	Salary

REFERENCES (Please include those persons familiar with your occupational background and abilities.):

Full Name	Address (give street, city, state)	Title

Any other information that should be known in the consideration of this application:

____

____

____

I hereby affirm that the information on this form is accurate and correct.

Date: ______________ Signature: ______________________________________

(B) for custodial and/or clerical

Name: ______________________________ Telephone: ______________

Address: ____

______________________________________ Zip: ______________

Social Security Number: ______________ Date of Birth: ______________

Position Desired: ____

PREVIOUS EXPERIENCE (Please begin with last position held.):

Dates (from-to)	Employer (Name and Address)	Number of Years

QUALIFICATIONS (List schools attended, courses taken, certifications and/or licenses held, etc.):

____

____

____

REFERENCES (Please list those persons who can testify to the quality of your work.):

Name	Address	Position

In your own words explain what you have to offer as an employee of the Rock Township Board of Education:

____

____

____

Are there any factors the Board should know in making its decision:

____

____

____

I hereby state that the information in this application is correct and accurate.

Date: ______________ Signature: ______________________________

APPLICATION

(C) for paraprofessional aide

Name: ______________________________ Telephone: ______________

Address: ____

____ Zip: ____________

Age: ____________ Social Security Number: ________________________

Position for which you are applying: ________________________________

EDUCATION (Please begin with highest level attained.):

School (give name and location)	Dates (from-to)	Degree or Certification

PREVIOUS EXPERIENCE RELATED TO EDUCATION (Include names, dates, places.):

____

____

____

EXPERIENCE IN OTHER FIELDS (Include names, dates, places.):

____

____

____

REFERENCES (Include those who can testify to your character and ability.):

Name	Address	Title

Are there any facts that should be considered in reviewing your application:

____

____

____

Why do you think that you should be hired as a paraprofessional by the Rock Township Board of Education:

____

____

____

I hereby attest that the facts presented in this application are accurate and true.
Date: ____________ **Signature:** ________________________________

. . .Non-Availability of Position

Dear Mr. Fortner,

We are in posession of your application for the position of vice-principal of Haskin Junior High School. We regret to inform you that the position for which you applied is no longer available.

When we originally advertised the position, it was because we had been advised that the current holder of the position would be going on extended medical leave, and a replacement was needed. Due to an unexpectedly rapid recovery following surgery, however, the vice-principal will be able to resume his duties in September.

While we are happy for his recovery, we regret any inconvenience this may have caused you. You may rest assured that we will keep your application in our active file, and should this or a similar position open up in the future, we shall consider you in contention for it.

Thank you again for applying.

Sincerely,

. . .Notice of Intent to Review

Dear __________________________,

This is to inform you that we shall shortly initiate a review of your application for the position of____________________________.

We shall advise you of place and time for your interview.

ROCK TOWNSHIP BOARD OF EDUCATION

APPRECIATION (See Also: CITIZENSHIP; QUALITY; SECRETARY; STUDENT COUNCIL; THANKS; VOLUNTEERS; YEARBOOK)

. . .Certificate of

ROCK TOWNSHIP HIGH SCHOOL

This Certificate is Presented

to

____

in grateful appreciation for

____

____

Presented this ______ day of _____________________________, 19 ___

__________________________, (title) ______________

. . .Letters of

(A) to an administrator

Dear Mr. Tanner,

Thank you so much for allowing our student dramatics classes to visit your school and perform for your primary grades. From the comments I have received it is evident that everyone profited from the experience.

We'd like you to know how much we appreciate your continued cooperation. Your graciousness in allowing us to visit your school has been so helpful that it has become part of our dramatics curriculum. Your kindnesses and cooperation are deeply appreciated by all concerned.

If there is any way in which we may reciprocate, please feel free to call upon us.

Sincerely,
J. Benson

(B) to a student

Dear Bob,

The recent Student Carnival was a huge success and an event upon which I have received many compliments from parents, faculty and students on how well-organized it was and how smoothly and efficiently it ran.

I told them, as I tell you now, that a great deal of that credit must go to you. As student organizer, you performed your tasks with a professionalism and enthusiasm which inspired those around you to give that little bit extra which spelled success.

I wonder if you know how much we appreciate your efforts? Your hard work, your dedication and your selfless giving have benefited the entire school, I am certain that the student body and the faculty must be as appreciative as I am.

On a personal note, I am proud and happy that you are a student in this school.

With my best regards,
J. Benson, Principal

(C) to a teacher

Dear George,

How often it is that what we do goes unnoticed by our peers. Often, we feel that we must be working in a vacuum. Such, however, is not the case in regard to your activities. Your recent actions on behalf of the school and the student body are appreciated far beyond our ability to acknowledge them.

Your guidance of the Student Council during the recent difficulties caused a potentially troublesome situation to be handled in a logical, precise and peaceful manner to the approval of all concerned.

It is with a deep sense of appreciation that I acknowledge your abilities, concern and dedication.

And, may I add a personal 'Thank You.'

Sincerely,
J. Benson

ASP (Alternate School Program) (See Also: ACCOUNTABILITY; BEHAVIOR; DISCIPLINE; SUSPENSION)

. . .Assignment of a Student to

ALTERNATE SCHOOL PROGRAM

Students who are suspended from the regular school program will be assigned to the Alternate School Program and will report to the A.S.P. Room with their homework, books and materials.

Students will be assigned to the Alternate School Program for at least three days. During this time they will stay in the A.S.P. Room. Luncheon orders will be taken and delivered from the cafeteria or students may bring lunch. These days will be used for intensive work. Students are expected to cooperate with the teacher. If this fails to occur, their time in the program may be extended or they may be suspended.

. . .Notification to Parents of Student's Placement

Dear ______________________________,

This is to inform you that your son/daughter, ______________________,
has been placed in the Alternate School Program for a period of ________ days.

This action has been taken for the following reason(s):

____

____

____

While in the A.S.P. Room your son/daughter will be under the supervision of Mr. Jonathan Keeler. Mr. Keeler has had experience with Alternate School Programs for many years, and he will do all in his power to make your child's stay a profitable one.

You are urged to discuss this with your child in order that this placement may be to his or her ultimate benefit.

If you have any questions, please call 234-5678 and arrange for an interview.

Sincerely,

J. Benson, Principal

. . .Notification to Parents of Student's Re-entry

Dear ________________________________,

On________, ________, 19___ your son/daughter,__________________,
will be returning to regular classes from our Alternate School Program.

While in the A.S.P. Room your child did the following work:

____

____

____

When your son or daughter re-enters regular classes, it is important that you be supportive of efforts to improve behavior and vigilant that the behavior which occasioned the placement does not occur again.

If you wish to discuss this matter further, please call me at 234-5678 to arrange an interview.

Sincerely,
J. Keeler,
Director of A.S.P.

. . .Notificaton to Teachers of Student's Placement

Date: ____________________

Dear ________________________________,

_________________________________ has been placed in the Alternate School Program for a period of______ days. This time will begin on_______ and end on _______.

Please provide whatever classwork you can for this period in order that the student may make profitable use of the time spent in the Alternate School Program.

Thank you very much for your cooperation.

Sincerely,
J. Keeler, A.S.P. Supervisor

Assignment in A.S.P. made by: ________________________________

...Notification to Teachers of Student's Re-entry

Dear ______________________________,

This is to inform you that ______________________________ will be returning to regular classes from A.S.P. on ______________________________.

He/she should have all the work you assigned during placement in the Alternate School Program.

Sincerely,
J. Keeler, A.S.P. Supervisor

...Request for Work Letter

Dear Faculty,

I am currently attempting to develop a resource bank of materials to be used for students in the Alternate School Program. As you know, the first responsibility of students in the A.S.P. Room is to complete the assignments from their regular classroom teachers. Many times, however, this work does not take up an entire day.

What I am trying to do is create units of work in various subject areas which will be of positive value to the students I have.

I am asking for your help. To accomplish what I have planned I need whatever you can offer in the following areas: 1.) books in your subject area and grade level, 2.) ditto master books to reinforce classroom topics, 3.) lists of essential vocabulary words in each subject area, 4.) a list of areas which could use basic reinforcement work, 5.) any ideas or suggestions you might have. You know what your students need–please tell me.

You are the people who deal with the A.S.P. student daily. I wish to return that person to you a *little* bit better than when he or she was sent to me. I will be very grateful for whatever help you can offer. Thank you very much.

Sincerely,
Joe Keeler, A.S.P. Supervisor

...Sample Student Evaluation Sheet

ALTERNATE SCHOOL PROGRAM

Student Evaluation

Name of Student: ______________________

Dates of Placement: ______________________

Reason for Placement: ______________________

____

Work Completed
During Placement: ______________________

____

This is the ______ time the student has been placed in the program. With 10 as highest and 1 as lowest, I have rated the student as follows:

Accepts responsibility for own actions. . . ______

Attitude toward authority. . . ______

Attitude toward school. . . ______

Attitude toward Alternate School Program. . . ______

Initiates own activities. . . ______

Makes good use of free time. . . ______

Peer acceptance. . . ______

General Comment:

____

____

____

Supervisor: ______________________

Date of Evaluation: ______________________

. . .Sample Yearly Evaluation Form

ALTERNATE SCHOOL PROGRAM

School Year: ______________________

Number of Students who have used the Program: ______

Number of Placements: ______________________

Number of Students with more than one Placement: ______________

Number of Students with a single Placement: ______________

Number of Parent contacts: ______________

Number of Parent Interviews: ______________

ASSEMBLIES

Examples of Student improvements: ____________________

____

____

General Comments: ____________________

____

____

A.S.P. Supervisor: ____________________

Principal: ____________________

Date: ____________________

ASSEMBLIES (See Also: CALENDAR; GRADUATION; JUNE; OPENING PROCEDURES)

. . .Assignment of Assembly Schedule

YEARLY ASSEMBLY SCHEDULE

Each teacher shall be responsible for one (1) assembly during the school year. Please fill in the following form by placing your name next to the time you prefer to give your assembly. Placement is on the first-come-first-serve basis. The number one (1) after a month indicates the first half of the month (from the 1st through the 15th) while a two (2) indicates the second half (from the 16th through the last). When this form has been completely filled, it will be copied and distributed to the staff as a reminder of due dates.

Date	Teacher	Date	Teacher
Sept. (2)		Feb. (1)	
Oct. (1)		Feb. (2)	
Oct. (2)		Mar. (1)	
Nov. (1)		Mar. (2)	
Nov. (2)		Apr. (1)	
Dec. (1)		Apr. (2)	
Dec. (2)		May (1)	
Jan. (1)		May (2)	
Jan. (2)		June (1)	

. . .Memo to Teachers on

MEMO

To: ALL TEACHERS
From: J. BENSON, PRINCIPAL
Re: ASSEMBLIES

Everyone likes assemblies—the students enjoy them and, from comments I've heard, so do the faculty. Assemblies have a definite place in Education as an instrument for the social growth of the student. They are not merely a "time to get out of class."

It is important, therefore, that we impress upon our students the proper behavior during an assembly, and it is equally important that all teachers sit with their classes and supervise behavior during the entire program.

I know that I can count upon your cooperation in this matter, and I look forward to some fine assemblies in the future.

. . .Policy on

We believe that assemblies are an integral part of the education of the children in our schools. We believe that they are a means for teaching social interaction in group situations as well as broadening the educational and cultural background of all students.

We also believe that all assemblies should be of such a nature as to provide information and entertainment to the viewers which are within the accepted limits of community standards. We also believe that no student or group of students should be made to feel slighted, neglected or outcast because of the content of any assembly.

All assemblies should be beneficial to all attending.

. . .Procedures for

ASSEMBLY PROCEDURES

The following procedures will apply to all assemblies:

1. All teachers will wait until called to the assembly over the public address system.

2. Teachers in rooms 100, 101, 102 and 103 will enter by Door D and take seats in sections M, N, O, and P.
3. Teachers in rooms 104, 105, 106 and 107 will enter by Door C and take seats in sections I, J, K, and L.
4. Teachers in rooms 200, 201, 202 and 203 will enter by Door A and take seats in sections A, B, C, and D.
5. Teachers in rooms 204, 205, 206 and 207 will enter by Door B and take seats in sections E, F, G, and H.
6. Teachers will sit with and supervise their classes during the assembly.
7. Upon completion of the assembly, teachers will wait until their section is dismissed by word from the stage.
8. Teachers will supervise their classes going to and coming from the assembly.
9. Emergencies in the assembly will be handled by the teacher in whose class it occurs, and the student or students shall be taken out the nearest exit.
10. In the event of teacher absence, the above procedures will be handled by the substitute. Regular teachers will assist in the supervision of those classes whenever possible.

ATTENDANCE (See Also: ABSENCE; ADDRESS; CLASS; FACULTY MEETINGS; OPENING PROCEDURES; REPRESENTATION)

. . .Memo on Attendance Procedures

MEMO

To: ALL TEACHERS
From: J. BENSON, PRINCIPAL
Re: ATTENDANCE PROCEDURES

In order to improve the procedures for taking attendance and to eliminate the possibility of class cutting, the following procedures will be implemented:

(1) All Home Room teachers will take attendance and send the attendance cards of those absent to the main office at the conclusion of Home Room Period. Students who report after morning exercises should have their cards sent to the main office in a special envelope marked "Tardy."

(2) In the main office all attendance will be correlated and an Attendance Bulletin published. The Bulletin shall contain the names of students absent or tardy listed alphabetically, boys and girls, and by grade. The number after a name indicates the number of consecutive days absent, while a "T" indicates a tardy student and the time listed when the student reported to school. This Bulletin shall be delivered to teachers during Period 3.

(3) Teachers shall take attendance in all classes and record the names of absent students.

(4) At the end of the day, teachers will check their class absences against the Attendance Bulletin. Any student who was absent from class and whose name does not appear on the Attendance Bulletin is to have his or her name placed on a separate sheet which is to be turned in to the office at the end of the school day.

(5) That list shall be checked and returned to the teacher with a disposition of each case, as "absent . . .not on list; sent home . . .ill; cut class; etc." It will then be up to the teacher involved to initiate the proper disciplinary procedures where warranted.

. . .Sample Attendance Card

ATTENDANCE CARD

Name: ____

Grade: _____ **Home Room** ________ **H. R. Teacher:** ________________

ABSENT – "X" on date **Tardy – Date circled**

Sept.	Oct.	Nov.	Dec.	Jan.	Feb.	Mar.	Apr.	May	June	Weekday	Key
--	3	--	--	WV	--	--	3	1	--	Mon.	CD–Columbus
--	4	1	--	3	--	--	4	2	--	Tues.	Day

ATTENDANCE

Sept.	Oct.	Nov.	Dec.	Jan.	Feb.	Mar.	Apr.	May	June	Weekday	Key
--	5	2	--	4	1	1	5	3	--	Wed.	
--	6	3	1	5	2	2	6	4	1	Thurs.	ED—Election Day
--	7	4	2	6	3	3	7	5	2	Fri.	
--	CD	7	5	9	6	6	10	8	5	Mon.	IS—In Service
6	IS	ED	6	10	7	7	11	9	6	Tues.	LB—Lincoln's Birthday
7	12	IS	7	11	8	8	12	10	7	Wed.	
8	13	TC	8	12	9	9	13	11	8	Thurs	MD—Memorial Day
9	14	TC	9	13	10	10	14	12	9	Fri.	
12	17	14	12	16	LB	13	17	15	12	Mon.	
13	18	15	13	17	14	14	18	16	13	Tues.	SV—Spring Vacation
14	19	16	14	18	15	15	19	17	14	Wed.	
15	20	17	15	19	16	16	20	18	15	Thurs.	TC—Teacher's Convention
16	21	18	16	20	17	17	21	19	16	Fri.	
19	24	21	19	23	WB	20	24	22	19	Mon.	TH—Thanksgiving Holiday
20	25	22	20	24	21	21	25	23	20	Tues.	
21	26	23	21	25	22	22	26	24	21	Wed.	
22	27	TH	22	26	23	23	27	25	22	Thurs.	WB—Washington's Birthday
23	28	TH	23	27	24	SV	28	26	23	Fri.	
26	31	28	WV	30	27	SV	--	MD	--	Mon.	WV—Winter Vacation
27	--	29	WV	31	28	SV	--	30	--	Tues.	
28	--	30	WV	--	--	SV	--	31	--	Wed.	
29	--	--	WV	--	--	SV	--	--	--	Thurs.	
30	--	--	WV	--	--	SV	--	--	--	Fri.	

										Possible Number of Days	
										Number of Days Absent	
										Times Tardy	

. . .Sample Part of Attendance Bulletin

ATTENDANCE BULLETIN

for

Friday, March 26, 19XX

Grade 10	Grade 11	Grade 12
BOYS	BOYS	BOYS
Adams, Tom (3)	Ajax, Andrew (1)	Bromton, Bill (2)
Ardley, Bruce (T-9:30)	Milton, Bill (6)	Buxer, Tony (10)
Banner, Joe (1)	Nester, James (T-9:05)	Junik, Joe (3)
Coleman, Dan (4)	Wafter, Tom (3)	Malin, Kenny (2)

GIRLS	GIRLS	GIRLS
Codely, Jane (T-9:11)	Kelton, Bev (4)	Lester, Paula (1)
Dennis, Mary (2)	Rastman, Carol (2)	Nunnel, Mary (T-8:57)
Enton, Brenda (2)	Teller, Jo Ann (1)	Porter, Jan (3)
Gunn, Julie (1)	Vix, Cindy (T-9:41)	Quillin, Tina (1)

AWARDS (See Also: CITIZENSHIP; HONOR ROLL; NATIONAL HONOR SOCIETY; SCHOLARSHIPS; SPORTS)

. . .Announcement of, to Local Newspapers

Ann Marie Denning, a senior at Rock Township High School, has been selected as the recipient of the Gordon Medal of Outstanding Citizenship. According to high school principal John Benson, this is the highest honor awarded to students at the school.

The medal, an annual presentation, is given to the senior student who has displayed the highest degree of good citizenship throughout his or her school career. Nominees are voted upon by students and faculty.

Miss Denning, who plans to attend Fairmont University in the fall, is currently president of the senior class. During her years at Rock Township High School she has been a member of the Student Council, a cheerleader, vice-president of the Student Welfare Organization and a member of the National Honor Society.

Miss Denning will receive the award during graduation procedures later this month.

. . .Announcement of, to Parents

Dear Mr. and Mrs. Denning,

It gives me great pleasure and a good deal of personal satisfaction to inform you that your daughter, Ann Marie, has been chosen to receive this year's Gordon Medal of Outstanding Citizenship.

Perhaps you are aware that the Gordon Medal is an annual award presented to that senior student at Rock Township High School who has best personified those qualities of citizenship and leadership that are reflective of the highest ideals of American society.

I am happy to report that Ann Marie was the outstanding choice of students and faculty alike. I personally feel that no finer choice could have been made.

The medal will be presented during graduation ceremonies. Meanwhile, may I congratulate you on this singular honor which your daughter so richly deserves.

Sincerely,
J. Benson, Principal

. . .Announcement of, to the School Newspaper

Mr. Benson today announced that all the votes have been counted, and the winner of this year's Gordon Medal of Outstanding Citizenship is senior Ann Marie Denning.

This medal, given each year to the one senior who has displayed outstanding citizenship during his or her years at Rock Township High, is voted by the students and faculty.

We all know Ann Marie from her work with the Student Council, her vice-presidency of the Student Welfare Organization, and her cheering on of our team to victory.

Ann Marie will be given the medal by Mr. Benson during graduation exercises.

B

BACK-TO-SCHOOL NIGHT (See Also: ADULT EDUCATION; ALUMNI; OPEN HOUSE)

. . .Announcement to Parents

AN INVITATION

How would you like to see your wife or husband try to fit into your child's school desk? You'll have a ringside seat to this outstanding event if you will accept our cordial invitation to attend our Back-to-School Night on Wednesday, November 9, 19XX at 8:00 p.m.

There will be a brief meeting of the Parent-Faculty Association and a short state-of-the-school report, but the major part of the evening will be spent following your son's or daughter's schedule of studies and meeting with the faculty.

We are looking forward to meeting the parents of our students.

. . .Follow-Up Letter to Those Involved

Dear __________,

How can I begin to tell you how much I appreciate your efforts in making our recent Back-to-School Night such an outstanding success?

The many positive comments I have received concerning the smooth functioning, informativeness and congeniality of the evening reflect a genuine feeling on the part of all attending that something positive and "real" was happening.

It is evident that everyone involved had a profitable and enjoyable evening, and part of the credit for it must go to you. Your involvement made the evening the success it was.

Thank you for being there, for giving of yourself and for creating a Back-to-School Night which will be pleasantly remembered by all concerned.

Thank you,
J. Benson, Principal

. . .Program for

TO ALL PARENTS

Welcome to Rock Township High School's Annual Back-to-School Night! We hope you will enjoy the program that awaits you. Please take this opportunity to get to know your child's teachers, and don't forget to drop by the main office and introduce yourself. We'll be happy to meet you.

J. Benson, Principal

BACK-TO-SCHOOL NIGHT

8:00 – General Meeting in Auditorium; Explanation of Program.

8:30 – Program Begins. Parents will follow their son's or daughter's schedule. Each "period" will be seven minutes in length. Change of periods will be announced over the public address system:

8:30 – 8:37 – Period 1	9:20 – 9:27 – Period 5
8;40 – 8:47 – Period 2	9:30 – 9:37 – Period 6
8:50 – 8:57 – Homeroom	9:40 – 9:47 – Period 7
9:00 – 9:07 – Period 3	9:50 – 9:57 – Period 8
9:10 – 9:17 – Period 4	10:00 – Program Concludes

10:00 –Coffee, Cake and Conversation. There will be an informal get-together in the cafeteria to which you are all cordially invited.

11:00 – Good Night! We hope you enjoyed yourself! Come back soon!

BEHAVIOR (See Also: ASP; DISCIPLINE; REPRIMANDS; SUSPENSION; VANDALISM)

. . .Code of Behavior

The infractions listed below are sufficiently serious to result in immediate suspension:

VIOLENCE

1. Fighting
2. Bullying or harassing another person

OBSCENITY

3. Profane or obscene language

VANDALISM

4. Major vandalism or behavior resulting in police action

INSUBORDINATION

5. Willful disobedience

Students suspended from school are not permitted to participate on varsity teams or attend school functions during the dates of their suspension.

To insure fair treatment and consistency, demerits will be assigned for certain offenses. These can be worked off by signing up in the main office in advance, and parental permission is necessary. Weekly work periods after school will permit students to contribute to the life of the school through preparing bulletin boards, painting, murals, planting bulbs, etc. One after-school period will erase one demerit. These work periods will be supervised by a staff member.

Student Responsibilities and Penalties for Noncompliance

HALLS AND STAIRWAYS	
1. Running	1 Demerit
2. Obstructing Hall Traffic	1 Demerit
3. Horseplay	2 Demerits
4. Littering	1 Demerit
5. Food in Halls	1 Demerit
6. In Halls During Class Time Without a Pass	2 Demerits
CLASSROOM	
1. Cutting Class	3 Demerits
2. Vandalism	3 Demerits or Suspension
3. Truancy	1 Week of Central Detention
CAFETERIA	
1. Not at Assigned Table	1 Demerit
2. Leaving Without a Pass	2 Demerits
3. Throwing Objects or Food	3 Demerits
4. Littering Area or Table	1 Demerit

. . .Letter of Policy to Parents

Dear Parents,

In answer to many parental inquiries, the following is the policy of the Board of Education on Behavior:

The Rock Township Board of Education has the authority to make reasonable and necessary rules governing the behavior of students in school. These rules will apply to all students going to, during, and returning from school and while on school-approved activities.

Teachers have the responsibility for maintaining a suitable environment for learning.

Administrators have the responsibility for maintaining and facilitating the educational programs. The principal is authorized by state statute to suspend students for cause. Rules and regulations shall be published and reviewed with students at the opening of each school year and will be posted in a prominent location within the school. Copies will be made available to students and parents upon request.

In order that infractions of the rules established for student conduct may be treated equitably and consistently, the Board has approved a disciplinary action schedule for the district's secondary schools. School administrators shall administer discipline within the guidelines of this schedule and other specific policies relating to student behavior adopted by the Board.

The intent of this schedule is to provide students with a definition of the limits of acceptable behavior and to equip school administrators for their disciplinary responsibilities. The schedule shall be interpreted by the principals and their designees in a manner which they deem just, given the circumstances of the individual case. Additionally, administrators shall have the authority to enforce other reasonable disciplinary actions which they find warranted by situations not covered in the disciplinary action schedule.

Hopefully, the policy quoted above will answer many question. If you would like any further clarification, please call me at 234-5678.

Sincerely,

J. Benson, Principal

. . .Principal's Message on

(A) to students

In any school it is necessary that rules and regulations be established for the safety and well-being of all. Each student is expected to recognize that the school's authority extends from within the building itself to the walls surrounding it, to the playgrounds, and to the buses and bus stops. Some of the more common rules are listed below:

1. Students are to follow the instructions of the teacher in the classroom.
2. Smoking, profanity and fighting are forbidden.
3. Students are not to engage in an action that is potentially or actually harmful to the safety of other students or adults (running in the halls, throwing an object, pushing or shoving, etc.).
4. Students are not to deliberately damage any school property.
5. Students are not to bring to school the following: radios, water pistols or any other type of "toy" gun, cigarettes or any other form of tobacco, firecrackers, matches, sharp or pointed instruments or any other dangerous object or substance.
6. Students with projects completed in shop areas may not take them home on school buses.
7. Students are not to leave the classroom without permission, cut classes, or be absent from school without proper reason.

In an effort to see that the rules are enforced in a fair and consistent manner, Rock Township High School has adopted a discipline system. The discipline system explains what is expected of each student and tells the student what will happen if a rule is violated. The purpose of the system is to help each student fully understand what is expected so he or she will not get into trouble.

BEHAVIOR

(B) to teachers

MEMO

To: ALL TEACHERS
From: J. BENSON
Re: BEHAVIOR

Behavior is everyone's concern. We have spent a goodly amount of time and trouble formulating a code of behavior which we all feel is meaningful, reasonable, and enforceable, and which will aid in the smooth functioning of our school. Now, therefore, it is essential that we *all* enforce the code uniformly. It is, in the long run, the consistency of discipline rather than its severity which make it the most effective.

Let us all resolve to consistently and uniformly enforce this excellent code which we have all worked so hard to attain.

. . .Samples of Introducing Change in Behavior Code

(A) exclusion of a rule

NOTICE

To: ALL STUDENTS
From: MR. BENSON
Re: GUM CHEWING

Recently, a number of teachers and parents have been working together for the good of the school and trying to come up with a code of discipline that is reasonable and effective.

One aspect of their review concerns the chewing of gum. Until now, students were not allowed to chew gum. The reason for this rule had to do with the way in which the gum was discarded. Gum stuck to a seat or under a desk is not fun, as any student with ruined clothes will tell you.

The committee feels, however, that the students of Rock Township High School are mature and reasonable enough to understand that concern for the rights of others must govern our actions.

I can agree with that statement, and that is why the rule against gum-chewing is suspended. We shall be studying the effects of this change in rules in the following weeks. If we observe common sense and a reasonable, caring attitude toward the comfort of others, there is no reason why the rule against gum-chewing cannot stay permanently abolished.

(B) Inclusion of a Rule

NOTICE

To: ALL STUDENTS
From: MR. BENSON
Re: RUNNING IN THE HALLS

I had a very unpleasant task yesterday. I had to take a student to the hospital who had a broken arm which she received when she was knocked down by two students who were running in the halls. Nor is this the first time that something like this has happened. Indeed, this is the third time since the beginning of the year that a student has been injured due to someone running in the halls.

Therefore, I feel it is necessary to publicly state that henceforth running in the hallways of Rock Township High School will not be tolerated. I am directing all teachers to send to me all students found running in the hallways. Possible consequences to the violation of this rule may include detention, suspension of privileges, and, if the case is serious enough, suspension from school.

I know that I can count on the cooperation of the students of this school in implementing this very necessary rule.

(C) seasonal

NOTICE

To: ALL STUDENTS
From: MR. BENSON
Re: SNOWBALLS

It's cold outside, and in a short time snow will be covering the ground. The very thought of it brings visions of skiing, sledding and . . . (here it comes) . . . snowballs. There isn't a person in the school who is not aware that a new snowfall brings with it the temptation to throw snowballs.

Unfortunately, we are also aware that snowballs can be a real hazard. A snowball tossed at the windshield of a school bus could cause an accident. A snowball hitting someone in the face could occasion anything from a bloody nose to the loss of an eye. A moment of careless pleasure could result in a lifetime of suffering.

Therefore, as stated in the Student Handbook, the throwing of snowballs is forbidden on school grounds. I am certain you can understand the importance of this rule, and that disciplinary action will not be needed.

BIDS (See Also: ACCEPTANCE; APPLICATION; VENDORS)

. . .Acceptance of

Date: ____________________

Dear ______________________________,

Please be advised that at the __________, 19____ meeting of the Rock Township Board of Education your bid of $________ was accepted for the following item(s):

QUANTITY	STOCK NO.	ITEM	DELIVERY DATE

All deliveries are to be made to the Central Supply Office. It is essential that all deliveries be made on or before the delivery date. If there is any reason why delivery cannot be made on time, you are required to notify the Rock Township Board of Education immediately.

Sincerely,

. . .Rejection of

Date: ____________________

Dear ______________________________,

We regret to inform you that at the ________________, 19________ meeting of the Rock Township Board of Education your bid for ________

____

was rejected for the following reason(s): ______________________

____

The winning bid was ______________________ and was submitted by ______________________.

Thank you for your interest in our school system. You will be advised of future bids.

Sincerely,

. . .Soliciting for

Date: ______________

TO ALL CONCERNED:

The Rock Township Board of Education announces that bids are invited on stage lighting equipment according to the following specifications:

1. A dimmer panel and board consisting of eight (8) channels at 2400 Watts per channel shall be installed and operational.
2. Eight (8) ante-proscenium lights of 750 Watts each shall be installed and operational.
3. Two (2) 1500 Watt traveling spots with diaphragm, single control cutoff and eight (8) gels shall be delivered and functional.
4. All electrical work is to be done by qualified electricians and must meet the specifications and standards of the electrical code of Rock Township.
5. Delivery and installation must be made by September 1, 19XX.

The bid itself must be submitted according to the following directions and specifications:

1. All bids are to be on your company letterhead and must list each item and service separately.
2. All bids must be received by 5:00 p.m. on Tuesday, March 21, 19XX.
3. Bids should be submitted in an envelope marked, "Bids on Stage Lighting" and delivered or mailed to Mr. Thomas Callerson, Rock Township Board of Education, 123 Crescent Road, Rock Township, ______________.

Bids will be opened and recorded at 8:00 p.m. on Wednesday, March 22, 19XX in the Business Office of the Rock Township Board of Education, 123 Crescent Road, Rock Township, ____________. The awarding of this bid shall be made at a regular meeting of the Rock Township Board of Education within thirty (30) days of the opening of bids.

Sincerely,

BI-LINGUAL EDUCATION (See Also: EXCHANGE STUDENTS; LANGUAGE; MINORITIES)

...Evaluation of

Evaluation of the Bi-Lingual Education Program

ROCK TOWNSHIP HIGH SCHOOL

For the School Year 19XX – 19XX

During the first school year of the implementation of the Bi-Lingual Education Program, the following results were achieved.

1. The grades of the students involved increased an average of 36.325% (See Sheet A) over the previous year's average.
2. The average daily attendance improved an average of 29.76% (See Sheet B).
3. The incidence of disciplinary infractions requiring action by the Main Office declined an average of 64.7% (See Sheet C).
4. The involvement of non-English speaking parents has increased 275% (See Sheet D).
5. The students involved have indicated on a questionnaire that they sense a greater degree of "belonging" through the program (See Sheet E).
6. Several leaders of the non-English-speaking community have openly praised Rock Township High School for endeavoring to meet the needs of their constituents (Letters Attached).

Submitted this ________________ day of ________, 19____________

Signature: ______________________________

Title: ______________________________

. . .Notice to Parents

(NOTE: The following should be translated into the particular language before being mailed to the non-English-speaking parents of the students involved.)

Dear Parents,

We are beginning a new program at Rock Township High School in September, and we would like to enroll your child.

The program which is called 'Bi-Lingual Education' is an attempt to meet the needs of those students whose first language is ______________ rather than English. All too often, such a student may not do as well in school as he is capable of doing because all subjects are taught in English, and the student has difficulty in understanding because of that language barrier.

This program hopes to solve that problem by providing instruction in the first language while attempting to improve English skills.

You are invited to a meeting at 8:00 p.m. on Thursday, April 26, 19XX in the Rock Township High School Auditorium. At this meeting, the Program Director, will discuss the program. ______________________ speaks______________ fluently and will give his program in__________.

We want your children to get all the education they can, and we feel that this program may be part of the answer.

Please come to this meeting and let us talk about the future of your children.

Sincerely,
J. Benson, Principal

BOARD OF EDUCATION

(See Also: DEMONSTRATIONS; FINANCIAL; ISSUES; MEDIATOR; NEGOTIATIONS...And All Statements of Policy)

. . .Congratulations to a New Member

Dear Mrs. Jordan,

Please accept my congratulations on your recent election to the Rock Township Board of Education. You have before you a task equal to your talents as you work for the ultimate goal of the best possible education for every student in Rock Township.

I wish you success in your endeavors and pledge my cooperation in working toward common educational goals.

If I may be of service, please do not hestitate to call upon me.

Sincerely,

J. Benson, Principal

. . .Message to Public

ROCK TOWNSHIP BOARD OF EDUCATION

The control of the Rock Township School District lies with its Board of Education which has been duly constituted and is governed by the state's educational statutes. The Board exercises its powers through the adoption of bylaws and policies for the organization and operation of the school district and is responsible for district operation through its chief executive officer, the Superintendent of Schools.

The Board consists of nine members. Each year three members of the Board are chosen by the community for a full three-year term at an annual election held on the first Tuesday in March. To qualify to represent the community-at-large, the candidate must be a citizen and resident of the district for at least two years and must be able to read and write. Board vacancies occurring by resignation, expulsion, or death are filled by a majority vote of the Board within two calendar months of the vacancy. Other vacancies or those not filled within the prescribed time are appointed by the County Superintendent of Schools. A Board member does not receive compensation for services.

All citizens have the right to advance notice of and attendance at all public meetings of the Board of Education. Announcements of meetings may be found at the front entrance to the Board of Education Office, 123 Crescent Road, at each of the 15 schools within the district, and once a year in local newspapers. The following descriptions of the types of meetings conducted by the Board have been prepared to help the community understand the operation of the Board.

Regular Public Meetings

Required by law to be held at least once a month, this is a meeting at which formal and official actions are taken by the Board of Education. The Rock Township Board usually holds such meetings on the first and third Wednesday of each month, the first to handle all items requiring official action and the second to authorize payment of bills. At these meetings there is time set aside for the public to speak and bring their concerns to the attention of the Board. However, if a resident wishes to speak on an agenda item prior to a vote being taken, a written request to do so must be submitted in advance to the Board president and a majority of the Board must agree to hear the request at that time.

Committee of the Whole Meetings (Workshop Meetings)

The purpose of a Committee of the Whole Meeting is to discuss issues and formulate motions to be acted upon at the next regularly scheduled meeting of the Board. No formal action is taken at such a meeting. Although the community may attend meetings of this nature it cannot participate in any of the discussions nor is time set aside for the public to speak. However, if a resident feels that a concern should be considered by the Board, the resident can request permission to speak, in writing, subject to approval by the majority of the Board.

Special Meetings

Special Meetings are those established by state statutes such as public hearings on school budgets, a proposed building referendum, etc. The community may attend and speak at all such special meetings, prior to formal action being taken by the Board.

Emergency Meetings

Emergency meetings may be called without advance notice being given to the community, but discussion and action are restricted to the item causing the emergency. A resolution setting forth the reason for the emergency must first be adopted by the Board.

Public Exclusion at Meetings

The community, as permitted by law, will be excluded from meetings or portions of meetings when items to be discussed might jeopardize the public interest or infringe upon the rights of an individual or individuals. Such an exclusion would include collective bargaining or negotiations sessions, employment termination evaluation and/or discipline of any present or prospective employee, and sessions in which information, if disclosed, would invade the personal privacy of an individual. The Board, however, must take formal action at a public meeting.

Agenda and Minutes

Agenda for all meetings are posted at the front entrance of the Board of Education Office and in the district's 15 schools. Minutes are available during normal working hours and copies of meeting notices and agenda are mailed at the request of a resident at a cost of 50 cents per page. An initial deposit of $10.00 is required from a resident who wishes to be placed on the mailing list.

BOOKS (See Also: LIBRARY; TEXTBOOKS)

. . .Book Fair

(A) announcement of

ADOPT A BOOK

There will be hundreds of needy books
at the
Third Annual
Rock Township High School
BOOK FAIR

Take a book home! Read! Relax! Enjoy! There are bargains by the score, so come early and stay late. Start that library now!

Friday Evening, May 14, 19XX from 8 to 11 p.m. at the
Rock Township High School Library.

SEE YOU THERE!

(B) procedures for

MEMO

To: ALL MEMBERS OF THE ENGLISH DEPARTMENT
From: NANCY RASLIN, CHAIRPERSON
Re: PROCEDURES FOR BOOK FAIR

On Friday evening, May 14, 19XX from 8 to 11 p.m. we will be holding our third annual Book Fair, The following are the procedures for this event:

1. During Period Eight on Friday afternoon each English teacher will send the books that have been collected in homeroom to the library. I shall be there to accept the books and begin to arrange them.

2. As soon as school is over, I would appreciate all the help—make that HELP!—you could give in setting up. Even a few minutes of your time would be greatly appreciated.
3. All department members will report no later than 7:45 p.m. and will take up posts as follows: Mr. Mintner, Ms. Kerrin, Mrs. Harvey and Mr. Simon will be the cashiers (Please see me to get the cash boxes and Sales Report Sheets.) while Mr. Hartly, Mrs. McGrath, Ms. Halser, Ms. Bretner and Mr. Hines will circulate among the book stalls, helping where needed.
4. Upon closing of the doors at 11:00 p.m., the cashiers will return cash boxes and Record Sheets to me.
5. Thank you in advance for all your help. I know that you will make this Book Fair as successful as those in the past.

(C) sales report sheet

BOOK FAIR SALES REPORT

Name of Salesperson: ____________________

Number	Title	Price	Total	Running Total

This is page ________ of ________

Total this page: ____________

Running Total: ____________

. . .Book Record List

(A) individual

BOOK RECORD SHEET

Book: ____________________ Publisher: ____________

Price: ________ Grade in which book is used: ____________

BOOKS

Date Issued: ____________________ Date Returned: ____________________

N — — New E — — Excellent G — — Good F — — Fair P — — Poor

New — — Full Value; Excellent — — 80%; Good — — 60%; Fair — — 40%; Poor — — 20%

PUPIL TO WHOM ASSIGNED	NUMBER OF BOOK	CONDITION WHEN ISSUED	CONDITION WHEN RET'D	FINES REMARKS

(B) school-wide

BOOK LIST

School: ____________________ Principal: ____________________

Subject	Title	Publisher	No. of Copies	Grade Used

. . .Request for

BOOK REQUEST

Name of Teacher: ____________________

Department: ____________________ Date: ____________________

Grade or Subject: ____________________ Room Number: ____________________

I hereby request that the following books be sent to the location listed above:

No. of Copies	Title, Publisher, Edition

Signature: ____________________

. . .Books to be Discarded

ROCK TOWNSHIP PUBLIC SCHOOLS

Book Discards

Principal: ______________________ School: ______________________

Date: ______________________

(   ) Discarded Books   (   ) Rebound Books   (   ) Surplus Books

(Please check the appropriate category)

NUMBER	PUBLISHER	TITLE OF BOOK	YEAR	AUTHOR

BUDGET (See Also: ...Those Activities or Items Requiring Budgets, such as FIELD TRIPS, Budget Form For...Etc.)

. . .Guidelines for Preparation of

To: ALL COORDINATORS, DIRECTORS AND SPECIALISTS
From: J. BENSON
Re: BUDGET PREPARATION

The following guidelines are to be followed in the preparation of your 19XX–19XX Budget:

1. Distribute all forms as soon as possible.
2. Request your teachers to return all forms no later than Monday, October 20, 19XX.
3. Categorize all requests by budget account categories on summary sheets:

2304.05	Contracted services, repairs
2305.05	Instructional supplies
2306.05	Teachers in-state travel and expenses
2406.05	Textbooks (all books except workbooks)
2504.05	Library book binding
2505.05	Library books, magazines

2506.05	Library travel, postage
2604.05	AV contracted services, repairs
2606.05	AV materials
2704.05	Guidance contracted test correcting
2705.05	Guidance supplies
2706.05	Guidance travel, expenses, printing
3205.05	Health (clinic) supplies
3206.05	Health (clinic) travel, postage, etc.
3370.05	Field trips
3515.05	Athletic and intramural supplies
7306.05	New equipment
7406.05	Replacement of equipment

4. Fill in a summary sheet for each of the categories in #3 above.

5. Check that all items are in proper categories.

6. Check arithmetic carefully.

7. All totals above last year's amounts must be explained thoroughly in writing. Unrealistic requests will be returned for trimming. All programs, old or new, and large individual items need written explanations. Small, miscellaneous items (under $10 each) may be combined and listed as follows:

   – miscellaneous laboratory supplies such as test tubes, beakers, clamps, etc. $50.00

   – other sewing supplies such as pins, needles, thread, tape and buttons. $45.00

8. Turn in all forms arranged by budget categories, carefully checked and totaled, no later than Monday, October 27, at 8:55 a.m. Attach summary sheet on top. Include all sheets, even if blank.

. . .Notice of

MEMO

To: ALL PRINCIPALS
From: THOMAS SMITH, SUPERINTENDENT
Re: BUDGET–IT'S THAT TIME AGAIN!

This year the pressure is really on for an early completion of the budget–at least the non-personnel items and requests for new positions.

I would like to have your budget for the Central Office review by November 15th of this year.

I can understand how difficult this will be. If you have any special problems, please call me. This, again, is going to be a tough year because of cuts in state aid. I feel that the climate is bad for program expansions or requests for new positions which cannot be specifically justified by increased enrollments. However, there seems to be a good deal of community support for improvement in Music programs. This will be an item on the agenda of the next principals' meeting.

Good luck!

. . .Notice to Parents

To All Parents:

The enclosed information has been compiled to give the community of Rock Township some background information on the 19XX–19XX school budget, prepared by the Board of Education and presented to the voters at the Annual School Election, Tuesday, March 6th. The polls will be open from 2 to 9 p.m.

The Board of Education has put together a budget which is within a 7.05 per cent ceiling, not an easy task considering continued improvement needs and ever-rising operational expenses.

We offer this information to the community so that informed voters may go to the polls. If you have any questions about the material, you may call the office of Public Information during normal working hours. The telephone number is 123-4567, Extension 255.

We appreciate the time you will take in reading this information, and we hope that you will pass it on to a neighbor when you are finished.

Table I – Cost of Education 19XX–19XX*

CURRENT EXPENSE

State Average	$1897.69 per student
State Region 4 Average	$1906.87 per student
County Average	$1907.54 per student
State Assessment	$2261.36 per student
Rock Township	$1594.32 per student

Table II – California Test of Basic Skills

	Rock Township District Grade 5			National Grade 5
19XX	Reading	Language	Arithmetic	5.8
	6.3	6.4	6.3	5.8

* Prepared by the State School Boards Association

Although we continue to spend below the State and County average in per-pupil cost in current expense, our elementary students are achieving substantially higher scores in reading, language and in math than the national average.

The program improvements on the elementary level are bringing results. Parents who have children in both the elementary and secondary schools tell me they wish their students now in the high school had had the program their younger children are now receiving.

Well, now they can. The same process is planned to be installed in our secondary schools. Be aware that the process will not turn around secondary education overnight. The elementary progress has taken us over the long haul. I perceive a similar experience for grades 7-12.

If our school budget is approved again this year by our voters, we will be able to assure our secondary students the same benefits.

Sincerely,
Thomas Smith
Superintendent of Schools

. . .Notice to Teachers

MEMO

To: ALL STAFF MEMBERS INVOLVED WITH BUDGET MAKING
From: J. BENSON, PRINCIPAL
Re: NEXT YEAR'S BUDGET

I have been directed by the Superintendent to start the budget process as soon as possible. I guess that means NOW! I know how time-consuming the process will be for all of us, but I also know that we are fortunate in being able to make real contributions in terms of real needs as we know them. So let's start with our performance objectives. What do we need to achieve them–*really* need? State aid is being cut. We must be realistic. We cannot ask for anything simply because it would be nice to have. Here we go!

1. Please read *carefully* the instructions on every form. They vary.
2. Please inventory your equipment and *specialized* supplies. Remember: equipment lasts until it wears out or is broken, like a textbook or a barometer. Specialized supplies are white rats or litmus paper. General supplies like chalk, paper, etc. are inventoried in the supply room for the entire school. Use any system you desire as long as the item is described along with the amount *you now have.* I know the year has just started, but if we do this each year in September, it will give us a good rough idea of how much we need. Check with other department teachers to avoid gaps and duplication.
3. Include a justification statement for each program or group of items on the reverse side of the form. Your Department Head can help you with this. If a program or group of items are included in several forms, it is unnecessary to repeat the justification. Merely cite the form on which the justification was written. Without this being done properly, the program items may be eliminated.
4. Include the cost for each program or item plus 5% for inflation and shipping and then round it off to the next higher five dollars (e.g. a $24.75 item plus 5% = $25.99; rounded off, this is $30.00).
5. Use a descriptive name for each item or program, such as "Athletic Equipment–hockey sticks," or "Film–Russia Today." Each of these would appear on a different form for a different budget category.
6. Do not include names of publishers or manufacturers. *This is not a requisition.* It is a request for money to be appropriated.
7. Be certain to include everything needed. Money not requested for typewriter covers will not be appreciated.
8. Turn in completed budget request forms to your Department Head by Monday, October 20.
9. After each request has been reviewed by your Department Head and by me, the total budget will be typed in book form. It will then be reviewed by the Central Office. The total District budget will then be submitted to the Board of Education which, in turn, will scrutinize each category before it is approved. We can then start ordering approved items in April for delivery after July 1 of the new fiscal year.

10. Increased requests over last year's amounts must be thoroughly substantiated, *especially* if it appears that an amount will be unexpended in a given category at the end of the budget year.

BUILDING (See Also: CLEANUP; CUSTODIAL SERVICES; MAP OF THE SCHOOL; WASTE)

. . .Building Condition Report (Teachers)

BUILDING REPORT

ROCK TOWNSHIP HIGH SCHOOL

Date: ______________________________ **Room:** ____________________

1. Physical condition of building needing attention:

Room #	Repairs

2. Any other circumstances that should receive the attention of the office—i.e.: cleaning, etc.

Teacher Signature: ________________________________

. . .Custodian's Building Condition Report

Building: ____

Head Custodian: ____

For the Month of ____________________, 19 __________

Conditions which have been corrected: ____

____

____

Conditions in Need of Correction: ____

____

____

Potentially Dangerous Situations: ____

____

____

Vandalism: ____

____

____

Signature of
Head Custodian: ______________________

. . .Granting Request to Use Building

PERMIT FOR USE OF SCHOOL BUILDING AND GROUNDS

This is to certify that the ______________________________

______________________________ has been reserved for

____

From ______________________ Until ______________________

On the Date(s) ______________________________________

At a Total Charge of __________________________________

CUSTODIANS ASSIGNED: REMARKS:

______________________ ______________________

______________________ ______________________

______________________ ______________________

Board of Education
Rock Township

Date: ______________________ by: ______________________

NOTE:

The holder of this permit should read carefully all "Rules and Regulations."

There must be one uniformed person on duty for each 100 people present.

There must be sufficient fire and police protection to uphold law and order for Special Events.

Schools WILL NOT be available when school is in session, on Election Day or during special school elections.

If a school function conflicts, school activities will have preference, and you will be notified.

When All-Purpose Rooms or Auditoriums are requested, kindly notify the Board of Education if chairs will be required, etc.

Special service of custodians is not to be expected unless arranged at the time of the request.

No smoking in school buildings.

A CERTIFICATE OF LIABILITY INSURANCE must be filed before the building is used.

. . .Improvement to Building Form

ROCK TOWNSHIP HIGH SCHOOL

Improvement of Building for the Year July 1, 19 ________ to June 30, 19 ________

Your Name: ____________________________________ Room: ____________

Department: ___________________________________ Date: ____________

DIRECTIONS: Include repair or replacement items such as fan motors and drapes or repair and maintenance of the building itself, such as concrete work, windows, painting, etc. and renovations such as removal or addition of partitions.

PRIORITY CODE: VHP = very high HP = high MP = medium LP = low

Priority	Program or Item	Quantity	Item Cost	Total Cost

. . .Refusing Request to Use Building

Date: ________________

M ________________________________

____

____

Dear ________________________,

Please be informed that your request to use (Name of Building) ______________________________ on (Date) ______________ has been denied because of the following reason(s): ______________

____

____

We regret if this has caused you any inconvenience. If you have any questions or wish further clarification, please call me at 123-4567.

Sincerely,

. . Requesting Use of Building

REQUEST TO USE SCHOOL BUILDING

Name: ____

Name of Group or Organization: ______________________

Building Requested: ____________________________________

Date Requested: ____________________ Time: From ________ To __________

Describe Activity: ______________________________________

____

Approximate Number of People to Use Building: ____________

Name and Address of Person to Contact regarding the Disposition of This Request:

Name: ____________________________ Telephone: ______________

Address: ____

_______________________________________ Zip ______________

I hereby state that the information in this application is true and accurate and that, if approved, I will abide by the rules and regulations for the use of public school buildings as set down by the Rock Township Board of Education.

Date: ______________ Signature: ___________________________

BULLETIN (See Also: BULLETIN BOARD; CALENDAR; HANDBOOK; NEWSLETTER; NEWSPAPER; PUBLIC RELATIONS)

. . . Form for Placing a Notice on the Daily Bulletin

DAILY BULLETIN NOTICE

The following message is to be included in the Daily Bulletin on the following date(s):

______________ ______________ ______________ ______________

NOTICE:

Teacher's Signature: ______________________________

Please place this form on Mrs. Bordon's desk BEFORE 1:30 p.m. of the day preceding publication.

. . .Memo of Criteria for Daily Bulletin

MEMO

To: FACULTY
From: J. BENSON, PRINCIPAL
Re: CRITERIA FOR NOTICES ON DAILY BULLETIN

I am really pleased that so many of you are using the Daily Bulletin, but before we start publishing a major newspaper each day, I feel I'd better remind you of the criteria to which we all agreed for the placement of a message on that Bulletin.

Simply put, notices on the Bulletin are restricted to those messages which pertain to the functioning of the school and the educational process. News of testing, meetings, guidance matters, budget deadlines, etc. can appear in the notices, while requests to car pool, the get-together at the Willsford Inn, and Do-You-Want-To-Adopt-A-Kitten notices should go on the Office Bulletin Board or on the Faculty Room wall.

Seriously, let's use some common sense and keep the Daily Bulletin within manageable limits.

BULLETIN BOARD

(See Also: BULLETIN; CLASS; MAP OF THE SCHOOL; SCHEDULE...And All Items Posted on Bulletin Boards, such as HONOR ROLL, Etc.)

. . .Form for Placing Notice on Office Bulletin Board

OFFICE BULLETIN BOARD

Date of Request:______________________________

I would like to place the following message on the office Bulletin Board:

Dates of Placement: FROM ____________ TO ____________

Signature of Person
Making Request:____

. . . .

Dear____________________________,

Your request to place a message on the Office Bulletin Board from ____________ to ____________ has been:

( ) Granted ( ) Denied for the following reason(s):

J. Benson, Principal

. . .Hall Bulletin Board Assignment List

To All Teachers:

Please fill in the form below as to which time you prefer to put up a display on the Front Hall Bulletin Board. It's strictly first-come-first-serve, so if you really have a preference, better sign up now. All assignments run from the 15th of one month through the 14th of the next month.

DATE	TEACHER	THEME OF BULLETIN BOARD
Sept.-Oct.		
Oct.-Nov.		
Nov.-Dec.		
Dec.-Jan.		
Jan.-Feb.		
Feb.-Mar.		
Mar.-Apr.		
Apr.-May		
May-June		

BUS (See Also: DISMISSAL PROCEDURES; FIELD TRIPS)

. . .Bus Card

ROCK TOWNSHIP HIGH SCHOOL

Name: ____________________________ Grade: __________

Assigned Bus: ____________________________

Bus Stop: ____________________________

Date: __________ Signature: ____________________

. . .Bus Passes

ROCK TOWNSHIP HIGH SCHOOL

Late Bus Pass

Student: ______________________________ Date: ____________

Late Bus (Circle One): A B C D E

Signature of Teacher: ______________________________

. . .Bus Reassignment Notice

NOTICE OF BUS REASSIGNMENT

Dear ______________________,

This is to inform you that your son/daughter, ________________,
a ______ grade student at ______________________ School,
has been reassigned to a new school bus effective ________________,
19 ______.

OLD SCHEDULE:

Bus Number: ______________ Time: ______________

Bus Stop: ______________________________

NEW SCHEDULE:

Bus Number: ______________ Time: ______________

Bus Stop: ______________________________

This reassignment has been scheduled for the following reason(s):

____

____

Please call 123-4567 if you require any further information.

Sincerely,

. . .Notice of Possible Removal

__________, 19____

Dear ______________________,

This is to inform you that your son/daughter, ________________,
a ______ grade student at ______________________ School,
is currently being considered for removal from bus transportation.

This review is being made for the following reason(s):

____

____

We urge you to discuss this situation with your child. If the situation continues, we shall have no alternative but to remove your child from school bus transportation for a specified amount of time.

You may call us at 123-4567 if you wish further clarification.

Sincerely,

. . .Notice of Removal

Dear________________________,

We regret to inform you that your son/daughter,______________, a______ grade student at ________________________School, is suspended from the use of the school bus from________ to ________ ______________, 19 __________.

This action is taken for the following reason(s):

____

____

We notified you of the possibility of this action on ____________ ______________, 19 __________. Unfortunately, the situation was not corrected, and the above action is taken.

If you should wish further clarification, please call me at 123-4567.

Sincerely,

. . .Request for Use of

Date__________________, 19___

School:__________________

Name:____

Grade and/or Subject:________________________________

I hereby request the use of the school bus(es) as follows:

Date:____

Time: From______________________ To______________________

Number of Students:______________ Number of Teachers:______________

BUS

Place of Departure: ______________________________

Destination: ______________________________

Purpose of Trip: ______________________________

____

Expenses to be borne by ( ) Group ( ) Board of Education

(Teachers are reminded that the trip must be directly related to the education of the students in order for the Board of Education to assume costs.)

. . .Statement of Bus Conduct

The importance of proper conduct while waiting for, boarding, riding or disembarking from a bus cannot be overemphasized. Any behavior that distracts the bus driver instantly endangers all. In the interests of safety, all students should understand and parents are urged to impress upon their children the necessity for strict compliance with the following rules:

1. Students are to remain well out of the roadway while waiting for the bus.
2. Getting on and off the bus should be done in an orderly manner.
3. Students are to remain seated while the bus is in motion.
4. No part of the body should ever be extended outside the bus.
5. Aisles should be kept clear at all times.
6. Conversations should take place in normal tones of voice. A sudden scream or yell is especially dangerous.
7. Nothing should be thrown either in or from the bus.
8. Smoking on the school bus is strictly forbidden.
9. Crowding, pushing, shoving, etc. are not only unnecessary, but dangerous as well.
10. Attitudes of helpfulness and cooperation will do much to insure safe and comfortable bus transportation for all.

> NOTE: Attention of students and parents is directed to the State School Law which states in part that, "A student may be excluded from bus transportation for disciplinary reasons by the principal, and his parents shall provide for his transportation to and from school during the period of such exclusion."

Buses will leave the school grounds shortly after dismissal. For those engaged in supervised after-school programs, late buses will be provided and are scheduled to leave the school grounds at 3:15 p.m.

Late buses will run every day, Monday through Thursday of each week.

C

CAFETERIA (See Also: CLEANUP; LUNCH; WASTE)

. . .Cafeteria Supervision Assignment Sheet

CAFETERIA SUPERVISION

Five teachers are scheduled for each lunch period. One teacher will supervise tables 1, 2 and 3, and a second will cover 4, 5 and 6, and so on. One teacher will maintain general supervision and assist where needed. All rules of cafeteria behavior are in effect.

Lunch	Tables				
Period	1-2-3	4-5-6	7-8-9	10-11-12	General
A	Mr. Jones	Miss Hansen	Mr. Torun	Mr. Smith	Mrs. Kerr
B	Mrs. Eddy	Mr. Yost	Miss Kern	Mrs. Jerrod	Mr. Winter
C	Mrs. Kerr	Mr. Jones	Miss Hansen	Mr. Torun	Mr. Smith
D	Mr. Winter	Mrs. Eddy	Mr. Yost	Miss Kern	Mrs. Jerrod

. . .Statement on Cafeteria Behavior

Rock Township High School has four lunch periods scheduled into its daily school program with approximately one quarter of the student body in attendance at each. Accordingly, Rock Township High School expects that all of its students will conduct themselves properly during lunch periods, practice good table manners and abide by the following rules:

1. Enter and leave the cafeteria at a walk.
2. Form and keep a single line at each service area.

3. Go through the serving line one time only. The doors leading to the serving areas will be closed as soon as the last student in line has been served.
4. Be seated and remain seated at your table until dismissed by the teacher in charge.
5. Leave the cafeteria during lunch period only with the permission of the teacher in charge.
6. Refrain from pushing, jostling and asking luncheon neighbors for money.
7. Conversation at lunch tables is not only permitted, but desirable. However, loud and boisterous talk, yelling, screaming, etc. are definitely not acceptable.
8. Special note is made of the rule that students are not to throw any object–no matter how small, for however short a distance.
9. Students are not to take food of any kind from the cafeteria.
10. Leave the table clean and suitable for luncheon use by other students.

CALENDAR (See Also: ASSEMBLIES; BULLETIN; JUNE; SEPTEMBER)

. . .Of Events for Parents

EVENTS FOR PARENTS

BACK TO SCHOOL NIGHT–Wednesday, October 23, 19XX

An opportunity to meet your child's teacher and to follow the daily schedule.

NEW TECHNIQUES IN FOREIGN LANGUAGES–Thursday, November 1, 19XX

Mini-lessons for parents in contemporary foreign language techniques.

MATH-SCIENCE NIGHT–Wednesday, November 14, 19XX

Parents take the role of students for a night of scientific experiments and seminar discussions with math teachers (Math seminars at 7:00; experiments 8:00-10:00 p.m.).

CALENDAR

CONTINENTAL BREAKFAST FOR PARENTS–Saturday, December 3, 19XX

State of the School Briefing. A brief one hour (10-11 a.m.) breakfasting and hearing about Rock Township High School's goals and programs from the principal. Lots of opportunities for questions and suggestions.

MEET THE BOARD CANDIDATES–Date to be announced (February)

Board members and candidates for the Board present their platforms and answer questions.

MARKET FAIR–Thursday, March 20, 19XX

Sponsored by the English and Social Studies Department. This evening features a book fair and flea market of obsolete treasures and student-made objects, as well as a chance to familiarize parents with the materials and programs of these departments.

DRAMA PRESENTATION "CAMELOT"

Thursday, March 27, 19XX–2:30 p.m.
Friday, March 28, 19XX–8:00 p.m.
Saturday, March 29, 19XX–8:00 p.m.

POTPOURRI OF ACTIVITIES–Thursday, April 25, 19XX

The Activity Arts and Physical Education Departments join in sports exhibitions, fashion shows, art shows, foods, metal, wood and small engine demonstrations.

. . .Of Professional Activities

To: ALL MEMBERS OF THE PROFESSIONAL STAFF
From: THOMAS H. SMITH, SUPERINTENDENT
Re: PROFESSIONAL ACTIVITIES–OPENING OF SCHOOL

The schedule for the "Professional Days" preceding the start of actual school sessions for the school year is as follows:

Monday, August 14	– 9:30 a.m.–Secondary Principals–Discipline and Attendance Procedures.
Wednesday, August 16	– Elementary principals will return to duty. Each principal will develop the schedule of the building secretary. Check with Mr. Hemming to complete staffing needs.

Thursday, August 17	– Registration for new pupils–9:00 a.m. to
Friday, August 18	– 11:00 a.m. and 1:00 p.m. to 3:00 p.m.
Tuesday, August 22	– 9:30 a.m.–Elementary principals at Central Office–Early Strategies, New Programs, etc.
Wednesday, August 23	– 9:30 a.m.–Secondary principals at Central Office.
Wednesday, August 30	– Administrative Council meets in Central Office.
Thursday, August 31	– *The high school and junior high schools* will be open from 9:00 a.m. to 3:00 p.m. for those Department Supervisors to come in and meet with new teachers. Teachers new to the secondary schools are invited to visit with their departments. *The elementary schools* will be open from 9:00 a.m. to 3:00 p.m. and all teachers new to the district are invited to visit their assigned buildings and review assignments with the principal.
Friday, Sepetember 1	– Teachers are to report to their assigned buildings at 8:30 a.m.
Tuesday, September 5	– Orientation Day for Kindergarteners: Morning session pupils–9:00-10:00 a.m. Afternoon sessions pupils–10:30-11:30 a.m. The building principals will arrange the schedule for teachers not involved with the orientation program.
Wednesday, September 6	– All schools will open at regularly scheduled times.

. . .Of School Year

ROCK TOWNSHIP PUBLIC SCHOOLS

SCHOOL CALENDAR FOR 19XX-XX

Friday	September 1, 19XX	Professional Day
Monday	September 4, 19XX	Labor Day Holiday
Tuesday	September 5, 19XX	Professional Day and Kindergarten Orientation
Wednesday	September 6, 19XX	All District Schools Open

CALENDAR

Monday	October 9, 19XX	Schools Closed for Columbus Day
Tuesday	October 10, 19XX	In-Service Day K-12
Wednesday	October 11, 19XX	Schools Closed
Thursday	November 2, 19XX	Schools Closed for State Teacher's Convention
Friday	November 3, 19XX	Schools Closed for State Teacher's Convention
Monday	November 6, 19XX	Schools Closed for Conferences and In-Service
Tuesday	November 7, 19XX	Schools Closed for Election Day
Thursday	November 23, 19XX	Schools Closed for Thanksgiving Day
Friday	November 24, 19XX	Schools Closed for Thanksgiving Recess
Friday	December 22, 19XX	Schools Closed at End of Day–Winter Recess
Tuesday	January 2, 19XX	All Schools Open at Regular Time
Monday	January 15, 19XX	Schools Closed for Martin Luther King Day
Monday	February 12, 19XX	Schools Closed for Lincoln's Birthday
Monday	February 19, 19XX	Schools Closed for Washington's Birthday
Thursday	April 12, 19XX	Schools Closed at End of Day–Spring Recess
Monday	April 23, 19XX	All Schools Open at Regular Time
Monday	May 28, 19XX	Schools Closed for Memorial Day
Friday	June 22, 19XX	Schools Closed at End of Day

POSSIBLE NUMBER OF DAYS

	Students	Teachers		Students	Teachers
September	18	20	February	18	18
October	19	20	March	22	22
November	16	17	April	15	15
December	16	16	May	22	22
January	21	21	June	16	16

Total for Students – 183
Total for Teachers – 187

NOTE: Days when schools are closed for emergency purposes will be made up at the end of the school year or by reducing vacation time.

Any such action will be in accordance with R.T.E.A. contractual obligations.

. . .Of Sporting Events

ROCK TOWNSHIP HIGH SCHOOL
FOOTBALL SCHEDULE

All home games are played on the athletic field. All games start at 2:00 p.m. unless otherwise indicated.

H = Home Game A - Away Game

DATE	OPPONENT	PLACE
September 23	Kennett Township	A
September 30	Ballminster	H
October 7	Round Ridge	A
October 14	Hays Township	A
October 21	Framton	H
October 27*	Cranshaw	A–8:00 p.m.
November 4	Merkin Township	H
November 11	St. Patrick's	A
November 18	Multonville	H
November 23**	Kellerton	H–11:00 a.m.

* Special Friday Night Game at the Cranshaw High School Stadium at 8:00 p.m.

** Thanksgiving Day Game at Home at 11:00 a.m.

CAREER (See Also: ADULT EDUCATION; ALUMNI; EMPLOYMENT; JOB; WORKING PAPERS; WORK-STUDY PROGRAM)

. . .Career Day

(A) follow-up letter to those involved

Dear ______________________________,

Please accept my thanks and the thanks of the student body for making our recent Career Day such an outstanding success. I am sincere in saying that we could not have done it without you. Your interest in our school, your understanding, and your expertise all contributed to the making of a memorable and informative Career Day for our students.

I hope that you are in some way aware of the contribution you have given and the impression you made upon our students.

I do hope that I may call upon you for future Career Days.

Thank you again for all your help.

Sincerely,
J. Benson, Principal

(B) notice to parents concerning

Dear Parents,

On Thursday, April 23, 19XX we shall be holding a "Career Day" at Rock Township High School. This is a program in which members of the professional and business community come to school and talk to the students concerning their various careers and the requirements and expectations of each. It is hoped that this will lead to informed choices of careers by our students.

If you should wish to attend this activity, please call the school at 234-5678, and we will make arrangements for your visit.

Sincerely,
J. Benson, Principal

(C) program for

CAREER DAY PROGRAM

Students have signed up to attend three programs and have been given passes to specific classes. Below is a list of the speakers and the rooms in which they will appear. At the beginning of Period 5, students will report to the first program on their schedule. At the bell they will proceed to the second, and at the bell ending that period, they will proceed to the final program. Attendance will be taken by the teacher in charge.

Have a good day!

CAREER	ROOM	EXPERT	CAREER	ROOM	EXPERT
Radio	100	Mr. John Bell	Modeling	200	Ms. Linda Martin
Beauty	101	Mrs. W. Harris	Accounting	201	Ms. S. Lenze
Mechanic	102	Mr. J. Telser	Grocer	202	Mr. W. Jenkins
Army	103	Capt. L. Hansen	Electrician	203	Mr. S. Norton
Writer	104	Mrs. K. Wens	Engineer	204	Mrs. A. Sesten
Police	105	Sgt. B. Thomas	Doctor	205	Dr. M. Simon

CAREER	ROOM	EXPERT	CAREER	ROOM	EXPERT
Insurance	106	Mrs. E. Kristen	Lawyer	206	Ms. G. Benata
Merchant	107	Mr. R. Gainor	Druggist	207	Mr. H. Lenser
Teacher	108	Mr. J. Benson	Repairman	208	Mr. D. Pease
Construction	109	Mr. Singler	Public Relations	209	Mrs. G. Barnett
Technician	110	Mr. W. Harten	Secretary	210	Mrs. S. Garry

(D) request to participate in

Dear ______________________________,

We could use your help. We are planning a "Career Day" to be held at Rock Township High School on Thursday, April 23, 19XX. During this activity we invite various business persons, professional persons and community leaders to come to our school and speak to our students concerning the careers they have chosen. These volunteers explain to our students the requirements for the career, what they may expect from the career (both good and bad), and give some personal insights from their own experience. We have found in the past that our students are greatly impressed by the speaker who presents the "inside story" of a career from a personal point of view. We know that this day is instrumental in helping our students choose their future careers.

May we count upon you to join us on that day? We know our students would enjoy listening to you, and we are certain that you will find the day rewarding.

Please call me at 234-5678 and let me know your decision. We would like to have you in our school, and we thank you for considering our request.

Sincerely,
J. Benson, Principal

. . .Career Education

(A) evaluation of program

CAREER EDUCATION

SCHOOL YEAR: ____________________

NUMBER OF	FALL	SPRING	TOTAL
Courses Offered			
Teachers Needed			
Students Involved			
Field Trips			
Outside Speakers			
Students Passed			
Students Failed			
Boys Taking Course			
Girls Taking Course			

COMMENTS FROM STUDENTS: ____________________

____

COMMENTS FROM PARENTS: ____________________

____

TEACHER COMMENTS: ____________________

____

Date: __________ Signature: ____________________

(B) notice to parents concerning

Dear Parents,

As you know, it is time for your son or daughter to select those courses which he or she will take next year at Rock Township High School. Among the courses listed on the selection sheet given to your child is a new one to be started in September entitled "Career Education." We would like to explain this a bit more fully.

We all live in an age when new career opportunities are opening up every day. Indeed, jobs exist today that were not dreamed of when you and I were young. At the same time, unemployment is at an all-time high. Part of the problem lies in the fact that many of these jobs have specialized requirements, and many applicants are simply not prepared.

This is where a course in Career Education could be of help to your son or daughter; by learning what careers are available and what each career requires in regard to preparation for it. In this way, it is hoped that the student may make an intelligent, informed choice regarding his or her future career choices.

We urge you to consider this course for selection by the student.

Sincerely,

CERTIFICATION (See Also: DEGREES; REFERENCES)

. . .Notification of Receipt

Date: ____________________

Dear ____________________,

This is to inform you that we are in receipt of your certification as follows:________

____

As soon as it has been processed and copied by us, it will be returned to you.

Thank you for your cooperation.

ROCK TOWNSHIP BOARD OF EDUCATION

. . .Request for

Date: ____________________

Dear____________________,

As you are aware, your appointment to the position of ____________________

____________________required certification as follows: ____________________

____

To date we have not received your certification. Please see to this matter immediately. Your certification will be returned to you upon processing by our office.

Thank you for your cooperation.

ROCK TOWNSHIP BOARD OF EDUCATION

CHAIRPERSONS (See Also: DEPARTMENTAL MEETINGS; UNIT CO-ORDINATION)

. . .Evaluation of

EVALUATION

CHAIRPERSON: ______________________________

DEPARTMENT ______________________ DATE: __________

NUMBER OF TEACHERS IN DEPARTMENT: ______________________

FOR THE SCHOOL YEAR 19___ – 19___

Check YES or NO for each of the following. If NO is checked, explain on a separate sheet.

ITEM	YES	NO
Met all deadlines		
All reports completed		
All observations completed		
Budget adequately prepared		
Held all required meetings		
Requisitions and forms completed		

OBSERVED RAPPORT BETWEEN CHAIRPERSON AND MEMBERS OF DEPARTMENT: ______________________________

____

____

WAYS IN WHICH CHAIRPERSON HAS MET PERSONAL OBJECTIVES: __________

____

____

OUTSTANDING ACTIVITIES OF THE DEPARTMENT: ______________

____

____

PERSONAL COMMENTS: ______________________________

____

____

Signature of Evaluator: ______________________

Signature of Chairperson: ______________________

. . .Job Description

(A) committee

MEMO

To: FACULTY
From: J. BENSON, PRINCIPAL
Re: COMMITTEE CHAIRPERSONS

From time to time it will be necessary to form committees and to appoint chairpersons of those committees. It shall be the duty of the chairperson to:

1. Assume responsibility for steering the committee to the completion of its assigned task.
2. Assign meetings when necessary for work and study.
3. Assign tasks in the committee.
4. See to it that proper minutes are taken of each meeting.
5. Be responsible for providing informal reports of progress to the principal.
6. Prepare and present a final report in writing of the findings or results of the committee's work.

It is hoped that this delineation of duties will simplify and define the tasks of all committee chairpersons.

(B) department heads

MEMO

To: ALL DEPARTMENT HEADS
From: J. BENSON, PRINCIPAL
Re: DUTIES

In reply to a number of requests, the following is a delineation of the duties of Department Chairpersons:

1. The Chairperson shall prepare and submit to the principal the annual budget for the department and all teachers within that department.

2. Chairpersons shall observe and evaluate each member of the department as follows: Tenured Teachers once per semester; Non-Tenured Teachers twice per semester. A copy of each evaluation shall be submitted to the principal.
3. Chairpersons shall keep account of textbooks and equipment used within the department and shall be responsible for replacement, repair and/or ordering.
4. Chairpersons shall conduct monthly departmental meetings to insure the implementation of curriculum.
5. Chairpersons shall keep those records as required by the main office including but not limited to percentage of promotion sheets, textbook usage forms, failure notices, etc.
6. Chairpersons shall distribute, collect and turn into the main office those forms, papers, cards, etc. as required.
7. Chairpersons shall receive and act upon complaints and suggestions of department members, immediately forwarding to the office any difficulties which cannot be amicably settled within the department.
8. Chairpersons shall submit an annual report of doings within the department.

CHILD STUDY TEAM (See Also: LEARNING DISABILITIES; PSYCHOLOGICAL SERVICES; REFERRAL; RETENTION; SPECIAL EDUCATION; UNIT COORDINATION)

. . .Request for Services of

CHILD STUDY TEAM

Request for Services

DATE:____________

NAME OF CHILD:____________________________ BIRTHDATE:____________

ADDRESS:______________________________________ PHONE:____________

SCHOOL: ____________________ GRADE:________TEACHER:_____________

REASON FOR REFERRAL:

A. Describe the child's school behavior and academic functioning that are of concern to you (specific examples are more helpful than generalized statements):

B. What have you been trying so far in handling the problem(s)?

C. To what extent are the child's parents aware of the problem?

SPECIALIZED SERVICES PROVIDED CURRENTLY OR IN PREVIOUS YEARS (e.g., speech therapy, specialized counseling, physical therapy, visual training, tutoring, individualized prescriptive or supplemental instruction):

PERTINENT CUMULATIVE FOLDER INFORMATION (e.g., retention; persistent problems; strong points; etc.):

PERTINENT HEALTH INFORMATION (to be filled in by school nurse):

Most recent screening (dates and results):
Visual:
Auditory:
Other recorded medical information:

SIGNATURE OF PRINCIPAL:________________________________

. . .Status Report Form

STATUS REPORT

TO: ________________________________ DATE: ____________

(Name of School)

FROM: ____

(Team Member Sending Memo)

RE: ____

(Student's Name and Grade)

Dear ____________________,

In response to your referral, I have been assigned to evaluate this student.

I shall try to keep you informed as to the progress of my evaluation.

If you have any additional information or any questions, please:

1. leave a message for me with your school secretary, and I will try to see you on my regularly scheduled day at your school; or
2. call me at 345-6789 and, if I am not in, leave a message with my secretary.

Thank you for your help.

Signature: ______________________________

CITIZENSHIP (See Also: ACHIEVEMENT; APPRECIATION; AWARDS; DISCIPLINE; HONOR ROLL; LEADERSHIP; RIGHTS AND RESPONSIBILITIES)

. . .Award for Good Citizenship

Date: ____________

To Whom It May Concern:

Be it known that

____

a _______ grade student at

ROCK TOWNSHIP HIGH SCHOOL

is awarded this certificate for

OUTSTANDING CITIZENSHIP

and particularly for

____

____

Awarded by: ______________________________

____

. . .Letter of Appreciation for

Dear Bob,

As principal of Rock Township High School it is often my unpleasant duty to contact students for disciplinary reasons. It fills me with happiness, therefore, to be able to write to you to compliment you on your very fine record in school.

At a time when the darker side of human nature is exploited in every newscast, it is gratifying to know that in students such as you is demonstrated the finest which mankind hopes to attain.

I would just like you to know that your fine citizenship at Rock Township High School is deeply appreciated by all of us.

May your future hold happiness and success.

Sincerely,
J. Benson, Principal

CLASS (See Also: ATTENDANCE; BULLETIN BOARD; CUTTING; LESSON PLANS; STUDENT TEACHER; SUBSTITUTE TEACHER; TEACHER AIDE)

. . .Record Form

CLASS RECORD

Month:________________________ Subject: ______________________

STUDENT	DAILY GRADE	MONTHLY AVERAGE

. . .Rules of the Class

1. Students are to be on time for class or have a pass explaining their tardiness. Unexcused tardiness is not permitted.
2. Always be polite. Extend courtesy and aid to those around you. Use words like "Please" and "Thank you." Try never to embarrass anyone.
3. If you wish something, raise your hand and wait until you are recognized by the teacher. Then ask fully and completely.
4. Homework is due on the day for which it was assigned. Late homework will be penalized if there is no acceptable reason why it is late.
5. The bell does not dismiss the class–the teacher does.
6. Whenever there is a guest in our room, whether a teacher or student, that guest is to be treated with respect.
7. You are here to learn. If you do not understand something–ask.
8. It is your responsibility to make up work after an absence. The same goes for missed tests and assignments. I will not go to you–it is your responsibility to ask me.
9. Extra help will be available to anyone who wishes it. Please see me, and we will arrange a convenient time.

10. You are not likely to be allowed to throw things around or generally "mess up" your home. It is expected that you will take pride in your school as well. Before leaving the room, each student is responsible for cleaning the area around his or her desk.

11. The class will proceed in an orderly fashion. Consequently there will be relative quiet unless otherwise instructed. If you wish to speak, raise your hand, and you will be recognized.

12. If you need to use the lavatory or see the nurse, come to my desk and ask quietly.

13. Obscene, profane or vulgar language, hitting anyone, mocking anyone, destroying property, cheating and bad manners WILL NOT BE TOLERATED AT ANY TIME.

14. All the rules of the school apply.

IF EVERYONE COOPERATES, THERE IS NO REASON WHY WE SHOULD NOT HAVE A HAPPY AND PRODUCTIVE SCHOOL YEAR.

. . .Schedule of Student Assignments

(A) in class

CLASS ASSIGNMENT SCHEDULE

SUBJECT	MONDAY	TUESDAY	WEDNESDAY	THURSDAY	FRIDAY
	22	23	24	25	26
Math	homework		homework		homework
English			composition		spelling
Science				report	
History		test			
Civics				debate	
Art		sculpture			
Music	report				

(B) out of class

OUTSIDE ASSIGNMENT SCHEDULE

STUDENT	MONDAY	TUESDAY	WEDNESDAY	THURSDAY	FRIDAY
Adams, Kelly	Office Aide 10-11:15		Office Aide 9-10		Office Aide 11-11:30
Carren, Tom		Trumpet Lesson 1-2		Trumpet Lesson 1-2	
Dorin, Bill	Reading Lab 2:15-3	Reading Lab 9:15-10	Reading Lab 10-10:45		
Lorsky, Mary	Nurse's Aide 9-10			Nurse's Aide 9-10	Nurse's Aide 10-11

. . .Student Work Assignment Sheet

WORK ASSIGNMENT SHEET

For the week of _________ to ________ , 19 ______

TASK	STUDENT	TASK	STUDENT
Windows	Bill Howard	Board	Sally Emmons
Paper	Jill Lacy	Art Supplies	Jack Kelton
Books	Mary Hunt	Monitor	Bobby Chorter
Homework	Tim Intor	Bulletin	Kelly Greene
Basket	Judy Rich	Milk	Stuart Lansley

Alternate (if any listed student is absent): Randy Maslow

CLEANUP (See Also: BUILDING; CAFETERIA; LUNCH; WASTE)

. . .Message to Students

MEMO

To: ALL STUDENTS
From: J. BENSON, PRINCIPAL
Re: CLEANUP DAY

As your teachers may have told you by now, Friday of this week has been designated as Cleanup Day. On that day Homeroom Period will be extended for 20 minutes in order that students may clean out lockers and desks. There will be extra refuse baskets in the hallways and you are reminded that all trash is to find its way into those baskets. After all, we want to keep our school clean, even on Cleanup Day.

Students are to report to Homeroom and await word from the office before beginning cleanup operations.

Let's make this Cleanup Day the smoothest-running, best ever.

. . .Note to Teachers

MEMO

To: ALL TEACHERS
From: J. BENSON, PRINCIPAL
Re: CLEANUP DAY

As you know, Friday has been designated as Cleanup Day for the entire school. Several large trash baskets will be placed throughout each hallway. It is imperative that teachers impress upon students that what they clean out of their desks and lockers should be placed *in* these baskets and not on the floor, as this latter action somewhat negates the purpose of the day.

I know I can count on your supervision and cooperation.

CLERICAL SERVICES (See Also: SECRETARY; SUPPLIES)

. . .Request for

REQUEST FOR CLERICAL SERVICES

Name: ____

Date: ______________ Grade or Subject: ______________________

I hereby request the following clerical service(s):
Nature of Service (Describe in Detail): ______________________

____

____

Date Service is Required: ______________________________

Where Required: ____________________________________

Reason For Requesting Clerical Aid: ______________________

Signature: ______________________

. . .Requisition Form for Supplies and Equipment

REQUISITION OF CLERICAL SUPPLIES

Name: ______________________ Date: ______________

School: ______________________ Position: ______________

I hereby requisition the following supplies for clerical use:

ITEM #	QUANTITY	DESCRIPTION

Place of Delivery: ______________________________

Date of Delivery: ______________________________

Signature of Person Making Request: ______________________

CLOSING OF SCHOOL (See Also: DISMISSAL PROCEDURE; EMERGENCY; FIRE DRILLS; JUNE; VACATION)

. . .Emergency Closing

EMERGENCY CLOSING OF SCHOOL

The following procedures are to be followed in cases where the school is to be dismissed earlier than the regular time:

1. Students will be notified via the Public Address System to get their coats and report to homeroom.
2. When students have reported to homeroom, attendance is to be taken, and a list of students suspected of cutting is to be sent to the office.
3. Rooms will be dismissed in sections via the Public Address System.
4. Under no circumstances are teachers to dismiss their classes prior to notification from the office via the Public Address System.
5. During the homeroom period and throughout dismissal, the following teachers are assigned to direct students to their homerooms and to assist during dismissal inside and outside of the building:

OUTSIDE	INSIDE
Mr. James – front (buses)	Miss Jacobs – Area between 200-205
Mr. Lee – " "	Mrs. Stevens – " 206-210
Mr. Warren – " "	Mrs. Kelly – " 100-105
Mr. Harte – Jay Rd. (buses)	Ms. Lane – " 106-110
Mr. Calter – " "	Mrs. Hanks – West Wing Exit
Mr. Innis – " "	Mr. Wender – South Wing Exit
Mr. Thomas – Parking Lot	Mr. Lenk – West Wing Bathrooms
	Mr. Kern – South Wing Bathrooms
	Mr. Leon – Shop Area
	Mr. Petrov – Gym Area

6. Upon dismissal of a homeroom the teacher in charge will go to the bus loading areas and assist with supervision.

. . .End of School Year

CLOSING OF SCHOOLS FOR THE SCHOOL YEAR 19XX-19XX

ALL SCHOOLS:

June 22 – Last day of school for students. School will close at the regular time.

June 23 – Last day for teachers. Procedures for the completion of all obligations will be made on a school level.

PRINCIPALS AND TEACHERS:

June 23 – Each principal will bring the following to the Central Office as soon as possible:

Registers
Statistical Reports
Enrollment Sheets (June)
Failure Notices
Tolls – Fines – All Other Reports

PAYDAYS:

The middle of June payday will be June 15th. The final check will be presented at the school to each teacher who is present on June 23rd. Checks for teachers who are absent on June 23rd shall be returned to the Central Office and will be mailed pending any necessary adjustment.

Those teachers on payroll deduction will make arrangements for summer payments by contacting the Teacher's Credit Union.

Home instructors are to get their time sheets and progress reports into Ms. Anderson's office by Tuesday, June 27, 19XX at the latest in order for the sheets to be processed and charged to the 19XX-19XX Home Instruction account.

PROMOTION, FAILURE AND RETENTION:

High School:

High School teachers shall fill out on a sheet of paper the names of the pupils in their assigned classes who have failed to pass, with explanation of the reason for such failure. The grade status of a high school student is determined by his success in passing certain numbers of points toward graduation.

CLOSING OF SCHOOL

Junior High Schools:

Junior High School teachers shall fill out on a sheet of paper the names of the pupils in their assigned classes who have failed to pass, with explanation of the reason for such failure. Promotion to the next grade level in the Junior High School, if the pupil is a seventh or eighth grader, is determined by conferences between the various teachers of a given pupil and administrative officials in accordance with Junior High School policy on retention.

Ninth grade students will have their status determined for the following year at the total number of secondary level credits they have passed. Ninth grade students are treated in the same way as senior high school students in this regard.

Elementary Schools:

Elementary teachers are asked to fill out only a list of pupils to be retained. Promotion lists or enrollment lists for the following year are filled out elsewhere. Promotion or retention at the elementary level is decided upon by the teachers, the principal, and the elementary supervisor, and often the parents of the child will be involved in this decision.

PERCENTAGE PROMOTION SHEET:

Each elementary school principal is to prepare a percentage promotion sheet for each grade level in the building; that is, Grade 5–enrolled 122, passed 116, retained 6–Percentage 95%.

In the Junior Highs and in the High School, a percentage promotion sheet is to be made by subject rather than by grade level; that is, English 9B, enrolled 100, passed 90, failed 10–Percentage 90%. This should be done by Department heads in the High School and Junior High Schools.

ENROLLMENT SHEETS IN THE ELEMENTARY SCHOOLS:

Enrollment sheets for next year should be made up at this time and handed to the principal. The principal will keep these enrollment sheets available in his desk. If the principal wishes to change the make-up of certain classes, this can be done readily. If there is no change, the enrollment sheets are ready to be handed out next fall.

PERMANENT RECORD CARDS:

Elementary Schools:

The classroom teacher is responsible for bringing the Permanent Record Card for each of her pupils completely up to date by the year's end.

Junior High Schools:

At the 7th, 8th and 9th Grade levels, bringing the Permanent Record Card up to date by the end of the year is the responsibility of the Guidance Department.

High School:

At the 10th, 11th and 12th Grade levels, the responsibility for bringing the Permanent Record Card up to date by year's end is that of the Guidance Department.

BOOK RECORD SHEETS AND FINES:

The record of books should remain in the possession of the individual school. If this is done, and books on which fines have been paid are subsequently returned by pupils, refunds can be handled through the school.

When fines have been collected, the building principal should turn over the complete amount of the fines to the Office of the Secretary of the Board of Education. The principal will receive, from the Secretary of the Board, a receipt for all such fines.

FINANCIAL RECORDS:

Records of school funds, and all papers concerning school funds, are to be turned in by the building principal to the Central Office when other reports are turned in. Information connected with the receipt or disbursal of school moneys should be placed in an envelope correctly marked with the school name, so that this information will be available to the school auditor.

TEXTBOOKS–SURPLUS–REBOUNDS:

Please refer to Business Office Bulletin #126, dated June 8, 19XX.

SUMMER ADDRESSES:

An envelope is provided for every teacher who will be returning in September, for the purpose of mailing the assignment sheet about the middle of August. After the teachers have self-addressed them, the envelopes should be put in alphabetical order and returned to the Central Office.

FINAL REPORTS AND RECORDS:

Final reports and records must be up to date before teachers leave. The Building Principal will turn in to this office the reports and records due here and will keep all other records in his or her office.

TITLE I TEACHERS:

All Title I teachers will work in accordance with the schedule distributed by Mrs. Carlson.

Best Wishes for a Happy Summer!

Jonathan T. Cronin,
Assistant Superintendent

. . .Inclement Weather

To: ALL PARENTS OF ROCK TOWNSHIP SCHOOL CHILDREN
From: OFFICE OF THE BOARD SECRETARY
Re: INFORMATION RELATING TO SCHOOL CLOSING AND TELEPHONE CALLING

This information on the subject of school closings due to weather or other conditions is intended to provide all parents with relevant information in this regard.

1. The decision to close school is made by 5:30 a.m.
2. The township fire sirens are set off at 6:30 a.m., 7:00 a.m., and 7:30 a.m.
3. The school closing announcement is broadcast by two radio stations:
   WUVW – 1234 AM – 81.2 FM
   KXYZ – 1345 AM – 82.1 FM
4. The switchboard of the Board of Education should not be called for confirmation of the closing. The decision to close is usually a day-to-day matter, so avoid calling for an answer on "tomorrow," as the switchboard when jammed (i.e. *200* calls an hour) restricts incoming and outgoing telephone calls.
5. Announcement or cancellation of non-school-hour programs and athletic programs due to inclement weather or other reasons is announced over radio stations WUVW and KXYZ once the decision is made by the proper authorities.
6. ABOVE ALL–DO NOT CALL THE ROCK TOWNSHIP POLICE DEPARTMENT ABOUT SCHOOL CLOSINGS. THE POLICE SWITCHBOARD, WHEN TIED UP BY THESE CALLS, CANNOT HANDLE ITS OBLIGATIONS TO RECEIVE AND

RESPOND TO POLICE EMERGENCY CALLS, FIRE EMERGENCY CALLS, AND FIRST AID EMERGENCY CALLS.

REMEMBER–Unnecessary calls prevent actual emergencies from being received.

CLUBS (See Also: EXTRA-CURRICULAR ACTIVITIES; LEADERSHIP; NEWSPAPER; YEARBOOK)

. . .Evaluation of

Name of Club or Activity: ______________________________

Evaluator: ______________________________ Date: ______________

Number of Students Involved in the Activity: ______________________

From What Grade(s): ______________ Faculty Advisor: ______________

Nature of Club or Activity: ______________________________

____

ITEM	NEEDS IMPROVEMENT	SATIS-FACTORY	GOOD	EXCEL-LENT
Rapport between advisor and student				
Student interest				
Involvement of most students				
Meeting needs of students				
Student loyalty to club				

COMMENTS: ____

____

____

Signature of Evaluator: ______________________ Date: ____________

Signature of Advisor: ______________________ Date: ____________

. . .Letter Soliciting Participation

AN OPEN LETTER TO ALL STUDENTS OF ROCK TOWNSHIP HIGH SCHOOL:

As we begin this school year I would like to remind you that a school is more than a building filled with classrooms, just as your educaton is more than a mark on a report card or a term paper. School is also the people who are in it, and your education continues with all the experiences you encounter in your school career.

Toward that end, I would like to draw your attention to the fine array of clubs and extra-curricular activities which are provided for you. Participation in these clubs can open up worlds of pleasure and fulfillment for you.

Take advantage of what the school has to offer, and you will look back on these days as happy and profitable ones for all concerned.

With best wishes for a great school year,

J. Benson, Principal

COMPLAINTS (See Also: ACCOUNTABILITY; DEMONSTRATIONS; PARENTS; PETITIONS; REJECTION; REPRIMANDS; SUGGESTIONS)

. . .Explanation of Procedures for

MEMO

To: ALL STUDENTS AND FACULTY
From: J. BENSON, PRINCIPAL
Re: COMPLAINT PROCEDURES

In any institution the size of Rock Township High School, it is inevitable that there will arise complaints on a number of subjects. If and when these arise, part of their solution lies in following certain procedures in each case. Therefore, whenever a legitimate complaint arises, the following procedures are to be taken:

1. Those with complaints should go to the Main Office and obtain a Student or Faculty Complaint Form.
2. This form is to be filled out, describing the complaint in detail, signed (unsigned forms will NOT be considered) and returned to Mrs. Zeller in the main office.
3. Within a week you will receive a reply from me regarding the disposition of your complaint.

4. If you disagree with that disposition, you may arrange for a personal conference.

Hopefully, these procedures will help give every person at Rock Township High School the opportunity to be heard.

. . .Reply to

COMPLAINT REPLY FORM

To: ______________________________

From: J. Benson, Principal

I have read your complaint dated ____________________ , 19____ concerning

____

____

The disposition of your complaint is as follows: ____________________________

____

____

____

I hope this meets with your satisfaction. If it does not, please arrange for a conference at a time of mutual convenience.

Date: ______________ Signature: ______________________________________

. . .Student's Form

STUDENT COMPLAINT FORM

Name: ____ Grade: ____________

Home Room: ______ Home Room Teacher: ______________________________

I would like to make the following complaint (Describe your complaint as fully as possible. Remember that FACTS and not OPINIONS are important.):

____

____

____

Date: ______________ Signature: ______________________________________

. . .Teacher's Form

TEACHER'S COMPLAINT FORM

Name: ______________________________

Grade and/or Subject: ______________________________

I would like to initiate the following complaint (The Faculty is reminded that those complaints tendered must be within the range of possibility of the Administration to correct and should not be within those frames of reference which require arbitration as outlined in the agreement between the Rock Township Board of Education and the Rock Township Education Association.):

____

____

____

____

Date: ____________ Signature: ______________________________

CONFERENCES

(See Also: COUNSELING; GUIDANCE; INTERVIEW; NEGOTIATIONS)

. . .Evaluation of

CONFERENCE EVALUATION FORM

DATE: ______________________________

PEOPLE PRESENT: ______________________________

____

REASON: ______________________________

____

OUTCOME: ______________________________

____

RECOMMENDATIONS: ______________________________

____

. . .Notice of Upcoming

Dear Parents,

The Guidance Department of Rock Township Junior High School will be scheduling students for High School courses on Tuesday, Wednesday and

Thursday, April 21, 22 and 23, 19XX. On those evenings from 7:30 to 10:30 p.m., we shall be holding conferences with students and their parents. Scheduling will be done at these conferences in order to allow all questions to be answered and to assure that everyone is satisfied with the final schedule.

You and your son/daughter, ________________________, have been tentatively scheduled for a conference with ________________________

on ________________________________, ____________________,

19______ at ________ p.m.

If this time is inconvenient, please call the Guidance Department at 345-6789 and arrange for an alternate conference time or date. You may also inform us if you wish us to proceed with the scheduling without a conference.

We look forward to seeing you soon.

Sincerely,

. . .Request to Come for

Dear Mr. & Mrs. ______________________,

__________________ to __________ on ____________________

has been set aside as the time I would like to confer with you concerning your child's progress. The conference will be held in the homeroom.

For scheduled conferences to be successful, the time limits set must be strictly adhered to. As the conference progresses, if you or I see that more time is necessary, we will arrange an additional appointment.

Sincerely,

______________________________ : Teacher

. . . . PLEASE DETACH AND RETURN PROMPTLY . . . .

( ) We shall attend the conference as scheduled.

( ) The time is inconvenient. I shall call the school office at 234-3232 and request another time.

______________________________ : Parent

CONFIRMATION (See Also: MEMO; NOTE PADS; PASSES; REPRESENTATION; SIGN-IN SHEETS)

. . .Form for Multiple Usage

To: ____

From: J. Benson, Principal

Date: ______________________

This shall confirm our:

( ) conversation
( ) meeting
( ) correspondence
( ) appointment
( ) conference

on (Date): ____
at (Time): ____
Re: ____
____
Comment: ____
____
____

. . .Of a Conversation

Date: ______________________
To: ______________________
From J. Benson, Principal

This shall confirm our conversation on ____________, 19___ at approximately ______________________

In that conversation we discussed the following:

____
____
____

Thank you for taking the time to talk.

CONGRATULATIONS

(See Also: ACHIEVEMENT; BOARD OF EDUCATION; DEGREES; JOURNALS; NATIONAL HONOR SOCIETY; PUBLICATION)

. . .To Faculty

Dear Faculty,

I felt I had to take this opportunity to congratulate you on the fine showing you made during our recent evaluation.

Your efforts were evident everywhere–in the smooth and efficient running of the classroom and the school; in the knowledge and social interaction of the students; in the professional attitude manifested by the entire staff; in the fine commendation provided us by the evaluating team.

The report of the team stands as a monument to your many hours of devotion and your professionalism.

You are to be congratulated on the attainment and implementation of the highest ideals of our profession.

Sincerely,
J. Benson, Principal

. . .To Students

To All Students,

Recently, we were visited by a team of people from the State Department of Education. As you are aware, these people observed classes, traveled throughout the school and spoke to many of you concerning the state of our school.

The report of these people has just reached me, and I am happy to say that we received a very fine evaluation indeed.

That is why I feel that I must congratulate you. In a very real sense, the success of the school is your success, for you are the school. Your attitude, your understanding and your academic abilities all contributed to the final outcome.

Please accept my congratulations on your fine showing. I look forward to working with you throughout the remaining school year.

Sincerely,
J. Benson, Principal

CONTRACT

(See Also: EXTRA-CURRICULAR ACTIVITIES; NEGOTIATIONS; NON-RENEWAL OF CONTRACT; VENDORS)

. . .Budget Form for Contracted Services

Contracted Services for the School Year July 1, 19XX to June 30, 19XX

Name: ______________________________ Room: __________

Department: ______________________ Number: __________

DIRECTIONS: Include all contracted services or any services which you think may become contracted items. These include repairs and maintenance of office machines, sewing machines, IA equipment, AV equipment, other instructional equipment, mop services and other building equipment services presently under contract. Please include justifications.

Annual Cost of Contract		Equipment or Item or Service
	GRAND TOTAL	

. . .Extra-Curricular

TO: ______________________

RE: Extra Contract Employment for the School Year 19XX-19XX

This is your extra contract as ______________________ in the Rock Township Public Schools for the school year in the amount of $ __________.

Thomas Smith,
Superintendent of Schools

- - - - - - - - - - - - Please Detach and Return to Central Office - - - - - - - - - - - -

( ) I hereby accept
( ) I respectfully decline

the extra contract as ______________________ in the Rock Township Public Schools for the school year in the amount of $ __________.

Date: __________ Signature: ______________________

. . .Professional Duties

TO:________________________________

RE: Employment for the School Year 19XX-19XX

At the meeting of the Rock Township Board of Educaton held on ______________, 19_____, you were approved for employment in the Rock Township Public School System for the school year 19___ - 19___, beginning September 1, 19____, and ending June 30, 19___, at a yearly salary of $_____________.

If it is your desire and purpose to continue in the employ of the Rock Township Board of Education for the school year listed, at the above salary, please sign and return the attached slip within the next two weeks.

. . . .

1. It is my desire and purpose to continue in the employ of the Rock Township Board of Education for the school year 19 ___ - 19___, beginning September 1, 19___ and ending June 30, 19___, at a yearly salary of $ _________________ in accordance with the action of the Rock Township Board of Education at the meeting held on _________________________, 19 __________.

2. According to the Board of Education policy, I hereby certify that before I drive a car on school property, said vehicle will be covered by liability and property damage insurance.

(Signed): ________________________________

(School): ________________________________

. . . .

OR:

3. It is my purpose to resign from the employ of the Rock Township Board of Education at the close of the present school year, and my resignation is herewith presented, effective as of that time.

(Signed): ________________________________

(School): ____________________________

CONVENTION (See Also: IN-SERVICE; PROFESSIONAL ASSOCIATION)

. . .Budget Form for

Name: ______________________________ Room: __________

Department: ______________________________

DIRECTIONS: Include all conventions (workshops, etc.) for which you wish to have paid travel, registrations, meals and lodging. Keep in mind the fact that each teacher has a limited number of professional days each year. Including all anticipated postage and/or printing costs.

ITEM	COST	DESTINATION AND EVENT
Workshops,		
Conventions,		
Etc.		
Postage		
Printing		
Professional		
Literature		
TOTAL		

. . .Notice to Faculty

MEMO

To: FACULTY
From: J. BENSON, PRINCIPAL
Re: CONVENTION

In a few days the convention of the state Education Association will be taking place. We are given released time for this annual event, and I urge you to attend. After all, we are never to old to learn, and we owe it to our students, our profession and ourselves to keep abreast of the latest developments in the field.

See you at the convention!

COUNSELING (See Also: CONFERENCES; GUIDANCE; INTERVIEW; PARENTS; REFERRAL; TUTORS)

. . .By Outside Agencies

Dear Dr. Mellinger,

We have been advised by the parents of Robert Henderson that he is currently undergoing psychiatric evaluation and counseling at your center pursuant to the conditions of probation set down by Juvenile Court Judge the Honorable Jamison T. Rath.

Also pursuant to that probationary order, a copy of your evaluation is to be sent to the Rock Township High School Guidance Department. Please address the report to:

Mr. Howard K. Lennel
Guidance Office
Rock Township High School
Rock Township,___________

We would also appreciate it if you would place the word "CONFIDENTIAL" on the envelope.

We stand ready to offer you whatever assistance you may require.

Sincerely,
Howard K. Lennel,
Director of Guidance

. . .Notification to Parents of

Dear Parents,

Rock Township High School, in an effort to meet the needs of its students, has a full staff of qualified and certified counselors in the Guidance Office who stand ready to aid students at any time with anything from personal and academic problems to scheduling and college placement.

COUNSELING

An individual student may request counseling on his own or such counseling may be instigated by parental request. As a matter of policy, each student is counseled at least once during each school year.

If you have any questions or if you should wish counseling for your son or daughter, please call the Guidance Office at 234-5678, Extension 12. We will be very happy to speak with you.

Sincerely,
H. K. Lennel,
Director of Guidance

. . .Report on

REPORT ON COUNSELING SESSION

Person Counseled: ______________________________

Session Number: ______________ Date: ______________

Place Held: ______________________________

Counselor: ______________________________

Persons Present: ______________________________

____

Problem(s): ______________________________

____

____

Disposition: ______________________________

____

____

Date of Next Counseling Session: ______________________________

Counselor's Comments: ______________________________

____

____

. . .Request for

Date: ______________________________

I request that the following student be seen for a counseling session:

Name of Student: ______________________________

Grade: __________ Home Room: ______________________________

Reason for Referral: ____

____

____

Should a report be sent? ( ) YES ( ) NO

If Yes, to whom? ____

____

Signature: ______________________________

Relation
to Student: ______________________________

COURSE OF STUDY (See Also: CURRICULUM; GOALS; MINI-COURSES; OBJECTIVES)

. . .Guidelines for Preparation

MEMO

To: COURSE-OF-STUDY COMMITTEE
From: J. BENSON, PRINCIPAL
Re: GUIDELINES FOR PREPARATION

As you begin your work on revising our course of study, I want to tell you how much I, personally, appreciate your efforts. I would also like to share with you a few guidelines which have proven helpful in the past.

1. A course of study must be within the legal requirements of the Statement Department of Education.
2. It should reflect the needs, standards and aspirations of the students, their parents and the community at large.
3. It should be direct and clear, avoiding language which is in any way confusing.
4. It must be usable and viable and within the possibility of implementation under existing budgetary limitations.

With these guidelines in mind and with your record of devotion to the ideals of Education, I know you will do an outstanding job.

. . .Principal's Message

The following course of study has been prepared after many long hours of investigation and study. It is designed to meet the needs of the students of Rock Township High School. If you will read it carefully with a thought toward the future, you will find that it offers a wide variety of choices intended for a complete education and preparation for future endeavors.

I sincerely hope that the students of Rock Township High School will take advantage of what is offered.

J. Benson, Principal

CURRICULUM (See Also: ACCOUNTABILITY; COURSE OF STUDY; GOALS; OBJECTIVES; PHILOSOPHY; UNIT COORDINATION)

. . .Form for Curricular Revision

REQUEST TO REVISE CURRICULUM

Date: ____________ Department: ______________________________

Person Making Request: ______________________________

Curriculum to be Revised: ______________________________

____

Section(s): to be Revised (Identify by page number, section letter and/or number.):

____

____

How Would it Be Revised: ______________________________

____

____

Explain the Need for this Revision: ______________________________

____

____

Would you be willing to work on this revision? ( ) Yes ( ) No

. . .Sample Section of

page 5

Language Arts

GRADE 3

I. Writing

A. Skills and Abilities

1. Using correct letter formation for capitals and small letters in manuscript writing.
2. Writing for freedom and ease.
3. Using manuscript writing to write one's own ideas.
4. Learning to space between letters and between words.
5. Bring slant manuscript to one space, but do not stress slant print.
6. Using correct letter formation for capitals and small letters in cursive writing.
7. Stress paper position, pencil holding, slide and slant in cursive writing–special care for left-handed students.
8. Taking pride in writing clearly, neatly and legibly.
9. Distinguishing appropriateness of handwriting for different occasions or purposes: rough draft, corrected copy, rewritten copy.

. . .Survey of Community Needs

Dear Parents,

In an effort to better meet the needs of the community it serves, Rock Township High School is in the process of revising its curriculum. Toward that end, we are requesting your aid. Of the ten statements below, would you please place the number one (1) before that statement you feel is the most important. Then place a number two (2) before the second most important, and place a three (3) before what you consider to be the third. There is space provided if you wish to include one of your own. Please feel free to make any comments you would like on the back of this sheet. Please return this sheet in the enclosed postage-paid envelope.

Sincerely,

J. Benson, Principal

- -

( ) Each child should be given a firm foundation in the basics of math, reading and English composition.

( ) Children should be given practice in critical thinking in order that they may make intelligent choices as adults.

( ) Children should develop an interest in and an appreciation for the Creative Arts both as participant and observer.

( ) Children should learn to tolerate and understand a diversity of cultures, races and nationalities other than their own.

( ) Children should be given a basis in physical fitness and a desire to pursue physical activity as an adult.

( ) Children should be made aware of various systems of political government and current political affairs.

( ) Children should be given a basis of morality along accepted non-denominational, philosophical lines.

( ) Children should learn all the ramifications of family living—economic, emotional and sexual.

( ) Children should have exposure to various careers in order that they may choose wisely when the time comes.

( ) Children should learn acceptable behavior in a variety of situations.

( ) ____

____

THANK YOU FOR YOUR COOPERATION!

CUSTODIAL SERVICES (See Also: BUILDING; CLEANUP; WASTE)

. . .Request for

NAME: ______________________________ DATE: __________

I hereby request custodial services as follows:

LOCATION	CONDITION WHICH REQUIRES CUSTODIAL ATTENTION

Signature: ______________________________

. . .Requisition Form for Supplies and Equipment

School: ______________________ Date: __________
Head Custodian: ______________________

I hereby request the following supplies and equipment for custodial care:

QUANTITY	ITEM #	DESCRIPTION	DATE NEEDED

( ) will pick up supplies ( ) please deliver to the school

Signature: ______________________

CUTTING

(See Also: ABSENCE; CLASS; DETENTION; PASSES; REFERRAL; TARDINESS)

. . .Class Cutting Form

Teacher: ______________________ Date: __________

PERIOD	ROOM	SUBJECT	ABSENT
1			
2			
3			
4			
5			
6			
7			
8			

Teachers are to record the names of absent students, check against the Absentee Sheet, and circle those names not on the sheet. This form is due in the Main Office at the end of the Teacher's school day.

. . .Of Assigned Detention

Teacher Reporting:____

Date:______________________

This is to report that ______________________________________,

Grade__________, was assigned detention on ___________________

for the following reason(s):_________________________________

____

____

He/She did not report to this assigned detention although attendance records indicate that the student was present in school.

. . .Policy on

The following shall be the school's policy on and procedures for identifying and dealing with the wanton cutting of class:

1. Daily attendance is taken by the teacher.
2. Suspected cutters' names are submitted to the office on the daily absentee sheet.
3. The office will verify the cuts and publish a cut list.
4. The teacher will complete an office referral indicating date and period of cut and previous action taken (e.g., parent called 2/23; detention assigned 2/25; etc.).
5. The student should receive no credit for the day's work unless it is made up to the satisfaction of the teacher.
6. Three (3) demerits will be assigned by the office.
7. Possible action for repeated violations include:
   A. Assignment to the Alternate School Program
   B. Five-day notice and a home visit by the Truant Officer
   C. Parent contact and conference in school
   D. Suspension from school in some instances

D

DEGREES (See Also: ACCEPTANCE; ACHIEVEMENT; APPLICATION; CERTIFICATION; CONGRATULATIONS; GRADUATION)

. . .Application for Acknowledgment of

Name: ______________________________ Date: ____________

School: ______________________ Grade and/or Subject: __________

Current Step on Salary Scale: ______________________________

Current Salary: ______________________________

Current Placement (i.e. BA; BA+10; MA+20; etc.): ____________________

New Degree Attained: ______________________________

Date Presented: ______________ Subject Area: ______________

Institute Granting Degree: ______________________________

Were Courses and/or Degree approved by the
Board of Education prior to taking: ( ) Yes ( ) No

New Placement on Salary Scale: ______________________________

. . .Congratulations on Attaining

Dear Mrs. Hendri,

How pleased I was to learn that you will be receiving a Master of Arts Degree at the commencement exercises of Holcroft University.

Your efforts in achieving this distinction are indicative of the drive, dedication and expertise which have marked your career at Rock Township High School and have made you such an outstanding teacher.

Please accept my heartiest congratulations on attaining your degree. I look forward to working with you in the future.

Sincerely,
J. Benson, Principal

...Letter of Acceptance of Honorary Degree

Dear Dr. Winter,

I was both pleased and humbled to receive your letter notifying me that you intend to present me with an Honorary Doctor of Humanities Degree at your college's commencement exercises. I was pleased to think that you would consider me for this honor and humbled to realize that this honor comes from as prestigious an institution as yours.

I shall be honored to accept this honorary degree in the name of the educators of our Township. I look forward to meeting you at the commencement exercises.

Sincerely,
J. Benson , Principal

DEMONSTRATIONS

(See Also: BOARD OF EDUCATION; COMPLAINTS; PETITIONS; PUBLIC RELATIONS)

...Policy of the Board on

The Board of Education recognizes the right of citizens to peaceful dissent. It feels, however, that the key word is "peaceful," and any demonstration, dissent, etc. that destroys property or threatens physical harm to any person is little more than vandalism and in no way may be classified as "peaceful dissent."

Therefore, should a demonstration or other overt form of dissent occur, the following steps shall be taken:

1. The principal shall immediately call the Central Administration Offices and inform them of what has occurred.
2. The principal shall wait for a representative of the Board of Education. They shall then address the student demonstrators, trying to determine the grievances of those individuals.
3. Student leaders are to be invited to discuss the matter with the Board Representative. All other students are to be invited to return to class.

4. Whatever the students choose to do, at this point all doors to the school will be locked, the understanding being that no student will be restrained from leaving the building, but, once outside, students will not be permitted to return.
5. Disciplinary action and/or further handling of the situation shall fall to the Representative of the Board of Education.
6. The only exception to the above procedures shall be if there exists a situation which obviously threatens the safety or well-being of the school and/or its occupants. In such a case (i.e., a fire set in the school; students throwing bricks through the windows; etc.), outside civic authorities are to be called before notifying the Board of Education.

. . .Report on

To: ROCK TOWNSHIP BOARD OF EDUCATION
From: J. BENSON, PRINCIPAL OF ROCK TOWNSHIP HIGH SCHOOL
Re: DISTURBANCE OF MAY 27, 19XX

1. At 9:37 a.m. I was informed by Mr. Thomas Merton, a physical education teacher at the school, that a number of students had left class and were gathering on the side of the hill to the north of the school.
2. At 9:40 a.m., having ascertained that, while noisy, the group was not overtly destructive, I notified the Board Office and was informed that a representative would arrive shortly.
3. At 9:47 a.m. Dr. Ralph Crenshaw, Assistant Superintendent of Schools, arrived, and we walked to the place where the students had assembled.
4. At 9:51 a.m. we reached the students who numbered approximately 75. Both Dr. Crenshaw and I spoke to the students and attempted to ascertain the reasons for the walkout.
5. By 10:08 a.m. we had discovered that 1.) there was no apparent leader, 2.) it was a particularly warm day, and the classrooms were uncomfortably hot, and 3.) the students felt that the rooms should be air-conditioned.

6. Dr. Crenshaw spoke with the group and explained the alternatives to and ramifications of their actions. At 10:15 a.m. I requested the students to return to class, informing them that the doors would be locked by 10:30 a.m.
7. By 10:30 a.m. all but seven (7) students had returned to class. Those seven students were informed that they were considered to be cutting class, and if they did not return, they would be treated as such.
8. By 10:35 a.m. four additional students returned to class. The three remaining students left school grounds. The names of these students were referred for disciplinary action.
9. By 10:40 a.m. all had returned to normal.

DEPARTMENTAL MEETINGS (See Also: CHAIRPERSONS; FACULTY MEETING; IN-SERVICE)

. . .Agenda for

ENGLISH DEPARTMENT MEETING

Thursday, November 14, 19XX

AGENDA

2:30–2:40	–Minutes of last meeting, correspondence sent and received.	–Ms. Talman
2:40–2:45	–Report of Textbook Committee	–Mr. Neri
2:45–3:05	–Instructions for Budget Preparation; New Budgetary Requirements; Explanation of New Budget Form	–Mrs. Rassler
3:05–3:10	–Questions and Answers	–All
3:10–3:15	–English Department Holiday Party	–Mr. Harrington

. . .Evaluation of

ENGLISH DEPARTMENT MEMO

To: ALL DEPARTMENT MEMBERS
From: K. RASSLER, CHAIRPERSON
Re: EVALUATION OF DEPARTMENTAL MEETINGS

May I ask your help? I'd like you to fill out the following questionnaire and return it to my mailbox by Friday, June 16, 19XX. Please do not sign your name, and please be honest in your answers. It is my sincere hope that this evaluation will lead to improved departmental meetings in the future.

1. Using 1 as the worst and 10 as the best, how would you rate our meetings this year? 1. __________
2. Have the day and time of the meetings been convenient? 2. __________
3. Have the meetings been an aid to you in the running of your classes? 3. __________
4. Have the meetings been informative, providing insights you could not have gotten elsewhere? 4. __________
5. Did you have an opportunity to ask all the questions you wanted to ask? 5. __________
6. Did everything you wanted to discuss get covered? 6. __________
7. Did the chairperson monopolize the time or deny time to anyone? 7. __________
8. Was your "paper work" made easier by our meetings? 8. __________
9. What one thing about our meetings would you improve: __________

    ____

    ____

10. Any Comments? ANYTHING: ______________________________

    ____

    ____

. . .Notice to Department Members

ENGLISH DEPARTMENT MEMO

To: ALL MEMBERS OF THE ENGLISH DEPARTMENT
From: K. RASSLER, CHAIRPERSON
Re: DEPARTMENT MEETING

We will be holding our monthly departmental meeting on Thursday, November 14, 19XX in Room 207 from 2:30–3:15 p.m.

This meeting is extremely important since it concerns our budget allotments. Since we are all interested in having enough supplies to last the year, I look forward to seeing you all this Thursday afternoon.

DETENTION (See Also: CUTTING; DISCIPLINE; REFERRAL; TARDINESS)

. . .Notice to Office of Assignment

NOTICE OF ASSIGNED DETENTION

____________________________ , a _________ grade student has been assigned detention by me on __________________ , 19 ___ because ________

____

____

Date: ____________ Signature: __________________________________

. . .Notification of Parents

Dear ______________________ ,

Your son/daughter _________________________ is being kept after school on ____________________________ because:

( ) Lessons poorly prepared or not done
( ) Inattention in class
( ) Work not done on time
( ) Unsatisfactory test score
( ) Poor attitude in class
( ) Absenteeism
( ) Frequently comes to school without books, pencils, etc.

( ) Other: ______________________________

____

____

The length of the detention will be 40 minutes after the close of school. If you have any questions, please call 253-8725 and ask to speak to me.

Sincerely,

____

Teacher

. . .Policy on

DETENTION

Students may be asked to stay after school for special help, to work off demerits, or for teacher and central detention. Students are expected to tell their parents twenty-four hours in advance of the date that they will be staying after school. All students are responsible for reporting at the time and place designated.

. . .Reminder Form

DETENTION REMINDER

This is a reminder that you have been assigned detention on ______________

______________, 19 ______________ in Room ________

with ______________________________.

Date of Reminder: ______________________________

Student Signature: ______________________________

Teacher Signature: ______________________________

DISCIPLINE

(See Also: ASP; BEHAVIOR; CITIZENSHIP; DETENTION; FAILURE; PARENTS; REFERRAL; REPRIMAND; SUSPENSION; VANDALISM)

. . .Code of Discipline

(NOTE: Under BEHAVIOR we have covered discipline procedures for behavior *within* a school. Discipline also extends to the school grounds and should concern itself with the safety of students coming to and going from school. The following discipline code is reflective of that latter philosophy.)

OUTSIDE SCHOOL RULES

Bicycles

Main Building

1. Walk bicycles inside the barricades
2. No DOUBLE riding
3. Ride bicycle on right sidewalk going toward Baily Street
4. Stop at Baily Street and obey the crossing guard
5. Bicycles going up Boulder Road stay to the right

Bicycles

Center

1. No DOUBLE riding
2. Park bicycles in racks along west wall of Center Building
3. NO foolish riding around Center Building Parking Lot

Walkers

1. Stay on cement walk coming out of the building
2. Walk on the left hand side going to Baily Street
3. No running into streets
4. Stop and obey the crossing guard at Baily Street
5. Walkers going up Boulder Road cross by the barricade on Peter's Place and walk up the left hand side of Boulder Road to Chamber's Drive
6. Only students living in Westwood Development are to go that way

Playground Rules

1. No throwing objects (such as tennis ball, football, etc.)
2. NO pushing or fighting
3. At the bell, line up quietly and obey the teachers and patrol on duty
4. No rough play or running on the playground

. . .Letter to Parents Concerning Infractions

Dear ________________________ ,

We regret to inform you that your son/daughter,__________________ ______________, a _____________grade student at Rock Township High School, has been referred to the office for disciplinary action on a number of occasions, and we felt that you would want to be appraised of the situation.

During the period from _______________ to _______________ your son/daughter was referred for:______________________________

____

____

____

We are certain that you must be as concerned about this situation as we are. May we suggest that a conference might prove beneficial for all concerned. You may call 234-5678 to arrange for a meeting.

Sincerely,
J. Benson, Principal

. . .Notice of Improvement

Dear ________________________ ,

We are pleased to inform you that your son/daughter ______________ a ____________ grade student at Rock Township High School, has shown improvement in his/her behavior and attitude toward discipline. Specifically: ______________________________

____

____

We are happy to be able to report this improvement, and we thank you for your cooperation in this matter,

Sincerely,
J. Benson, Principal

. . .Notice to Student

To: ______________________________

Grade: ______________ Home Room: ______________

In the period from ______________ to ______________ you have been referred to the office for disciplinary reasons on ________ occasions.

If this pattern continues, it could have serious consequences in your life.

Please come to the Guidance Office and arrange for an interview immediately, but no later than ______________________.

Counselor: ______________

. . .Referral Form

DISCIPLINARY REFERRAL

Student's Name: ______________________ Date: __________

Grade: ______________________ Teacher: ______________

NOTICE TO PARENTS

1. The purpose of this report is to inform you of a disciplinary incident involving the student.
2. You are urged to both appreciate the action taken by the teacher and to cooperate with the corrective action initiated.

REASON(S) FOR REFERRAL:

( ) Class Disruption
( ) Cutting Detention
( ) Cutting Class
( ) Lack of Cooperation
( ) Inappropriate Language
( ) Smoking on School Grounds
( ) Insubordination
( ) Safety Violations

( ) Fighting
( ) Destructive to School Property
( ) Unprepared for Gym
( ) Rude; Discourteous
( ) Misconduct in Cafeteria
( ) Truancy
( ) Other (Please Comment): ______________________

____

____

ACTION TAKEN PRIOR TO REFERRAL:

( ) Consulted Counselor
( ) Changed Student's Seat
( ) Telephoned Parents
( ) Gave Corrective Assignment
( ) Held Conference With Parent
( ) Detained Student After School
( ) Held Conference With Student
( ) Other (Please Comment):

____

____

____

PRESENT ACTION AND RECOMMENDATION(S) (For Office Use Only):

( ) Case Referred to ______________
( ) Student Suspended
( ) Placed on Restricted List
( ) Student Will Make Up Time
( ) Parent Conference Requested
( ) Talked to Student–Warned
( ) Other (Please Comment): ______________________

____

____

For Office Only–Number of Referral for This School Year: ______________

DISMISSAL PROCEDURES

(See Also: ABSENCE; BUS; CLOSING OF SCHOOL; JUNE; MAP OF THE SCHOOL; VACATION; YEAR-END REPORT)

. . .Early

EARLY DISMISSAL

In the event of early dismissal from school for whatever reason, the procedures for normal dismissal shall be followed with the following exceptions:

1. Teachers in Rooms 200–212 will proceed to the bus loading areas and supervise the leaving of all buses.

2. Teachers in Rooms 100–112 will supervise the halls and see to it that ALL students leave the building within five minutes of the dismissal.
3. Five minutes after the early dismissal, the custodians will lock all doors except the exit by the main office.
4. Teachers may leave five minutes after the last child has left the building.

. . .Final Day of School

MEMO

To: ALL FACULTY
From: J. BENSON, PRINCIPAL
Re: DISMISSAL PROCEDURES FOR THE LAST DAY OF SCHOOL

In order to insure a safe and rapid dismissal on the final day of school, the following procedures and assignments have been developed. The cooperation of the entire faculty is imperative for its success. I know that I can count on you.

1. General Information:
   A. No students are to be sent to the library or out of any classroom without a pass from the teacher.
   B. Lavatories will not be open during periods 7 and 8.
   C. Once students are outside, all interior doors (except for the door by the main office) will be locked.
2. From the beginning of Period 8 until 15 minutes after dismissal, the following staff members are assigned as follows:

FIRST FLOOR:

Mr. Bartrum	Exit 11 (Near Shop Area)
Mrs. Colfax	Exit 10 (Near Nurse's Office)
Mr. James	Exit 7 (Gym Corridor)
Mr. Kerrington	Exit 8 (Near Side Parking Lot)
Mr. Lennel	Exit 1 (Main Door)
Mr. Hartnett	Exit 4 (Near Room 112)
Mrs. Wenz	Exit 2 (Across from Guidance)
Miss Johnson	Exit 3 (Near Room 108)

Mrs. Farrel	Exit 6 (Near Room 107)
Mr. Carlson	Exit 5 (Near Library)
Mrs. Houseman	Exit 12 (Near Room 101)

SECOND FLOOR:

Mrs. Marks	North Stairs Exit (Near Room 200)
Mrs. Geller	Center Stairs Exit (Near Room 205)
Mrs. Palusi	South Stairs Exit (Near Room 212)

OUTSIDE:

Mr. Quinn	Side Parking Lot
Mrs. Innes	Front Parking Lot
Mrs. Renner	Front Parking Lot
Mr. Dalton	Front of Building

3. Dismissal Procedures:
   A. On a staggered schedule, rooms will be dismissed via the Public Address System or in person by an administrator.
   B. Teachers are to ACCOMPANY their classes to the outer doors specified, and then are to take their assigned bus duty posts.
   C. Once outside, no student will be permitted in the building.
4. Dismissal Schedule:

FIRST DISMISSAL:

Rooms 200, 201, 202, 203, 204, 205, 206	–Center Stairs ONLY to Exit 3 and out
Rooms 207, 208, 209 210, 211, 212	–South Stairs ONLY to Exit 4 and out

SECOND DISMISSAL:

Rooms 100, 101, 102 103, 104, 105 106	–Exit 3 ONLY
Rooms 107, 108, 109, 110, 111, 112	–Exit 2 ONLY

THIRD DISMISSAL:

Gyms, Shop Classes, and All Activity Arts Rooms	–Main Door ONLY

5. Bus Duty Posts:

FRONT OF BUILDING:

Ms. Yarrow
Mr. Manners
Mrs. Falthough
Mr. Keats
Mrs. Hunt
Mrs. Melville
Mr. Calle
Mr. Kranmer
Mr. Vickers
Mrs. Tanner
Ms. Halley

ROUND RIDGE ROAD:

Mr. Jacobs
Mr. Jordan
Mrs. Baily
Mr. Shelly
Mrs. Todd
Mrs. Arran
Mr. Geld
Mrs. Lansing
Mrs. Monk

. . .Normal

DISMISSAL PROCEDURES

1. The bell ending the school day shall ring at 2:45 p.m.
2. Bus Duty teachers will lock their rooms and report to their assigned bus loading areas where they will supervise until all buses leave.
3. After School Hall Duty teachers will supervise in the halls. By 2:50 p.m. all students are to be either out of the building or engaged in extra-curricular activities, detention, or extra help.
4. All teachers will help to supervise students leaving the building.

DRESS CODES (See Also: BEHAVIOR; HANDBOOK)

. . .Example of Legal Dress Code

DRESS CODE

In the matter of hair style, The Board of Education recognizes that students have the right to exercise judgment so long as they do not:

1. Present a danger to their health and safety, or the the health and safety of the staff and student body;

2. Cause an interference with school work or create a classroom disorder;

With regard to student dress, the Board of Education specifies the following policy:

1. Students shall not wear clothing deemed to be a safety hazard with regard to the activity being undertaken.
2. Dress which restricts the student from doing his or her best work is discouraged.
3. Styles that create or may create a classroom disturbance are not permitted.
4. Articles of clothing which cause excessive wear or damage to school property are not permitted.
5. Wearing apparel which may be a health hazard to the student is not permitted in school without a doctor's permission.

. . .Policy on

POLICY ON DRESS AND GROOMING

It is the purpose of the Board of Education in the matter of student dress and grooming to enhance the health and safety of the students and to avoid distractions to the educative process. It is neither the intention of the Board of Education to usurp parental prerogatives for determining appropriate grooming and dress for their children, nor to use style, fashion, or taste as a sole criterion for exclusion from instruction.

DRINKING OF ALCOHOLIC BEVERAGES ON SCHOOL GROUNDS

(See Also: BEHAVIOR; BUILDING; DISCIPLINE; HANDBOOK; POLICE AND JUVENILE AUTHORITIES; REFERRAL)

. . .Notice to Parents

Dear ______________________ ,

Please be informed that on____________________, 19 ___, your son/daughter______________________________, a ___________ grade student, was reported to the main office for the possession and/or consumption of alcoholic beverages on school grounds. Specifically:

____

____

____

As you may be aware, this is a violation of the policy set down by the Rock Township Board of Education.

That policy sets a three-day suspension as punishment for the offense, and your son/daughter is hereby suspended from school on __________,
____________, and ___________, 19 _________.

You are urged to discuss this matter with your child. If you have any questions, please call me at 234-5678.

Sincerely,
J. Benson, Principal

. . .Policy on

While the Rock Township Board of Education recognizes that alcoholic beverages may be a part of the social interaction of many adults, it is also aware that the students are not adults, and that the school building and grounds are public buildings. As public buildings they are subject to Rock Township Municipal Code 27:18-46. Therefore, the consumption and/or possession of alcoholic beverages on school grounds shall not be allowed. Adults who violate this policy shall be subject to the Municipal Code mentioned above; students will receive a three-day out-of-school suspension and parents will be notified of the reason for the suspension.

DRUGS (See Also: BEHAVIOR; DISCIPLINE; HANDBOOK; MEDICAL; POLICE AND JUVENILE AUTHORITIES; REFERRAL; SUSPENSION)

. . .Notification of Parents

Dear ____________________________,

We regret the necessity of having to contact you on a very serious matter. On______________________________, 19 ______ , your son/daughter, ______________________________________, a__________grade student at our school, was referred to our office for the illegal possession and/or use of drugs. Specifically:____

____

____

As we are sure you are aware, this is a violation not only of the Board of Education policy, but of civil law as well.

Your son/daughter is hereby suspended from school pending action of the Board of Education. You and your son/daughter have certain legal rights in these actions, and you are requested to call 234-5678 at your earliest convenience to arrange for a conference.

May we hear from you soon?

Sincerely,
J. Benson, Principal

. . .Policy on

The possession and/or use of a controlled dangerous substance, narcotic, and/or other illegal drug or drugs as defined by State Law 29: 33-14 and 29: 33-15 are illegal and therefore prohibited on school grounds. Students found in possession of, or using, the aforesaid substances shall be suspended forthwith from school until such a time as the Board of Education shall act upon the case. The parents of the offending student shall be notified of their legal rights, and due process shall be followed. The Board reserves the right to call in outside civil authorities where it deems it appropriate.

E

EDITORIAL (See Also: NEWS COVERAGE; NEWSLETTER; NEWSPAPER; NEWS RELEASES; PUBLIC RELATIONS)

. . .Answering Editorials

(A) in local newspaper

Dear Sir:

In the Thursday, November 14, 19XX issue of the *Rock Township Register*, your editorial entitled "Toward Tomorrow" called for increasing courses that were geared for "the needs of tomorrow's citizens," specifically the introduction of courses in computer technology and programming. Your editorial further stated that Rock Township High School must be "held accountable" for this "disturbing lack of foresight."

As principal of Rock Township High School, I feel that I would indeed be derelict in my duties if I did not answer your comments and clear the air of an obvious misunderstanding. Some four years ago the courses which you mention were proposed by curriculum committees and subsequently approved by the Rock Township Board of Education. The only obstacles were the hiring of qualified teachers and the purchase of a computer commensurate with the needs of the classes.

As you are undoubtedly aware, the budget has been defeated for the past four years running. Each defeat entailed a reappraisal of monetary allotments, and the outlay for the computer courses had to be weighed against possible cuts in the basic curriculum. Surely, your newspaper is not suggesting that we cut back courses in basic English and math. No one wants that. At the same time, the courses you suggest will be possible only when there is a sufficiency of funds to allow for their implementation.

I fail to see, therefore, how you can hold Rock Township High School responsible for not offering courses which are beyond our fiscal possibility to offer.

Sincerely,
J. Benson, Principal
Rock Township High School

(B) in school newspaper

I am happy to have this oportunity to answer the editorial in the last issue of "The Rocket." In that editorial it was charged that the administration of this school did not take student opinion into account when making decisions. I feel that it is my duty to answer this charge.

In making decisions relative to the good of Rock Township High School, it has always been the policy and the practice of the main office to solicit opinions from the students, to advise them of the situation requiring change, and to involve students in the decision-making process wherever possible. Toward those ends we have placed suggestion boxes in the main office and guidance office, and all signed suggestions are answered. We have a process for making a complaint as well. The student council (which represents the student body) has been consulted on all matters that include the students of this school. Moreover, there has been established a Student Advisory Committee whose functions include investigating student response to various suggestions and directives from the main office.

To me, all of this certainly spells student involvement in every possible manner. If, however, there are other constructive suggestions that the editors of "The Rocket" have to offer, I always stand ready to discuss the matter with them.

J. Benson, Principal

. . .Principal's Editorial in Student Newspaper

It is a great pleasure to be able to write this editorial in the first issue of "The Rock Township High School Rocket" for this school year.

"The Rocket" is *your* school newspaper. As such it reflects and reports on the happenings at Rock Township High School over the school year. We are all a part of it, since it is a mirror of all that we do. Years from now, when we look back upon the hours and days spent here, it will be publications like "The Rocket" that will aid our memories and help us recall the activities, events and functions, the happy and the sad, the troubles and the triumphs of our school careers.

Let us, then, do everything in our power to support "The Rocket" and its efforts on our behalf. Make sure you get every issue. Read it, contribute to its efforts, and if you should disagree with any of its opinions or editorials, there is an opportunity for you to answer those statements by writing letters to the editor.

I know that my office will always be open to members of "The Rocket's" staff. I also hope that all students will cooperate and take advantage of all that is offered in this fine publication.

J. Benson, Principal

EMERGENCY

(See Also: ADDRESS; CLOSING OF SCHOOL; FIRE DRILLS; LESSON PLANS; MEDICAL; POLICE AND JUVENILE AUTHORITIES; VANDALISM)

. . .Emergency Information Card

To All Parents,

For your child's welfare, will you please fill in the following form and return it to school as soon as possible. This information will remain confidential and will only be used in the event that an emergency situation occurs involving your child.

J. Benson, Principal

. . . .

Student's Name: ______________________________

Address: ______________________ Home Telephone: __________

______________________________ Zip __________

Bus: __________ Home Room: ______ Grade: ______________

If not at home, where can the parents be reached?

Father: ______________________________

______________________________ Telephone: __________

Mother: ______________________________

______________________________ Telephone: __________

If you cannot be reached, please list the names of two persons (relatives, neighbors, etc.) who will assume temporary care of your child until you are available:

Person: ____________________

____________________ Telephone: __________

Person: ____________________

Any present conditions or allergies which should be known: __________

____

____

Your Child's Doctor: ____________________

____________________ Telephone: __________

Please read and sign the following statement:

In the case of an emergency situation such as an accident or serious illness, I understand that the school shall attempt to contact me. If I cannot be reached, I authorize the school to contact the doctor listed in this form and follow the doctor's directions. If the doctor cannot be contacted, I authorize the school to take whatever steps seem necessary.

Date: __________ Parent or Guardian: ____________________

. . .Emergency Procedure Form

Dear Parents or Guardians,

For the sake of your child's safety and well-being, will you please take time now to fill out the form below and return it to the school as soon as possible.

J. Benson, Principal

- -

If an emergency should occur involving my child, I wish the following procedures to be followed (Please place "1" before the action you wish to be taken first, place "2" before the action to be taken next, etc. If you do not wish a certain action performed, merely leave it blank.):

( ) Give first aid

( ) Contact School Nurse

( ) Call First Aid Squad and transport to ____________________ Hospital

( ) Call Doctor __________ at ____________________

( ) Call Mother at ____________________

( ) Call Father at ____________________

EMERGENCY

( ) Call neighbor (friend, relative) at ______________________________

( ) Bring child to ______________________________

( ) Other: ______________________________

____

Date: ____________ Parent or Guardian: ______________________________

. . .Emergency Situation Procedures

In the event of an emergency situation, all staff members will be notified via the Public Address system with the words "BUILDING CHECK."

Upon this notification, the following procedures will be followed:

1. TEACHERS IN ALL INSTRUCTIONAL ROOMS INCLUDING THE LIBRARY:
   A. Search desks, closets, file cabinets, etc.
   B. Send a student to the office with a note indicating the room number, the date, the teacher's signature and the words "ALL CLEAR."
   C. The office will check off these notes against a master list.
2. TEACHERS ON DUTY ASSIGNMENTS OTHER THAN THE CAFETERIA ARE TO REPORT TO THE MAIN OFFICE FOR ASSIGNMENT.
3. SHOULD A SUSPICIOUS OBJECT BE DISCOVERED:
   A. Never touch or move the object.
   B. Evacuate the instructional area.
   C. Notify the office that you have evacuated Room #____. This will be sufficient indication to the office that the entire school must be evacuated.
4. EVACUATION PROCEDURES ARE THE SAME AS FOR A FIRE DRILL.
5. GENERAL REMARKS:
   A. Please remain calm under all circumstances. Failure to do so may result in student panic and possible physical injury to students or staff.
   B. "ALL CLEAR" or "I HAVE EVACUATED ROOM #___" must be sent to the office immediately.

. . .Report on Emergency Situation

STUDENT ACCIDENT REPORT

Please report accidents to the office immediately. This report must be turned in on the same day as the accident. Thank you.

Student: ______________________________

Grade: ______________ Home Room: ______________

Date of Accident: ______________ Time of Accident: ______________

Location of Accident: ______________________________

Description of Accident: ______________________________

____

Description of Injury: ______________________________

____

What was the student doing at the time of the accident: ______________

____

Name and title of person supervising student at time of accident:

____

Signature: ______________________________

EMPLOYMENT (See Also: CAREER; JOB; WORKING PAPERS; WORK-STUDY PROGRAM)

. . .Employment Information Form for Students

STUDENT EMPLOYMENT INFORMATION

Name: ______________________________ Date: ______________

Grade: __________ Age: __________ Date of Birth: ______________

Home Address: ______________________ Telephone: ______________

______________________________ Zip: ______________

Experience (List jobs held): ______________________________

____

____

Type of Job Desired: ______________________________

____

Hours and Days Willing to Work: ______________________________

____

Wages Expected: ______________________________

Do you have working papers: ( ) Yes ( ) No

If the job requires working papers,
would you apply for them? ( ) Yes ( ) No

Do you have a means of Transportation?
( ) None ( ) Car ( ) Bicycle ( ) Family/Friends

Any statement you would like to make concerning your abilities and/or employment:

____

____

. . .Request for

EMPLOYMENT REQUEST

Name: ______________________________

Address: ______________________________

______________________________ Zip ______________

Telephone: ______________________________

This is to inform you that I am actively seeking employment on a ( ) Full Time ( ) Part Time ( ) Summer–Full Time ( ) Summer–Part Time basis. I shall be available beginning ______________________, 19 ________

Date: ______________ Signature: ______________________________

EQUIPMENT (See Also: SUPPLIES; TEXTBOOKS)

. . .A-V Equipment Budget Form

BUDGET FORM FOR AUDIO-VISUAL MATERIALS

Name: ______________________________

Department: ______________________________ Room: ______________

DIRECTIONS: Include the two general categories listed below. Do NOT include film rentals, field trips, or maps.

I. RAW MATERIALS: Example: Unexposed film, flash bulbs, blank video tape, etc. Please include justification.

TOTAL COST	ITEM	QUANTITY

II. PREPARED MATERIALS: Example: Filmstrips, records, prepared cassette tapes, prepared transparencies, etc.

TOTAL COST	ITEM	QUANTITY

GRAND TOTAL (Parts I and II): ______________________

. . .Equipment Replacement Form

Replacement of Equipment for Year: ______________________

Name: ______________________________________ Room: ______________

Department: __________________________________ Date: ______________

DIRECTIONS: Include replacement items of a permanent nature, usually costing above $25. A justification of need for each item or program must be written on the reverse side of this sheet. Absence of a justification statement or placement of an item on the wrong forms may result in the item being eliminated.

PRIORITY CODE: VHP = Very High HP = High MP = Medium LP = Low

PRIORITY	PROGRAM OR ITEM	QUANTITY	ITEM COST	TOTAL COST
			Total This Page	
			Grand Total	

. . .New Equipment Requisition Form

New Equipment for Year: ______________________

Name: ______________________ Room: __________

Department: ______________________ Date: __________

DIRECTIONS: Include NEW equipment, both instructional and other, such as furniture, machinery, etc. EQUIPMENT is usually interpreted as items which cost $25 per item or more and will have a useful life of two years or more. A justification of need for each item or program must be written on the reverse side of this sheet. Absence of a justification statement or placement of items on wrong forms may result in the item being eliminated.

PRIORITY CODE: VHP = Very High HP = High MP = Medium LP = Low

PRIORITY	PROGRAM OR ITEM	QUANTITY	ITEM COST	TOTAL COST
			Total This Page	
			Grand Total	

EVALUATION

(See Also: ACCOUNTABILITY; OBSERVATION; REPORT CARDS; SPECIAL EDUCATION; STUDENT INFORMATION; STUDENT TEACHER; YEAR-END REPORT)

. . .Guidelines for

PROFESSIONAL STAFF PERFORMANCE EVALUATION

The ultimate focus or purpose of supervision is the promotion of pupil growth through the improvement of instruction.

The purposes of teacher evaluation are:

A. To provide each teacher with an appraisal of professional strengths and weaknesses and total performance as an employee of the Board of Education.

B. To provide information that will aid the individual teacher to overcome weaknesses and more effectively utilize strengths.

C. To provide a basis for the improvement of instruction and pupil achievement.

D. To establish a total record of performance over a period of time, which upon review can show demonstratively whether professional strengths and weaknesses have improved or declined.

Improvement of instruction can and does result from in-service education, curriculum development, and the evaluation of the teacher's performance regarding the total education of the child. Evaluation of teachers is a *part* of the total supervisory process and is an essential responsibility of the school administration.

. . .Of Administrators

EVALUATION OF ADMINISTRATORS

It is the policy of the Board of Education that each employee of this system holding an administrative position shall be evaluated annually by his or her immediate supervisor.

The Superintendent shall prepare an evaluation form and procedures for the conduct of all evaluations that are mutually agreeable to the administrators.

The Superintendent shall report annually to the Board of Education on each administrator's performance.

. . .Of Self

SELF-EVALUATION

The following is an aid for self-analysis. Indicate by a check in the appropriate column that category which best describes you.

	NEVER	SELDOM	SOME-TIMES	OFTEN	ALWAYS
1. Possesses competence and knowledgeability in his or her field of work, and strives toward continued professional self-improvement.					

	NEVER	SELDOM	SOME-TIMES	OFTEN	ALWAYS
2. Maintains physical capability, alertness, and emotional readiness to teach.					
3. Exhibits high standards of moral and ethical conduct, and employs a wholesome sense of humor in dealing with people.					
4. Is fair and impartial in the treatment of pupils and recognizes the dignity of the child.					
5. Exhibits an understanding and acceptance of individual differences among students and provides for those differences.					
6. Works well in communicating with parents.					
7. Contributes significantly to the total functioning of the school.					
8. Explores and openly evaluates new approaches to teaching.					
9. Is receptive to suggestions for improvement.					

. . .Of Teachers (3 Forms)

(A) first form

Teacher: ____________________ Date: __________

Subject: ____________________ Period Observed: __________

QUALITY	ACCEPTABLE	IMPROVEMENT NEEDED
Control of the Class		
Planning of Lesson		
Motivation of Students		
Enthusiasm for Subject		
Ability to Communicate Ideas		
Rapport With Class		
Sense of Humor Displayed		
Recognizes and Provides for Individual Differences		
Appropriate Use of Materials		

COMMENTS:

Number of Evaluation This School Year: ____________________

Evaluator's Signature: ____________________

Teacher's Signature: ____________________

(B) second form

Teacher's Name: ____________________ Date: __________

School: ____________________ Time of Day: __________

Grade and/or Subject: ____________________ Evaluation Number: __________

Status of Teacher: ( ) First Year ( ) Non-Tenured ( ) Tenured

EVALUATION

EVALUATION CODE: A = Acceptable N = Not Acceptable U = Unobserved

	A	N	U
Classroom Management			
Appearance of the Room:			
Arrangement and condition of materials and equipment			
Orderliness and cleanliness			
Ventilation and lighting			
Decorations and bulletin boards			
Routine Procedures:			
Distribution and collection of materials			
Group Dynamics			
Teacher-Pupil Relationships:			
Rapport and control of group			
Provides for individual differences			
Pupil Attitudes:			
Student interest and participation			
Tolerance and respect for others			
Presentation			
The Assignment:			
Development and clarity			
Motivation			
Pertinence			
Teaching Techniques:			
Materials			
Motivation and planning			
Aim of lesson developed and realized			
Procedure, tempo and flexibility			
Pertinence			
Characteristics of Teacher			
Personal:			
Enthusiasm and warmth			
Voice and language			
Professional:			
Knowledge of subject			
Knowledge of good teaching methods			

EVALUATOR'S COMMENTS:

TEACHER'S COMMENTS:

Evaluator's Signature: ______________________

Teacher's Signature: ______________________

(C) third form

Teacher: ______________________ Date: ____________

Grade and/or Subject: ______________________ Time of Day: __________

Evaluation Number: ______________ Evaluator: ______________________

ITEM	SATISFACTORY	UNSATISFACTORY
The Classroom:		
1. Temperature and ventilation		
2. Arrangement of furniture and materials		
3. Bulletin boards and decorations		
4. Illumination		
5. Neatness		
Instruction:		
1. Control of class		
2. Planning		
3. Communication		
4. Motivation		
5. Recognition of individual differences		
6. Use of materials		
7. Rapport with students		
Personal Characteristics:		
1. Receptiveness to student needs		
2. Voice		
3. Enthusiasm and humor		

EVALUATOR'S COMMENTS:

TEACHER'S RESPONSE:

Evaluator's Signature: ____________________

Teacher's Signature: ____________________

EXAMINATIONS

(See Also: FAILURE; GRADES; HONOR ROLL; PERCENTAGE OF PROMOTION SHEETS; REPORT CARDS; RETENTION)

. . .Memo to Teachers on

MEMO

To: ALL TEACHERS
From: J. BENSON, PRINCIPAL
Re: UPCOMING EXAMINATIONS

As a very new teacher I was once expounding about a test I had constructed which would, I assured everyone, ". . .keep them studying all night!" An older and considerably wiser colleague remarked that he was not aware that I was giving a test on the ability to memorize.

He was right, of course, and over the years I, like all of us, have come to know that a test should be a diagnostic tool used to find out where a student is academically. Indeed, we are all aware that an examination given to fail, or for that matter to pass, a student is as worthless as a test of someone's ability to memorize 20 facts in five minutes.

I know that I can count on you to make the upcoming exams incisive, meaningful and truly reflective of the fine education that has been going on all year.

. . .Notification to Students of

To: ALL STUDENTS
From: J. BENSON, PRINCIPAL
Re: FINAL EXAMS

Very soon you will be taking your final subject-area examinations for the current school year. A schedule of the times and places will be given to you during homeroom period, and a master list will be placed on the bulletin board outside the main office as well.

I wish you well in your exams, and I'd like to remind you that if you have kept up with your classes all year long, you have nothing to worry about in your final exams. Review your notes and study for them by all means, but remember that what you have learned over this year has become a part of you, a part that you should be able to represent quite well in a final examination.

I am confident that you will all do extremely well.

. . .Policy Statement on

Examinations serve useful purposes, but there are many pitfalls in their use that we must attempt to avoid. They should not be threats held over the heads of the students to make them work. There are obvious reasons why examination marks must be consistent with the marks given for the marking periods.

Teachers are reminded that examination marks are but a part of the student's academic progress indicators, and that the whole picture must be taken into account when formulating a final grade.

EXCHANGE STUDENTS (See Also: BI-LINGUAL EDUCATION; LANGUAGE; MINORITIES)

. . .Letter of Farewell

Dear Jose,

How quickly a year has passed. It seems just yesterday that I was welcoming you to Rock Township High School, and here it is time to say goodbye.

You have been with us for a year, and in that time we have had the pleasure to get to know you well. We shall carry the memory of you with us through the years to come. We shall remember your kindness, your willingness to help and your ability to put us all at ease. We shall remember your inquisitiveness, your sense of humor, and the general good will which has been felt by all of us who knew you.

We have lived, laughed and studied with you; we have known you as our friend; we shall miss you greatly in the days ahead.

Remember us in future years as we shall keep your memory alive in our minds.

Our best wishes for your continued success in all you do.

With best wishes,
J. Benson, Principal

. . .Letter of Welcome

Dear Manuel,

Welcome to the United States of America and welcome to Rock Township High School. For the next year you will be a guest in our country as well as a student in our school. We hope that the time you spend here will be a profitable time for all of us.

We have much to learn about your country and your people, and we look forward to an exchange of understanding. We hope that we, in turn, may be of service to you, and we invite you to call upon us if there is anything we can do to make your stay more pleasant.

My office is open to you at any time as are the complete facilities of Rock Township High School. Please make use of them, and please visit us and let us get better acquainted.

Please accept my very best wishes for a happy and successful school year.

Yours sincerely,
J. Benson, Principal

EXTRA-CURRICULAR ACTIVITIES

(See Also: CLUBS; CONTRACTS; EVALUATION; NEWSPAPER; PUBLIC RELATIONS; SPORTS; YEARBOOK)

. . .Contract for

To: ______________________
From: Rock Township Board of Education
Re: Extra-Curricular Contract

The Board of Education has awarded you an extra-curricular contract for the school year 19__ -19 __ as follows:

NATURE OF CONTRACT: ______________________________________

____

SALARY: ______________________________________

Please fill out the form below, sign it, detach and return it to the Central Office as soon as possible. Thank you.

ROCK TOWNSHIP BOARD OF EDUCATION

. . . .

( ) I hereby accept the extra-curricular contract for the school year 19__-19 __ as follows:

NATURE OF CONTRACT: ______________________________________

____

SALARY: ______________________________________

( ) I do not wish to accept this contract.

Date: ______________ Signature: ______________________________________

. . .Form Indicating Student Interest in

Name of Student: ______________________________________

Grade: ______________________ Home Room: ______________

Home Room Teacher: ______________________________________

I am interested in the following activity(ies):

( ) Newspaper	( ) Yearbook
( ) Drama Club	( ) Cheerleaders
( ) Stamp and Coin	( ) Twirlers
( ) Chess Club	( ) Pep Club

( ) Modern Dance Club

( ) Please send me more information.
( ) Please send me an application form.

Date:____________ Signature:__________________________________

. . .Philosophy of

We believe that in considering the totality of an education there are certain aspects of personality development and social interaction which fall outside the realm of academic curriculum.

We further believe that extra-curricular activities provide just such opportunities outside of the curriculum for meeting with a variety of situations requiring social interaction and engendering personality growth. Along with development of social and personal graces, involvement in wholesome activities guided by competent faculty advisors may often provide an opportunity for the development and nurturing of a sense of morality and justice that will stand the student in good stead in later life.

We, therefore, feel that the school should do all within its power to sponsor, promote, and encourage extra-curricular activities and participation in them by the largest possible number of students.

F

FACULTY MEETINGS (See Also: ATTENDANCE; DEPARTMENTAL MEETINGS; IN- SERVICE)

. . .Agenda for

MEMO

To: FACULTY
From: J. BENSON, PRINCIPAL
Re: FACULTY MEETING AGENDA

May 22, 19XX–3:15 p.m.–Library

3:15–3:30–MR. BENSON–Elaboration and Interpretation of State Proficiency Tests
3:30–3:35–MRS. HARRINGTON–Failure Notices for the School Year
3:35–3:45–MR. KENNERT–Report of the Discipline Committee
A. Effectiveness of New Referral Form
B. Progress on New Discipline Code
3:45–4:00–MR. GIANISI–Explanation of Proposed Salary Scale for 19XX–19XX

. . .Notification of Staff

MEMO

To: FACULTY
From: J. BENSON, PRINCIPAL
Re: FACULTY MEETING

This is the one you won't want to miss! Not only will there be a few surprises from the discipline committee, but the results of the state-wide test are in. If that isn't enough, Mr. Gianisi will be discussing next year's salary guide!

It's all happening on Wednesday, May 22, 19XX at 3:15 p.m. in the library. See you there!

. . .Policy on

FACULTY MEETINGS

for the school year

19XX–19XX

Pursuant to the agreement between the Rock Township Board of Education and the Rock Township Education Association for the 19XX–19XX school year, the following policy on faculty meetings shall be followed:

1. There will be ten regularly scheduled faculty meetings for the school year with two additional meetings which may be called at the principal's discretion.
2. The meetings will take place on the last Wednesday of the month. Should this day not be available, the meeting will be held on the Wednesday preceding the normally scheduled meeting.
3. The meeting shall begin within ten minutes of the end of the school day and shall not exceed the length of a regular period of class instruction.
4. A portion of time shall be set aside in each meeting for RTEA business.
5. Personal problems or those more judiciously handled on a one-to-one situation shall not be the subject matter of a faculty meeting.
6. An agenda for each meeting shall be published at least two days prior to the meeting.

Hopefully, if this policy is understood and implemented by all, our faculty meetings should continue to be both useful and dynamic.

. . .Report on

FACULTY SECRETARY'S REPORT
Faculty Meeting of May 22, 19XX

The meeting was called to order at 3:17 p.m. by Mr. Benson. He spoke of the results of the State-Wide Testing Program. He pointed out that Rock Township High School was in the top ten percentile for the state in overall standings and further elaborated on the composite scores of specific areas of instruction. Mr. Benson remarked on the fine showing of our students as being reflective of the quality of instruction.

At 3:33 p.m. Mrs. Harrington spoke of the pressure on the Guidance Office at this time of the year and the necessity of all teachers getting in the names of possible failures for the school year as soon as possible.

At 3:36 p.m. Mr. Kennert, chairperson of the Discipline Committee, reported that the new discipline referral form is proving effective in leading to quicker and more judicious handling of disciplinary cases. This is gathered from many teacher comments and the report of the vice-principal. Mr. Kennert further reported that teachers would soon be receiving a questionnaire from the committee. He asked that this form be filled out and returned as soon as possible, as it would serve as one basis for the revision of the Discipline Code.

At 3:47 p.m. Mr. Gianisi, the faculty representative of the Rock Township Education Association announced the new salary scale as approved by the Board of Education and the RTEA. A question and answer session followed.

Mr. Benson adjourned the meeting at 4:02 p.m.

Respectfully submitted,
Marion R. Haines,
Faculty Secretary

FAILURE (See Also: DISCIPLINE; EXAMINATIONS; GRADES; GRADUATION; REPORT CARDS; RETENTION; SUMMER SCHOOL)

. . .Failures for the School Year Form

Please fill in the form below and return it to the Guidance Office no later than Tuesday, June 20, 19XX at the end of the school day:

Name: ______________________ Date: ______________

Grade: ______________________ Subject: ______________

FAILURES FOR THE SCHOOL YEAR

STUDENT	GRADE FOR MARKING PERIOD 1	2	3	4	FINAL AVERAGE

REASON(S) FOR FAILURE:

Teacher Signature: ______________________

. . .Notice to Parents of Failure for Marking Period (2 Forms)

(A) first form

Dear Parent (or Guardian):

Your son/daugher, ______________________, Grade ________, is not doing satisfactory work in (subject) ______________ for the marking period which ends ______________.

The purpose of this report is to bring this situation to your attention in order that pupil, teacher and parents, working together, may seek to remedy the situation.

We are checking below some of the causes which seem to be contributing to his/her present difficulties:

( ) Absenteeism
( ) Unsatisfactory test scores
( ) Inattention in class
( ) Lessons poorly prepared or not done
( ) Poor attitude in class
( ) Work not done on time
( ) Frequently comes to school without books, pencils, etc.
( ) Other (Please Comment): ______________________________

____

____

In order to help the situation improve, a conference here at the school may be helpful. Please phone the school (756-0903) for a conference.

Teacher: ______________________

(B) second form

Marking Period Ends: ________

Dear Parents (or Guardians):

(Student) ______________________ Grade ______________________

( ) is in danger of failing (Subject) ______________________

( ) is doing passing work in (Subject) ______________________, but is capable of doing, and should be urged to do, better.

In order to improve the situation, he/she must:

( ) take responsibility for bringing all necessary materials to class.
( ) hand in assignments regularly and on time.
( ) improve the quality of assignments.
( ) take responsibility for finding out about and making up all assignments missed because of absence, trips, etc.
( ) give complete attention to the explanations and practice exercises in class.
( ) study more diligently and pass more tests.
( ) improve behavior in class.
( ) put extra effort into improving skills in ______________________.
( ) come for extra help.
( ) complete a major project.
( ) Other: ______________________________

____

____

FAILURE

Would you please:

( ) telephone the Guidance Office (234-5678, Ext. 12) for an appointment in order to discuss this more fully. If you prefer, you may arrange for a telephone conversation.

( ) sign and return this sheet to me.

TEACHER'S SIGNATURE: ______________________

. . .Notice to Parents of Failure for School Year

Dear ______________________,

We sincerely regret to inform you that your son/daughter, ________________,
a ______________ Grade student at Rock Township High School, is in danger of failing the following subject(s) for the current *School Year*:

SUBJECT	TEACHER

The teacher(s) involved have indicated the following as possible reasons for this situation: ____

____

____

We are as concerned as you must be about this very serious situation. If you would care to call me at 234-5678, Extension 12, I will be happy to set up a conference at your earliest convenience.

I do hope that we may be of service and can help to rectify this unfortunate situation.

Sincerely,
H. K. Lennel,
Director of Guidance

. . .Notice to Teachers on

To: ALL TEACHERS
From: GUIDANCE DEPARTMENT
Re: FAILURE NOTICES FOR 4TH MARKING PERIOD

Warning notices will be mailed at the end of the school day on Monday, May 22nd. The preparation and sending of failure notices is as follows:

1. Teachers are to obtain failure notices from the Guidance Office.
2. Teachers are to fill out the form in duplicate–one white, one blue–for each student who is not doing passing or satisfactory work in their course.
3. Please write the student's homeroom number and the homeroom teacher's name at the top of the notice on both copies.
4. Turn in completed forms to Department Chairpersons as soon as possible.
5. Department Chairpersons will check for completeness, legibility, etc. and submit the forms to the Guidance Office by the end of the day on Thursday, May 18th.
6. On Friday, May 19th, the Guidance Office will forward the blue copies to the proper guidance counselor and will "homeroomize" the white copies. The completed white copies will then be placed in the homeroom teacher's mailbox.
7. Homeroom teachers are to collate the completed white copies, obtain a sufficient number of stamped envelopes from Guidance, address them to parents via information obtained from attendance cards, seal and return the envelopes to the Guidance Office as soon as possible on Monday, May 22nd. The Guidance Office will be responsible for mailing the envelopes.
8. The 4th marking period ends June 23. (April 21–June 23).
9. INCOMPLETE POLICY: An INC (incomplete) should be given when a student has not done the work for a period in which the grade is given because of one of the following reasons:
    1. Extended absence due to illness.
    2. An emotional crisis (death–divorce)
    3. An extenuating reason which the teacher will discuss with Guidance and the Administration before giving the grade.

NOTE: It is assumed that all teachers understand that the issuance of a warning notice is a solicitation for a parental conference. Conferences with parents will be arranged for you by the Guidance Office at your convenience whenever possible. Any comments made on the warning notices should be consonant with good public relations practices.

FIELD TRIPS (See Also: BUS; PERMISSION SLIPS; VOLUNTEERS)

. . .Budget Form for

NAME: ______________________________ Room: __________

DEPARTMENT: ______________________________________

DIRECTIONS: Include all trips, local and out of district. Include justifications. Figure costs at ______ per mile and ______ per hour of waiting time; add 5% and round off to the next highest five dollars. Trips should be coordinated within a department.

EST. COST	NO. OF BUSES	NO. OF STUDENTS	DESTI-NATION	ROUND-TRIP MILES	TIME AT DESTI-NATION	PURPOSE
			--TOTAL--			

. . .Evaluation Form

FIELD TRIP EVALUATION FORM

(This form is provided for the teacher's personal records as an aid in evaluating and planning Field Trips.)

Date of Trip: ______________________________

Group Taken: ______________________________

Teachers: ______________________________

Nature of Trip: ______________________________

Bus Carrier: ______________________________

HOW WOULD YOU RATE:	LOW	2	3	4	5	HIGH
Bus Service						
Student Interest						
Simplicity of Arrangements						
Treatment at Destination						
Educational Value						

Would you take this trip again? ( ) Yes ( ) No

Why or Why Not?____

____

____

Overall Evaluation of Trip:____________________________________

____

____

. . .Guidelines for

FIELD TRIP PROCEDURES AND GUIDELINES

1. TRIP REQUEST: A trip request form is to be completed and turned in to the office for approval or disapproval. Requests must be made three (3) weeks before the date planned.
2. Parental permission slips, available in the office, must be signed by a parent and turned in to the teacher in charge at least one day before the proposed trip.
3. When any monies are involved, they should be collected by the teacher and turned in each day for safekeeping. All money should be collected at least two days before the trip. Requests for checks from the office must be made at least one day before you need that check.
4. In planning for a field trip, teachers will NOT purchase tickets, transportation, theater seats, etc. before receiving the money for these tickets from their students. Teachers will explain to their students when the trip is first proposed that paying his or her share of the costs will constitute a firm commitment. The teacher must explain that the money cannot be refunded unless the refund would not impose an additional burden on the other students and/or the school.

5. Alphabetical lists of students must be turned in to the office two days in advance of the trip. This will enable us to publish the list in the daily notices the day before the trip is scheduled.

6. The teacher in charge should obtain two copies of the daily notice on which the listing of students is published. The day of the trip, the teacher in charge must send one of these daily notices to the office after roll has been taken on the bus. Please indicate those who are absent and send this list to the main office immediately before departure. The second list should be kept by the teacher for use during the trip.

. . .Request Form

REQUEST FOR FIELD TRIP FORM

Teacher Making Request: ______________________________ Date: ______________

Grade and/or Subject: ____

Date of Trip: ____

Itinerary: ____

____

____

Teacher and/or Adult Chaperones (Please list yourself first.): ______________

____

____

Number of Students Going: _____________ Have Dates Been Confirmed: _______

Transportation by: ______________________________ Cost: ______________

- -

Dear ______________________________,

Your request for a field trip has been:

( ) Approved
( ) Not Approved for the Following Reason(s): ____________________

____

Date: ______________________________ Signature: ____________________

FINANCIAL (See Also: BOARD OF EDUCATION; NEGOTIATIONS; SALARY; SCHOLARSHIPS; VENDORS)

. . .Policy on Money in School

It is sometimes necessary for teachers to handle money in connection with some of the activities of the school. Monies collected from students are to be placed in a suitably labeled sealed envelope and given to the office for safekeeping. Please do not leave funds unguarded AT ANY TIME and in no event overnight in your room or desk. Your own valuables should be handled accordingly.

In the collection of monies, student treasurers are used for all regular activities according to school rules and regulations, but fines or payments for lost or damaged books, etc. are handled directly by the teacher who must furnish an account of the reason the money was collected. Teachers are to hand in the cash; personal checks will not be accepted. Receipts should be given and required when the transfer takes place.

. . .Support

FINANCING EDUCATION

The school budget is prepared each year by the board of Education and its chief administrators after a review of budget requests submitted by teachers, principals, special services personnel and other professional staff members. The budget consists of three main segments: current expense, capital outlay and debt service. The citizens of the Township vote annually on all of these except debt service, which is a fixed charge on bond issues previously approved by the voters. The school budget election is held in conjunction with the school board election. Prior to the election, a public hearing on the budget must be held and the proposed budget advertised, both in local papers and the district's official publication.

If the proposed budget is defeated by the electorate, it falls to the Township Committee to certify the budget, making whatever changes they may decree. Normally, the Township Committee and the Board of Education meet to study the proposed budget before the public hearing. In the event of defeat, the two bodies must meet within two weeks to confer on proposed cuts. The Board of Education has the right to appeal any cuts made by the Committee to the Commissioner of Education who may reinstate the appealed funds or a portion thereof.

FIRE DRILLS

(See Also: CLOSING OF SCHOOL; EMERGENCY; HANDBOOK; MAP OF THE SCHOOL)

. . .Evacuation Drill Report

FIRE DRILL REPORT

SCHOOL: ______________________________

DATE OF DRILL: ______________________________

START TIME: ____________ FINISH TIME: ____________

TOTAL TIME TO EVACUATE BUILDING: ______________________________

SPECIAL CIRCUMSTANCES: ______________________________

____

____

DATE: __________ SIGNATURE: ______________________________

TITLE: ______________________________

. . .Procedures for a Safe Fire Drill

FIRE DRILL (EVACUATION) PROCEDURES

A. SIGNAL–Repeated ringing of the fire drill bells.

B. GENERAL INSTRUCTIONS–

1. Books are to be left in rooms. Only valuables (pens, purses, etc.) are to be taken.
2. Under no circumstances are students to go to their lockers.
3. All windows and doors are to be closed but not locked.
4. All electrical and gas equipment should be turned off.
5. Pupils with physical disabilities are to report to the Main Office.
6. Teachers must take their roll books.
7. Ignore any bells during the fire drill.

C. PROCEDURES–

1. At the sound of the alarm, students are to form a double line in the classroom and await instructions.
2. The teacher will review the exit to be used and the line of march.

3. Pupils are to walk quickly in double lines in a compact group. Teachers are to be at the HEAD of the line.
4. The teacher and class are to proceed to the designated area.
5. ABSOLUTE SILENCE IS TO BE OBSERVED THROUGHOUT THE EVACUATION, THE WAITING IN THE DESIGNATED AREAS AND THE RETURN TO THE BUILDING.
6. While waiting for the signal to return to the building, teachers are to ACTIVELY SUPERVISE their students who are to remain together in a double line.
7. Returning to the building, pupils are to maintain a silent double line until they are seated in their classrooms.
8. *SPECIAL NOTE*: NO children, parents, visitors, teachers or other personnel are to remain in the building during a fire drill.

D. TEACHERS WITHOUT CLASSES–Personnel not specifically assigned an evacuation duty are to report to the outside main exit and await instruction.

. . .Procedures for Dealing With False Fire Alarms

To: ALL PRINCIPALS
From: OFFICE OF THE SUPERINTENDNET
Re: UNSCHEDULED FIRE DRILLS (FALSE ALARMS)

In the event that the Fire Alarm shall sound at an unscheduled time, the following procedures shall be implemented:

1. The school shall be evacuated according to regular fire drill procedures.
2. The Rock Township Police shall be called and advised that the alarm is unscheduled.
3. A representative shall be sent to the area in which the alarm originated (determined by the Fire Alarm Bell Code) and a determination made as to the nature of the alarm.
4. Upon the report of the representative, the Police shall be informed as to the nature of the alarm and whether outside aid shall be needed.
5. If the alarm is a false alarm, students shall be returned to class.

6. If the alarm represents a true emergency, students are to be moved to such positions where they will be out of danger and will not interfere with Firefighting or Emergency vehicles and personnel.
7. Principal shall immediately take steps toward the implementation of the above procedures.

. . .Statement of Policy

FIRE DRILLS

The signal for a fire or a fire drill is the repeated ringing of the fire alarm bells.

Signs are posted near the doorway of each room indicating the proper route for leaving the building. In addition, students will obtain from their teachers information regarding other procedures to be followed.

Students are to remain orderly, keep moving quickly and quietly and be prepared to follow any additional instructions that may be given to them by teachers during exit.

For safety reasons students are required to stand 300 feet from the building (so engines and hoses can get through).

Students will return to their classes when the signal has been given.

G

GIFTED STUDENTS (See Also: ACHIEVEMENT; GRADES; NATIONAL HONOR SOCIETY; SCHOLARSHIPS)

. . .Evaluation of (2 Forms)

(A) first form

CONTRACT EVALUATION FORM

Your Name: ______________________________ Contract Title: ____________

Date Approved: __________________________ Date Completed: ____________

Number of Weeks it Took and Why?: _____________________________________

____

1. Where did you get the idea for the contract?

2. Did you plan well? Why or why not?

3. Did you enjoy this contract? Is there more to learn about this subject? Do you think you will ever return to it?

4. Did you encounter any problems in the contract? What were they? How were they solved or did you solve them?

5. Did you accomplish your objective? Why or why not?

6. Did you learn something new? About yourself? About others?

(B) second form

PROJECT EVALUATION FORM

Student: ______________________________ Date: ______________

Evaluator: ____

Pleae check below each statement the word, phrase, or space which most closely corresponds with your evaluation. If none of the available comments apply, please write your own comments. If you are unable to judge an item, make no marks.

* *

1. Interest level throughout the project:
   ( ) Consistently High ( ) Improved ( ) Sufficient ( ) Dropped ( ) Low
2. Accepts responsibility for:
   A. Attendance and Punctuality
   ( ) Dependable ( ) Improved ( ) Sufficient ( ) Decreased
   ( ) Undependable
   B. Maintaining Project and Room:
   ( ) Dependable ( ) Improved ( ) Sufficient ( ) Decreased
   ( ) Undependable
3. States in writing the goals of study (Check what applies.):
   ( ) Challengingly ( ) Originally ( ) Realistically ( ) Specifically
   ( ) Measurably
4. Lists in writing the methods of doing study (Check what applies.):
   ( ) Clearly ( ) Realistically ( ) In Logical Order ( ) In Ample Detail
   ( ) Vaguely
5. Locates pertinent information from a variety of sources:
   ( ) Most Ably ( ) Improved ( ) Sufficient ( ) Least Ably
6. Organizes information and materials well:
   ( ) Consistently ( ) Improved ( ) Sufficiently ( ) Decreased
   ( ) Seldom
7. Organizes time wisely:
   ( ) Consistently ( ) Improved ( ) Sufficiently ( ) Decreased
   ( ) Seldom
8. Analyzes and criticizes (Such as: compares viewpoints, questions, judges, evaluates information, solves problems, uses logic, corrects errors, etc.):
   ( ) Consistently ( ) Improved ( ) Sufficiently ( ) Decreased
   ( ) Seldom
9. Creates; produces original product; thinks original thoughts:
   ( ) Consistently ( ) Improved ( ) Sufficiently ( ) Seldom
10. Works with little or no supervision:
    ( ) Consistently ( ) Improved ( ) Sufficiently ( ) Decreased
    ( ) Seldom

11. Amount of teacher guidance needed as project progressed:
( ) Less and Less ( ) Same as When Started ( ) More and More

12. Makes a final presentation which is (Check what applies.):
( ) Interesting ( ) Creative ( ) Well-Organized ( ) Unimaginative

13. Demonstrates increased general knowledge of study:
( ) Most Increase ( ) Moderate Increase ( ) Little Increase

14. Demonstrates increased depth of understanding (Example: learning a specialized vocabulary and adding own opinions.):
( ) Most Increase ( ) Moderate Increase ( ) Little Increase

15. Submits a written bibliography of sources utilized (Check any that apply.):
( ) Complete ( ) In Proper Form ( ) Incomplete ( ) None

16. Shares results with other students and teachers:
( ) Most ( ) High Moderate ( ) Low Moderate ( ) Least

17. Submits, throughout the project, evidence and evaluation of work done:
( ) Consistently ( ) Regularly ( ) Improved ( ) Sufficiently
( ) Irregularly

18. Demonstrates ability to evaluate how well the objectives were accomplished:
( ) Very Accurately ( ) Improved ( ) Sufficiently ( ) Poorly

19. Looks into suggestions which are offered:
( ) Consistently ( ) Sometimes ( ) Seldom

20. In making decisions about the project, the advisor gave:
( ) Too Much Help ( ) Sufficient Help ( ) Too Little Help

21. More decisions about the work were made in:
( ) Independent Study ( ) Regular Class

22. Regular class work has:
( ) Improved ( ) Remained High ( ) Remained Low ( ) Gone Down

23. Followed through to completion:
( ) No Pushing ( ) Some Pushing ( ) Much Pushing

I would evaluate this project as: ( ) Acceptable ( ) Unacceptable

On a separate sheet of paper, list any strengths and/or weaknesses inherent in the project itself, any evaluation of goals and methods accomplished, or other comments.

COMMENTS:

. . .Notice to Parents of Placement

Dear ____________________________ ,

We are pleased to inform you that your son/daughter,_______________, has been accepted for placement in our Gifted Student Program. He/she will begin classes on ________________________________.

You are requested to review the attached schedule and let us know if you have any comments. We look forward to working with you and _________________________throughout the coming year.

Sincerely,
H. K. Linnel,
Director of Guidance

. . .Notice to Parents of Program

Dear Parents,

This January we are beginning to prepare for our new Gifted Student Program which is slated to start in September. The program is intended to allow our students to reach their full potential.

We will be using several different criteria for student selection:

1. IQ test results.
2. Report Card Grades of past years.
3. Teacher recommendations.
4. Torrence Test of Creativity.
5. Metropolitan Reading Placement Test.
6. Parent recommendation.

Before any students are assigned to this new project, materials will have to be made ready for them. Besides the normal classroom supplies, we are asking for magazines, records and tapes of the classics, reading books, extra encyclopedias, etc, from our community.

The formation of the program has taken into consideration many different ways in which our children learn as well as the deep impact of the home upon a child's education. Consequently, the time schedules within our program will be far different from what they have been in the past (See attached Sample Schedule). Also, because of the difference in class assignments, we will be asking for the total support of the home. Periodic letters of progress will be sent from the student's advisor with replies required. Your input is essential to the success of our project.

There will be a meeting on Friday, January 29, 19XX in the school auditorium at 7:30 p.m. to explain all of the ramifications and goals of this project. All teachers, administrators and advisors to the program will be present. You are cordially invited to attend.

We hope to see you there.

Sincerely,
J. Benson, Principal

. . .Philosophy of Education of

In order to fully educate the gifted and/or talented student, we believe that certain criteria are essential to leading the student toward the recognition of his or her full potential.

Toward that end, all work assignments, enrichment activities, and scheduling having to do with the Gifted Student Program must meet with the following criteria:

1. Enlarging their worlds.
2. Exploring and exercising their minds.
3. Bringing them new and meaningful challenges.
4. Pinpointing their fields of interest.
5. Allowing them to be creative.

GOALS (See Also: COURSE OF STUDY; CURRICULUM; OBJECTIVES)

. . .District Goals

The following are the goals identified by all the schools in the district:

1. To acquire basic skills in obtaining information, solving problems, thinking critically and communicating effectively.
2. To learn to enjoy the process of learning and acquire skills necessary for a lifetime of continuous learning and adaptation.
3. To develop an understanding of a student's worth, abilities, potentialities and limitations.

GOALS

. . .Outcome Goals

The following are the outcome goals of education as identified by teachers, students and parents:

1. To acquire basic skills in obtaining information, solving problems, thinking critically and communicating effectively.
2. To acquire job entry level skills and, also, to acquire knowledge necessary for further education, so that it serves as basic universal application for ALL students: NO TRACKING OR BREAKDOWN INTO COLLEGE/NON-COLLEGE.
3. To learn to enjoy the process of learning and acquire skills necessary for a lifetime of continuous learning and adaptation.

. . .Process Goals

The following goals involve the process of education:

1. Teaching staff and administrative members of high quality.
2. Providing a stimulating environment that activates the student's interests in all aspects of the curriculum and motivates the student to seek his or her full potential.
3. Instruction which bears a meaningful relationship to the present and future needs and/or interests of pupils.

. . .Projected Goals for the School

The Board of Education sanctions and promulgates the following goals for education within the Township as a guide for its policy and other determinations. The public schools shall help every person to:

1. Acquire basic skills in obtaining information, solving problems, thinking critically, and communicating effectively.
2. Acquire the knowledge, skills, and understanding that permit his or her participation in a satisfying and responsible role on the job and as a consumer.

3. Learn to enjoy the process of education, and to acquire the skills necessary for a lifetime of continuous learning and adaptation to change, and wise use of leisure time.
4. Acquire a stock of basic information, covering the principles of physical, biological, and social sciences, the historical record of human achievements and failures, and current social issues, including knowledge of the environment.
5. Become an effective and responsible contributor to the decision-making processes of the political and other institutions of the community, state, country and world.
6. Acquire the ability to form satisfying and responsible relationships with a wide range of other people, including, but not limited to, those with social and cultural characteristics different from his or her own.
7. Acquire the capacities for playing satisfying and responsible roles in family life and society, including social customs, manners, morals, ethics and integrity.
8. Acquire the knowledge, habits and attitudes that promote personal and public health in physical, mental, and emotional maturity.
9. Acquire the ability and the desire to express himself or herself creatively in one or more of the arts, and to appreciate the esthetic expressions of other people.
10. Develop an understanding of his or her own worth, abilities, potentialities, and limitations.

GRADES

(See Also: ACCOUNTABILITY; EXAMINATIONS; FAILURE; GIFTED STUDENTS; PERMANENT RECORDS; REPORT CARDS; SCHOLARSHIPS; TUTORS)

. . .Notice to Teachers on Final Averages

The following information is intended to assist teachers in the determination of final averages:

1. The final average is to reflect the work done during the four marking periods. If a student entered our school late, please check with Guidance for the previous grades and incorporate them into the final average.

2. The letter grades given during each marking period are assigned the following numerical values:

   A = 8, B+ = 7, B = 6, C+ = 5, C = 4, D = 2, F = 0

3. Using these values, determine the final average by totaling the grades and referring to the table below:

YEARLY TOTAL	FINAL AVERAGE	YEARLY TOTAL	FINAL AVERAGE
32		21	
31	A	20	C+
30		19	
		18	
29		17	
28	B+	16	C
27		15	
26		14	
25		13	
24	B	12	C or D
23		11	(teacher judgment)
22		10	
		9	
		8	D
		7	
		6	

4. For yearly totals of 5 and below, teachers are to exercise judgment based on individual student merit as to whether a grade of 'D' or 'F' is to be given.

5. Please refer any questions to the Guidance Office.

. . .Philosophy of Grading

Marks serve several legitimate educational purposes–to inform parents how their child is perceived in school, socially and academically; to help the student see himself as a learner and set his goals for further areas of learning; to monitor the student for school placement; and to regulate the flow of pupils into various programs.

There are as many ideas about marks as there are students, teachers and parents. They are, at best, our only assessment of the achievement of the student.

Students are marked on recitations, tests, quizzes, papers, participation, and in some cases extra-credit work. Parents often question a teacher's grades. For this reason, it is wise to have approximately two grades a week for each student which assesses his or her work in a specific area. Since students often have an "off" day, many teachers, when averaging a student's grades, drop the lowest one (provided it is not an important project).

Teachers may be asked for the reasons for the failures each marking period, and the steps the teacher took during the period covered to see that the failure was averted. This is not for the purpose of "checking up" on the teacher, but is primarily to help in the education of the pupil and to keep the parents informed of what they can do for their children in their school work.

Halfway through each marking period warning notices will be sent to the parents of all students in danger of failing a subject in that marking period. A grade of "F" cannot be given on the report card unless a warning notice has been sent to the parents at least two weeks in advance.

It should always be remembered that marks should be given in relation to the ability of the student who is being marked. Marks on efforts alone should not be above "C," but a pupil who does as well as he is able, regardless of his or her accomplishments, should be passed. In subjects such as algebra, geometry, foreign language, stenography, etc., the pupil without the ability to do the work should be transferred to another subject. In this connection, it is the responsibility of each teacher to know the approximate ability of each student. Past records, test scores, etc. are available at the Guidance Office and should be used. Guidance Counselors are anxious to assist with any problems of placement.

. . .Sample Grade Report Form

GRADE REPORT

19___-19___

NAME: ____________________________ GRADE: ______________

HOME ROOM: _______________________ SUBJECT: ______________

TEACHER: ____

MARKING PERIOD	GRADE	CITIZENSHIP	WORK HABITS	TEACHER (initial)
1.				
2.				
3.				
4.				
Final				

TEACHER COMMENTS

MARKING PERIOD ONE:

Parent Signature: ______________________________

MARKING PERIOD TWO:

Parent Signature: ______________________________

MARKING PERIOD THREE:

Parent Signature: ______________________________

MARKING PERIOD FOUR:

GRADUATION

(See Also: ASSEMBLIES; DEGREES; FAILURE; JUNE; PERCENTAGE OF PROMOTION SHEETS; PERMANENT RECORDS)

. . .Invitation to

You are cordially invited to attend

THE GRADUATION CEREMONIES

of the

ROCK TOWNSHIP HIGH SCHOOL

Class of 19XX

on

Thursday, June 17, 19XX at 7:00 p.m.

ROCK TOWNSHIP HIGH SCHOOL ATHLETIC FIELD

In the event of inclement weather, ceremonies will be held in the Rock Township High School Auditorium at 7:00 p.m. In that case, attendance will be by invitation only, and this card will admit two people.

. . .Notice of Non-Graduation

Dear Mr. and Mrs. Brady,

It is my unhappy duty to inform you that your son, Adam, will not be graduating with his class in the June, 19XX ceremonies.

It is our policy to give every consideration to senior students, but, as I advised you in letters dated January 17, March 21, April 12, and May 6, 19XX, Adam's steadfast refusal to participate in class, to take any tests, or do any assigned work has led to such academic weaknesses that it is impossible for him to pass his required courses.

I hope that we may be able to help Adam to overcome this very serious situation. Hopefully, if Adam applies himself to summer school courses, he will be able to receive his diploma in September or sometime early next year.

We stand ready to provide whatever assistance we may. Please call upon us and advise us of your decision in this matter.

Sincerely,
J. Benson, Principal

. . .Principal's Address to Graduates

Tonight I have a gift for the graduating class of 19XX–my speech will be short.

I am keeping it short, because I fully realize how anxious you are to "get on with it." You are anxious to get those diplomas for which you have worked so hard; you are anxious to join your families and your friends to share your joy with them; you are anxious to get started with your plans for the future.

And this is as it should be, for a graduation, far from being an end, is the beginning of all your tomorrows. Over the past several years you have worked and studied, practiced and played, and grown–grown mentally as well as physically–and now you are here, ready to begin your lives as members of the adult community.

GRADUATION

For some of you this will mean a job and the responsibilities of family living. For others this will mean college and further years of study and preparation. Whatever course *your* future takes, it is my sincere hope that you will look back on your years here as having prepared you to meet and deal with the challenges that life will present.

On behalf of myself and the faculty and staff of Rock Township High School, I wish to each and every one of you the happiness of a productive life, the respect of your fellow human beings, and the love of your family. May the future be yours.

The best of luck and congratulations to the Class of 'XX.

. . .Procedures for

GRADUATION, 19XX

The following procedures for graduation must be followed by all students who intend to receive diplomas:

1. On Wednesday, June 16, 19XX, graduating Seniors will report to the Guidance Office to pick up their caps and gowns. You must sign for these items before you receive them.
2. On Thursday, June 17, 19XX, Seniors will report to the Girl's Gym by 6:30 p.m. Seniors are to bring their caps and gowns and be ON TIME. Anyone who is late will hold back procedures for all others. BE ON TIME!
3. Once in the Girl's Gym, students will change into their caps and gowns and line up as arranged at practice. Students are not to leave the Gym.
4. Mr. Weldman will be in charge of graduation. All problems are to be referred to him, and the students are to follow his directions.
5. Upon Mr. Weldman's signal, students will proceed to the athletic field and proceed with graduation ceremonies as rehearsed.
6. Upon completion of ceremonies, students will report back to the Girl's Gym where they will return caps and gowns and have their names checked off.
7. Students not returning caps and gowns will be charged the full price for them.
8. In the event of rain, the same procedures will be followed, except that the ceremonies will be held in the auditorium.

GUIDANCE (See Also: CONFERENCES; COUNSELING; INTERVIEW; PERMANENT RECORDS; REPORT CARDS; STUDENT INFORMATION; UNIT COORDINATION)

. . .Definition in Student Handbook

GUIDANCE DEPARTMENT

Each student in Rock Township High School will be assigned to a Guidance Counselor who will be more than willing to try to help the individul student with any personal or academic problem which may arise in school. Educational or vocational planning, course selections, and improvement of study habits are examples of some of the many areas with which counselors are glad to assist students.

Students who have appointments with their counselors will be given a "Guidance Slip" which is to be shown to the teacher when going to and returning from the Guidance Office.

Students (and their parents) are encouraged to use the facilities of the Guidance Department. Whenever a need arises, they should feel free to request a conference with a counselor and may arrange to do so through the Guidance Office Secretary.

The Guidance Office publishes a special booklet annually, detailing their services. It is given to each student.

. . .Notice to Parents of Services

Dear Parents,

The services of the Guidance Department are available to all students and their parents.

A number of counselors are assigned to each grade level, and they remain with the same students throughout their high school years. This is in keeping with the developmental approach to guidance which emphasizes the growth of the individual student. Counseling services are available on an individual and group basis both upon request and according to need.

The duties of the counselor fall into three areas: Working with students; working with the professional staff; and working with parents. Working with students includes counseling students on a referral or self-referral basis, administering and interpreting tests, planning and conducting orientation programs, and counseling students in selecting courses for the following year.

GUIDANCE

The counselor holds conferences related to student needs with the Child Study Team as well as with appropriate staff members. Each counselor consults with teachers in order to evaluate student progress, appropriate placement, and individual needs. The counselor works closely with curriculum committees, department chairmen, liaison committees as well as with psychologists, physicians and such community agencies as the Division of Childhood and Family Services, the Commission for the Blind, Teenage Psychiatric Center, etc. Counselors provide supportive services to the entire staff whenever appropriate.

The counselor participates in student-teacher-parent conferences and arranges meetings between parents and members of the Child Study Team. The counselor is available to interpret test results and review school records for parents in an attempt to help them make realistic educational and vocational plans for their child. Counselors also provide career and educational information and arrange for home instruction and tutoring.

It is our sincere hope that all students and parents will take advantage of these services.

Sincerely,
H. K. Linnel,
Director of Guidance

. . .Notice to Students

MEMO

To: ALL STUDENTS
From: GUIDANCE OFFICE
Re: STUDENT USE OF GUIDANCE OFFICE

The Guidance Office of Rock Township High School is open to all students. The Guidance Counselors are there to help you with all matters related to school. They can be a great help to you in planning your schedules, in dealing with academic problems, and in preparing you for college. Moreover, the Guidance Office can aid you in finding part-time jobs or in solving personal problems in a confidential atmosphere.

This is *your* Guidance Office. We hope that you will use it with confidence that it is there to help you and serve your needs.

H

HALL DUTY (See Also: LOCKERS; PASSES)

. . .Guidelines for

HALL DUTY

Teachers on Hall Duty are to be guided by the following instructions:

1. Each student in the halls during the time when classes are in session must have in his or her possession either a Hall Pass or a Library Pass.
2. Students found in the halls without a proper pass are to be escorted back to their classroom.
3. Check the Boys' or Girls' Rooms at least twice each period and more frequently if conditions warrant.
4. Patrol the assigned area at irregular intervals.
5. Become acquainted with any classroom situation where a substitute is teaching and offer cooperation and assistance if such seems desired and/or indicated.
6. Refer all visitors to the office for a visitor's pass and assist them if possible.
7. Assist those teachers who have special activities in progress—e.g., Field Trips, Health Examinations, Student Photographs, etc.
8. Students requiring disciplinary attention are to be referred to the Main Office.
9. Be available to substitute briefly for any regular classroom teacher who may find it necessary to leave the classroom.
10. Teachers are expected to be on duty during the entire period of assignment and are responsible for any activity that occurs in the hall during that time.

. . .Policy for Teachers on

GENERAL HALL SUPERVISION

Hall supervision is the responsibility of the entire staff. Each time that the student body is in the hall either in the morning visitation period, between periods, or at the end of the school day it is imperative that all staff members assist in hall supervision. Each staff member should be at the door to his or her room or at a lavatory if one is nearby. Students should be allowed to converse freely with their friends, but certain rules should be enforced. They are:

1. Stay to the right when walking in the halls.
2. No loud talking or yelling.
3. No running.
4. No pushing or shoving.
5. No destruction of school property.
6. Any other discipline rules that apply to the movement of student traffic in the halls.

In addition, when the warning bell rings in the morning, all staff members should be sure that any students in their immediate area move to homeroom quickly and quietly.

HANDBOOK

(See Also: BULLETIN; DRESS CODES; DRINKING OF ALCOHOLIC BEVERAGES ON SCHOOL GROUNDS; DRUGS; FIRE DRILLS: KEYS; MAP OF THE SCHOOL; PARENTS; SCHEDULE; TELEPHONE)

. . .Guide for Handbook Use

(A) by students

Welcome to Rock Township High School. We are glad to have you here. This handbook answers many of the questions you may have about the rules and activities here at Rock Township High. We hope that this will be helpful to you throughout the year. We are looking forward to helping you have a good school year, and we're always open to any suggestions you might have.

(B) by teachers

The purpose of this compilation of suggestions and regulations is to aid new teachers in adjusting themselves to the policies of the school; and to enable all teachers to have, in concise and readily available form, answers to those questions which come up each school year. Undoubtedly those rules will be changed from time to time as circumstances change, and as we improve by discussing our problems and by experimenting with new ideas.

. . .Principal's Message in

(A) student's

WELCOME! Whether you are a newcomer to our school or an "old-timer," we hope you will find this school year to be a memorable and exciting one. Cooperation is, of course, the key, and toward that end we suggest that you read this handbook thoroughly. It will tell you exactly what we expect of you and what services and benefits you may expect from the school. We hope that you will take both messages to heart.

May this year be one of the most rewarding in your school career.

J. Benson, Principal

(B) teacher's

In the past year our staff has had an opportunity to review some of our educational processes and assess their strengths and weaknesses. We have evidence of accomplishments for which we can be justly proud and some conditions which indicate the need for change. It is to our credit that we have had the courage to look critically at what we are doing. It remains for us to show the wisdom to make the appropriate changes.

During this period the need for consistency in policies and procedures becomes most evident. I hope that this professional handbook will be helpful in meeting that need. Please read it carefully to become familiar with its contents.

ɔod luck during the school year!

. . .Sample Table of Contents

TABLE OF CONTENTS

HONOR ROLL (See Also: APPLICATION; AWARDS; CITIZENSHIP; EXAMINATIONS; NATIONAL HONOR SOCIETY; PERMANENT RECORDS)

. . .Application for Inclusion

HONOR ROLL APPLICATION FORM

NAME: ____________________ DATE: ____________________

GRADE: ____________________ HOME ROOM: _______________

MARKING PERIOD (Circle One): 1 2 3 4

I AM APPLYING FOR PLACEMENT ON THE ( ) HONOR ROLL
( ) HIGH HONOR ROLL

Please fill in the following for the Marking Period:

SUBJECT	TEACHER	GRADE

UPON CHECKING THE ABOVE INFORMATION, YOUR NAME WILL BE PLACED ON THE APPROPRIATE HONOR ROLL.

. . .Policy on

Students will be named to the Honor Roll if:

A. They have at least a six-point average in all of their subjects. To compute this, please note the following numerals for letter grades.

A = 8; B+ = 7; B = 6; C+ = 5; C = 4; D = 2; F = 0

For example, if a student received A (8 points) in Social Studies, A (8 points) in English, B+ (7 points) in Science, B (6 points) in Math, C+ (5 points) in Physical Education, B (6 points) in Spanish, then his or her total would be 40 points. Divided by the number of subjects (6), it would equal 6.66 or a 6.7 average or a B+.

B. They pass ALL subjects.

C. An "Incomplete" is made up within 10 school days.

D. They meet the behavior requirements of nothing lower than a 3 in work habits or social attitudes. (These will be checked in special cases by Guidance.)

Marks in work habits and conduct are given according to a numerical system:

1–Excellent 3–Improvement Made
2–Satisfactory 4–Improvement Needed
5–Parental Conference Requested

. . .Sample Form

Rock Township High School

HONOR ROLL

Second Marking Period

GRADE 10	GRADE 11	GRADE 12
Arton, Beverly	Brock, Paul	Bimore, William–H
Callen, James–H	Eber, Evelyn–H	Carter, Kenneth
Dorto, Daniel	Evens, Frank–H	Cerni, Louis–H
Dyer, Robert	Farley, Cindy	Folks, David–H
Ginty, Helen–H	Hink, Jessica–H	Linder, Lauren–H
Marker, Helen–H	Kelley, Laura	Losser, James
Merton, Joanne–H	Larch, Peter–H	March, Harriet–H
Rassler, Harold	Norris, Cindy–H	Nally, Jill
Tunnig, Roberta–H	Nostin, Robert	Quinn, Brian–H
Walters, James	Padula, William	Short, Harold–H

"H"–Denotes High Honor Roll

HOSPITALIZATION (See Also: MEDICAL; NEGOTIATIONS)

. . .Notification of Change of Carrier

To: ALL EMPLOYEES OF THE ROCK TOWNSHIP SCHOOL DISTRICT
From: CENTRAL ADMINISTRATION BUSINESS OFFICE
Re: HOSPITALIZATION/MAJOR MEDICAL FOR 19XX–XX

As a result of negotiations with the various employee groups within the school district, the Rock Township Board of Education has agreed to a change in the hospitalization and major medical plans for the 19XX–XX school year.

As part of the transition it will be necessary for each employee to complete the two enclosed enrollment cards to assure the proper coverage is continued effective July 1, 19XX. The single-ply card will be for your hospitalization with the Medusa Hospitalization Plan, and the three-ply card will be for Medical and Major Medical coverage with the Johnson Life Insurance Company.

BOTH CARDS NEED TO BE COMPLETED IN FULL, SIGNED AND DATED AND RETURNED TO THIS OFFICE NO LATER THAN JUNE 1, 19XX.

The benefits booklet is in the process of being prepared and will be provided to each employee as soon as it is received from the carrier.

In order for the transition to run smoothly, we will need each employee's cooperation in returning the cards as quickly as possible. Please read the instructions on the cards carefully and contact this office if there are any questions.

. . .Notification of Policy in Effect

MEMO

To: ALL TEACHERS IN ROCK TOWNSHIP
From: ROCK TOWNSHIP EDUCATION ASSOCIATION
Re: HOSPITALIZATION

All teachers in the Rock Township Education Association are advised that the new hospitalization policy negotiated with the Rock Township

HOSPITALIZATION

Board of Education will go into effect on July 1, 19XX. By now, every teacher in the Township should have received a Hospitalization Identification Card. It is essential that you keep this card in your possession, as it is your proof of coverage and must be presented at time of treatment in a hospital.

Forms for Major Medical coverage must be picked up at the Office of the Board of Education, filled out and returned there.

If you have not received your card or if you have any questions regarding your hospitalization policy, please contact Mrs. Greer at the Board Office, 123–4567.

I

IDEAS (See Also: ACCEPTANCE; ISSUES; NEW POLICY OR PROGRAM; PHILOSOPHY; SUGGESTIONS)

. . .Acknowledgment of a Good Idea

Dear Mrs. Thomas,

I just finished reading the note you left for me. May I say that I think your idea is outstanding.

We have been looking for a solution to the study hall problem for some time, and it looks as if you have provided us with the answer. Your suggestions are not only sensible, but perfectly within the realm of realization as well.

Please set up an appointment with me so that I may thank you personally and further discuss your excellent idea.

Thank you for sharing your thoughts with me.

Sincerely,
J. Benson, Principal

. . .Gentle Denial of a Poor Idea

Dear. Mr. Bernard,

I have read with great interest your suggestions on improving the physical education facilities of our school. It is evident that a great deal of thought went into them and that you have the welfare of our students in mind. They are clear, precise, and do you a great credit.

This makes it all the more difficult for me to tell you that it is not possible to implement your suggestions at this time. Recent budgetary cutbacks, of which you may be aware, have necessitated a hard look at each dollar spent, and our prime concern must be for the maintenance of the academic curriculum. Consequently, it would not be possible to go ahead with the plans you have suggested.

I want to thank you, however, for sharing your ideas with me. I hope I will be hearing from you again in the near future.

Thank you for being so interested in the good of our school.

Sincerely,
J. Benson, Principal

. . .Soliciting New Ideas

MEMO

To: FACULTY
From: J. BENSON, PRINCIPAL
Re: NEW IDEAS

Too often, people come up with great ideas that go nowhere. They think, "Nobody would be interested in this!" or "Why bother? Who'd listen?" How sad this is, because when people begin to think this way their ideas die, and something that might have benefited many people is lost forever.

You are, after all, the people who know this school the best. Consequently, if you have any ideas about the functioning of it or any aspect of it, for that matter, I'd like to hear about it.

Please share your ideas with me. Everyone will profit from your knowledge, insight and expertise.

IDENTIFICATION (See Also: PERMANENT RECORDS; REPRESENTATION)

. . .Faculty I.D. Card

ROCK TOWNSHIP HIGH SCHOOL

FACULTY MEMBER:

NAME: ____________________

DEPARTMENT: ____________________

YEAR: ____________________

THIS CERTIFIES THAT THE ABOVE NAMED PERSON IS A CURRENT MEMBER OF THE FACULTY OF ROCK TOWNSHIP HIGH SCHOOL FOR THE CURRENT SCHOOL YEAR.

(PHOTO)

. . .Student I.D. Card

ROCK TOWNSHIP HIGH SCHOOL

–STUDENT IDENTIFICATION

(PHOTO)

Name: ____________________

Year: __________ H.R. ________

Address: ____________________

____

THIS CARD MUST BE PRESENTED, IF REQUESTED, UPON ENTRANCE TO CERTAIN ACTIVITIES RESTRICTED TO MEMBERS OF THE SCHOOL.

INQUIRIES (See Also: MEDICAL; PETITIONS; PROFESSIONAL ASSOCIATION; ZONING)

. . .Into Job Possibilities for Students

Dear Member of the Business Community,

There are many fine students at Rock Township High School who are honest, industrious and capable. Many of these teenagers are anxious and willing to join the working people of our community on a part-time basis. Jobs for these young people would not only provide them with additional income, but would give them experience, direction and responsibility that would become a valuable part of their education.

We were wondering if you, as a functioning member of the business community of Rock Township, had any part-time jobs in your establishment which might be filled by these young people. Not only would you be contributing to the growth of future citizens, but I am certain that you would find their performance satisfactory.

If you have any such positions available, we would appreciate hearing from you. Please call me at 234-5678, Ext. 12, and we can discuss whatever you have in mind. I am certain we can find the right applicant for you.

In the name of our students, I thank you for any and all considerations.

Sincerely,
H. K. Lennel,
Director of Guidance

. . .Into Position Availability

Dear Dr. Smith,

I have been a teacher in Rock Township for the past six years. During that time I took particular interest in improving the reading skills of my students. This, in turn, led me to graduate studies in the field of reading, particularly in the instruction of those students who are drastically below grade level.

Recently, I received my Master's Degree in Reading from Fairmont University. My concentration was in remedial reading instruction.

I am anxious to serve the needs of the students of Rock Township in this regard, and I was wondering about the possibility of utilizing my knowledge on a full-time basis.

I would greatly appreciate it, therefore, if you would be kind enough to inform me if you anticipate any openings in my particular field in the near future. Needless to say, I would be more than willing to fill out any applications required, come for interviews, or present any credentials you may deem necessary.

Thank you for your many past kindnesses and for all future considerations.

Very truly yours,
Mary D. Rodner

. . .Response to Inquiry

Dear Ms. Rodner,

Thank you for your letter of January 30, 19XX inquiring into the availability of positions in the field of remedial reading instruction in the Rock Township Public Schools.

I would like to congratulate you on attaining your Master's Degree and tell you that we are well aware of your fine record as a teacher in our school system.

We anticipate one opening in remedial reading for the 19XX-19XX school year. It will be on the Junior High School level. As you are aware, in the interests of fairness we must advertise the availability of this position and invite applications for it. Undoubtedly, there will be a number of applicants.

We shall, however, be very happy to consider your candidacy for the position. Please fill out the enclosed application and return it to the Central Office. Also, please call and arrange for a personal interview at your convenience.

Thank you again for your interest.

Sincerely,
Thomas Smith,
Superintendent of Schools

IN-SCHOOL SUSPENSION (See: ASP (Alternative School Program))

IN-SERVICE (See Also: ACCOUNTABILITY; CONVENTION; DEPARTMENTAL MEETINGS; FACULTY MEETINGS; JOURNALS; NEW POLICY OR PROGRAM; SCHEDULE; SUGGESTIONS)

. . .Announcement of

MEMO

To: FACULTY
From: J. BENSON, PRINCIPAL
Re: IN–SERVICE DAY

On Tuesday, October 14, 19XX, schools will not be in session in order that the entire Professional Staff may participate in a day of in-service training sessions to be held at Rock Township High School from 9:00 a.m. to 3:00 p.m.

A separate agenda will be published prior to the meeting, but I understand that many interesting and informative programs have been prepared for us by the In-Service Committee.

I look forward to sharing this day with you.

. . .Evaluation of Program

(A) individual session

EVALUATION OF IN-SERVICE SESSION

Name: ______________________ School: ______________________

Grade and/or Subject: ______________ Date: ______________________

Title of In-Service Session: ______________________________________

Please check your reactions to the following items:

ITEM	Excellent	Good	Satisfactory	Poor
1. Content of Session				
2. Manner in which Material was Presented				
3. Helpfulness of Session to You				
4. Received Answers to Your Questions				
5. Relationship of Instructor to Class				
6. Overall Impression of Session				
COMMENTS:				

(B) overall

EVALUATION OF IN-SERVICE DAY

Name: ______________________ School: ______________________

Grade and/or Subject: ______________ Date: ______________________

Please check the appropriate box for each of the following items:

WAS THE IN-SERVICE DAY:	YES	NO	SOMEWHAT
1. INFORMATIVE			
2. HELPFUL			
3. INTERESTING			
4. THOUGHT-PROVOKING			
5. WELL-ORGANIZED			
6. WORTHWHILE			

SHOULD WE CONTINUE FUTURE IN-SERVICE DAYS: ( ) Yes ( ) No

SUGGESTIONS FOR FUTURE IN-SERVICE SESSIONS: ______________________

____

COMMENTS: ______________________________________

____

____

. . .Interest Form from Staff

To the Professional Staff of Rock Township:

Since a day of in-service programs has become a regular part of our school calendar, we are anxious to present those programs from which the staff may most benefit. We would also like to present programs of significance and interest.

Toward that end, I would really appreciate it if you could take a few minutes to fill in the following form and return it to me as soon as possible.

Thank you for your cooperation. Your input is not only appreciated but necessary.

Laura Vitelli, Chairperson
In-Service Committee

. . . .

What area(s) would you like to see covered in the in-service sessions:

____

____

What specific areas would you like to see covered in depth:

____

____

Have you any suggestions relative to the smooth functioning of the day:

____

____

Have you any specific person or group whom you would recommend:

____

____

Date: ____________ Signature of Teacher: ____________________

. . .Request to Give

Dear Mr. Hartnett,

As Chairperson of the Committee for In-Service Sessions in Rock Township, I am constantly on the lookout for new and innovative approaches which would be of interest to the Professional Staff of Rock Township in various in-service sessions.

We have been informed by your principal, Mr. Benson, that you have been extremely successful in motivating and sponsoring creative writing on the part of those students who do not normally participate in such an activity. Mr. Benson speaks highly of your abilities and the results you attain.

I was wondering, therefore, if you would be willing to share some of your methods with your fellow educators in an in-service session held during the annual in-service day.

Please call me at home at 374-8694 any time after 6:00 p.m. and let me know if you would consider doing us this favor.

Personally, I hope you will.

Yours sincerely,
(Mrs.) Laura Vitelli, Chairperson
In-Service Committee

. . .Sample Program and Agenda

Dear Teachers,

Below is a schedule for our in-service day on Tuesday, October 14, 19XX at Rock Township High School from 9:00 a.m. to 3:00 p.m.

9:00	Meeting in the Auditorium
10:00	Coffee in the Cafeteria
10:30-12:00	Building Staff Meetings
12:00-12:45	Lunch in Cafeteria
12:45-3:00	Subject Area Meetings

The purpose of this day is to conclude the presentation of the Glasser approach to discipline (9:00-10:00), to arrive at commitment to a unified district-wide approach to discipline (10:30-12:00) and finally, to look at our goals, needs and priorities in each subject matter area in light of that commitment as well as in the light of other dictates of the subject.

Please review the attached pamphlets and be ready to discuss them with your fellow educators on Tuesday.

I hope that this will be an enjoyable and productive day for all.

Sincerely,
Barbara O'Neill,
Assistant to the Principal

. . .Scheduling of Meetings

IN-SERVICE DAY

October 14, 19XX

Room Assignments

SUBJECT AREA MEETINGS

ENGLISH	Group 1–200	Group 3–202
	Group 2–201	Group 4–203

If you wish to meet as one large group at the end of the discussion, please use the North end of the Cafeteria.

SOCIAL STUDIES:	Group 1–204	Group 2–205
	Group 3–206	

If you wish to meet as one large group at the end of the discussion, please use the South end of the Cafeteria.

MATH:	Group 1–207	Group 3–209
	Group 2–208	Group 4–210

If you wish to meet as one large group at the end of the discussion, please use the Library.

SCIENCE:	Group 1–100	Group 2–101
	Group 3–102	

If you wish to meet as one large group at the end of the discussion, please use the Girls' Gym.

* * * * * *

Rooms 211 and 212 have been reserved if the following subject areas wish to get together to discuss the topic further. The room assignments below are for the subject area listed.

MUSIC	103
ART	104
FOREIGN LANGUAGE	105
INDUSTRIAL ARTS	106
PHYSICAL EDUCATION	107
HOME ECONOMICS	108
BUSINESS EDUCATION	109

LIBRARIANS	110
NURSES	111
GUIDANCE	112

There are a few people in areas too small to form a group. If you are not listed, you may choose whichever group is most closely related to your specialization.

INSTRUCTION

(See Also: ACCOUNTABILITY; LESSON PLANS; MINI-COURSES; QUALITY; STUDENT TEACHER; SUBSTITUTE TEACHER; SUMMER SCHOOL; TEACHER AIDE)

. . .Improving the Quality of

The following is the policy of the Board of Education relative to staff development in order to improve the quality of instruction:

"Today's dynamic and rapidly changing society, with its tremendous accumulation of new knowledge and the attending obsolescence in some areas of practice, makes it imperative that all staff members be engaged in a continuous program of professional and technical growth in order that they may provide a quality educational program for all students being served by the Rock Township Public Schools.

"It is the policy of the Board of Education that a program of staff development be established to provide an opportunity for the continuous professional and technical growth of the staff through a program designed to meet documented needs.

"As a result of the operation of this policy, participants will have the opportunity to learn of developments and changes which will improve, expand and renew their skills, knowledge and abilities."

Following this policy, the Staff Development Committee has been meeting to determine its long-term objectives. It is our intent to keep you informed of our progress.

This Fall we will be surveying the staff in order to determine our priorities and directions. The following explanation of the scope and purpose of Staff Development is designed to give you some "food for thought" prior to our survey.

WHAT ARE SOME OF THE REASONS FOR A STAFF DEVELOPMENT PROGRAM?

1. District Policy
2. District and building goals
3. Individual training desires
4. Individual objectives
5. New skills for new programs
6. Professional renewal

WHAT ARE THE COMPONENTS OF STAFF DEVELOPMENT?

I. Institutional

The type of training or research necessary to meet the district or building goals to introduce new programs or otherwise serve an institutional need would be required, and in accordance with contractual arrangements. These activities might include:

1. In-service training
2. Visits in and out of district
3. Workshops
4. Conferences
5. Internships

II. Individual

To meet individual training desires either during non-school hours or during school hours with approval of the building administrator, programs would be voluntary and pursued independently. These might include:

1. Visits
2. Workshops
3. College or University courses
4. Teacher centers

If you have any thoughts you wish to contribute, would you please direct them to a member of the Staff Development Committee.

. . .Supplemental Instruction—Progress Report

SUPPLEMENTAL INSTRUCTION—PROGRESS REPORT

Name of Pupil: ______________________ Grade: __________

Address of Pupil: ____________________ Telephone: __________

______________________________ Zip: __________

School: ______________________ Date: __________

Instructor: ______________________________

In what subject(s): ______________________________

What does supplemental instruction replace: ______________________

____

Number of hours of supplemental instruction per week: ______________________

Day and time: ____

With whom have you conferred in the structuring of the program: ______________

____

Objective of supplemental instruction for this child: ____________________

____

SUBJECT (Reading, Math, etc.—Page numbers and skills being worked on, etc.): ____

____

____

TEACHER'S PROCEDURES (Teacher-made materials, methods and techniques used and which work best with student, tests given and items of interest):

____

____

STUDENT'S PROGRESS (Academic progress, attitude and physical condition): _____

____

____

FURTHER RECOMMENDATIONS: ______________________________

____

TERMINATION (Date of return to regular class, or moved, or date when instruction terminated, reason for, etc.):

____

INTERVIEW (See Also: CONFERENCES; COUNSELING; GUIDANCE)

. . . Interview Evaluation Sheet

INTERVIEW EVALUATION

Candidate: ______________________ Date: ______________

Interview for the Position of: ______________________________

Interviewer: ______________________________________

Please check the appropriate category:

ITEM	HIGH	VERY HIGH	SATIS-FACTORY	LOW	UNACCEPT-ABLE
1. Credentials					
2. Knowledge of Subject Area					
3. Reflects Philosophy of District					

ITEM	HIGH	VERY HIGH	SATIS-FACTORY	LOW	UNACCEPT-ABLE
4. Enthusiasm					
5. Originality of Ideas					
6. Apparant Affinity for Students					
7. Innovative Ideas					
8. Receptiveness to Suggestions					

Overall Impression: ______________________________

____

Comments: ______________________________

____

Recommendation(s): ______________________________

____

. . .Report on

REPORT ON THE INTERVIEW OF: ______________________________

FOR THE POSITION OF: ______________________________

DATE HELD: ______________ WHERE: ______________________________

INTERVIEWER(S): ______________________________

____

SUBJECTS DISCUSSED: ______________________________

____

STRONG POINTS OF CANDIDATE: ______________________________

____

AREAS OF CONFLICT: ______________________________

____

COMMENTS: ______________________________

____

RECOMMENDATION(S): ______________________________

____

Signature of
Head Interviewer: ______________

Please attach Interview Evaluation Sheet.

. . .Request to Come for

Dear ________________________,

In connection with your application for a position in the Rock Township Public Schools, please be advised that an interview has been arranged for you with ________________________ on ____________________ at (place) __________________________________ at (time)_____ .

If this time is convenient, please call 123-4567.

ROCK TOWNSHIP BOARD
OF EDUCATION

INTRODUCTION (See Also: NEWSLETTER; NEWS RELEASES; PROFILE SHEET; PUBLIC RELATIONS; VOLUNTEERS)

. . .Of a New Administrator

To: THE FACULTY OF ROCK TOWNSHIP HIGH SCHOOL
From: THOMAS SMITH, SUPERINTENDENT OF SCHOOLS
Re: YOUR NEW PRINCIPAL

I would like to take this opportunity to introduce Mr. John T. Benson, the new principal of your high school.

Mr. Benson was selected from a number of highly qualified candidates. He has taught for eight years, holds an M.A. in Administration and Supervision from Fairmont University, and has served as vice-principal of Talburg High School for the past seven years. He is an energetic, vital human being with a background of practical experience in education. I am certain that, with your cooperation, he will do an exemplary job.

. . .Of a New Faculty Member

Dear Faculty,

I'd like to introduce myself. My name is Mary Rodner, and I am the new remedial reading teacher here at Miller Junior High School. I have a Master's Degree in Reading from Fairmont University with a concentration in the instruction of remedial reading. Before coming to this position, I taught right here in Rock Township for six years.

Believe me, I know the time-consuming work that goes into effective teaching. I also know first-hand the exasperation and frustration involved in dealing with the student who is drastically below grade level in reading. In fact, it was just that feeling which led me into the study of reading.

Perhaps, in some small way, I may be of help. If you have any students who you feel could use my services, please refer them to me. I am in the process of reviewing records now, and very shortly I shall start a school-wide testing program. I want to work with you as a partner in the education of our students.

I am anxious to get started, and I look forward to getting to know you on a professional and on a personal level.

I'm glad to be here,
Mary D. Rodner

ISSUES (See Also: BOARD OF EDUCATION; IDEAS; PETITIONS; PUBLICATION; RIGHTS AND RESPONSIBILITIES; SUGGESTIONS; VOTING)

. . .Guidelines for the Presentation of

Within the scope of normal teaching, particularly on the secondary level, there may come times when the teacher shall present to his or her class certain issues, contemporary or classical, for its consideration and continued education.

When such issues are presented to a class it is expected that all sides of the question shall be presented without prejudice. Moreover, provision shall be made for the voicing of various opinions on the part of the students, and no student shall be made to feel slighted, outcast or inferior because of his or her beliefs.

In short, a complete presentation of all sides and a respect for the opinions of all are the keynotes to the presentation of issues.

. . .Policy on Issues and Academic Freedom

In considering a new course of study or a revision to an existing course the Board weighs, among other considerations, whether such course meets the Board's goals for children and whether it matches the maturity level of the students for whom it is intended. To insure that proposed curricula reflect these criteria, it is the policy of the Board to require that a guide be prepared for each approved course of study.

It is the responsibility of the Superintendent to see that the currently approved curriculum guides are applied in the schools of this district, and it is the responsibility of the teaching staff to utilize the material so provided as the core of the courses they have been assigned to teach.

The Board recognizes that some deviation from the assigned curriculum guide is necessary in the free exchange of the classroom. However, the Board specifies for the guidance of the Superintendent, and through his directives, the guidance of the staff, that any discussion of controversial issues in the classroom shall be conducted in an unprejudiced and dispassionate manner designed to foster a spirit of inquiry, and further that such discussion shall:

1. foster the educational process,
2. match the maturity level of students,
3. be consistent with the goals of the Board and the appropriate curriculum guide,
4. meet the standards of legal, educational and ethical responsibility which are necessary in connection with the successful operation of the public school system.

J

JOB (See Also: CAREER; EMPLOYMENT; WORKING PAPERS; WORK-STUDY PROGRAM)

. . .Request for Summer Job

SUMMER WORK REQUEST

STUDENT: ______________________________ DATE: __________

HOME ADDRESS: ______________________________________

______________________________________ ZIP: __________

HOME TELEPHONE NUMBER: __________________ GRADE: __________

I hereby authorize the Rock Township High School Guidance Department to inform me of any available summer jobs.

I AM WILLING TO WORK DURING THE SUMMER: ( ) FULL TIME
( ) PART TIME

DATES AVAILABLE: FROM ____________ UNTIL ____________

I WILL WORK: ( ) DAYS ONLY ( ) NIGHTS ONLY ( ) EITHER

I HAVE: ( ) OWN TRANSPORTATION ( ) TRANSPORTATION AVAILABLE
( ) PUBLIC TRANSPORTATION ( ) BICYCLE ( ) NONE

MINIMUM ACCEPTABLE HOURLY WAGE: ____________________

I HAVE: ( ) DRIVER'S LIÇENSE ( ) WORKING PAPERS
( ) SOCIAL SECURITY CARD

IS THERE ANYTHING THAT WOULD PREVENT YOU FROM WORKING THROUGH THE SUMMER (e.g., family vacation, etc.): ______________

IF "YES," EXPLAIN AND GIVE DATES UNAVAILABLE: ______________

____

ANY COMMENTS YOU WOULD CARE TO MAKE: ______________________

____

____

DATE: __________ STUDENT'S SIGNATURE: ______________________

. . .Schedule of Jobs

School: ____

Head Custodian: ______________________________________

JOB SCHEDULE OF

Custodian: ____

From ______________________ To ______________________

AREA	TASK	TIME

Special Duties: ______________________________________

____

____

Special Instructions: _________________________________

____

____

Break Times: 1st Half of Shift: __________ 2nd Half of Shift: __________

Lunch: From: ______________ To: ______________

Date: __________ Signature of Head Custodian: ______________________

Signature of Custodian: ______________________

JOURNALS (See Also: CONGRATULATIONS; IN-SERVICE; NEWS RELEASES; PUBLICATION; PUBLIC RELATIONS)

. . .Congratulations on Publication in

Dear Harry,

Last night I had the pleasure of reading your article, "Getting to the Gifted Child," in the May, 19XX issue of the State Education Association *Journal.* The insight which you possess into the problems of the gifted child coupled with your highly readable, conversational style makes for an enjoyable, informative article which will surely benefit every educator.

Please accept my congratulations on the publication of your article and let me also say how fortunate it is for me and the students that you are a part of our school.

Please keep writing–we need you!

Best wishes for continued success,
John Benson

. . .Inquiry Letter About an Article

Dear Editor,

In the May, 19XX issue of the State Education Association *Journal,* Volume XXII, Number 9, on pages 43-45, you published an article entitled "Getting to the Gifted Child" by Harold Thompkins.

Mr. Thompkins is a teacher in Rock Township High School of which I am the principal. I was very impressed with Mr. Thompkins' article, and I am certain that members of our Parent-Faculty Organization would appreciate reading it.

I was wondering if reprints of the article are available and, if so, what the costs involved would be? We would be ordering at least 200 copies. I would appreciate any information you would have on this possibility.

Thank you for your consideration.

Sincerely,
J. Benson, Principal

. . .Notice of Interesting Article in

MEMO

To: STAFF
From: J. BENSON, PRINCIPAL
RE: SOMETHING YOU SHOULD KNOW

I'd like to draw your attention to an article in this month's issue of the State Education Association *Journal.* Titled "Getting to the Gifted Child," this article on pages 43-45 was written by our own Mr. Harold Thompkins. The article examines methods of identifying and effectively educating the gifted and talented child. We are all aware of Mr. Thompkins' success in this area, and I am certain that we will all profit by sharing the insights in this article.

JUNE

(See Also: ASSEMBLIES; CALENDAR; CLOSING OF SCHOOL; DISMISSAL PROCEDURES; GRADUATION; VACATION; YEAR-END REPORT)

. . .Activity List for the Month of

MEMO

To: FACULTY
From: J. BENSON, PRINCIPAL
Re: ACTIVITIES FOR THE MONTH OF JUNE

The last month of school is traditionally a hectic time for everyone. In order that you may plan effectively, the following list of school-time activities is presented for your information:

DATE	ACTIVITY
Wednesday, June 2	Freshman Picnic–Tyson Park
Thursday, June 3	Modern Music Assembly–Period 6
Monday, June 7	Sophomore Picnic–Tyson Park
Wednesday, June 9	Field Day–Athletic Field
Friday, June 11	Junior Picnic–Tyson Park
Tuesday, June 15	Senior Picnic–Tyson Park
Wednesday, June 16	Graduation Practice–Seniors
Tuesday, June 22	Awards Assemble–Periods 6 and 7
Wednesday, June 23	Last Day of School

. . .Principal's Message Concerning

MEMO

To: FACULTY
From: J. BENSON, PRINCIPAL
Re: JUNE!

As the song so aptly states, "June Is Bustin' Out All Over!" Along with June comes the anticipation of summer and all that that thought conveys. Nor is this "Spirit of June" restricted to the student body. We are all touched by it, and with that knowledge comes the resolution that we all have to make a renewed effort to keep up the procedures of education which have served us so well throughout the year. We don't want our school "Bustin' Out All Over" like the month. I know I can count on you to see to it that education and reasonable discipline continue throughout these last days of school.

K

KEYS (See Also: HANDBOOK; LOCKERS; VACATION)

...List of Key Assignments

KEY ASSIGNMENTS

ROOM	LOCKERS From	LOCKERS To	DOOR SERIAL NO.	CLOSET SERIAL NO.	TEACHER
105	170	205	G287609A	K988975A	Mr. Marsden

...Procedures for the Collection of

To: ALL HOMEROOM TEACHERS
Re: COLLECTION OF LOCKER KEYS

On Monday and Tuesday, June 21 and 22, 19XX, locker keys will be collected during homeroom period by homeroom teachers. The following is offered as a guide for that collection:

1. Distribute the white key tags to all students in your homeroom. Have the students write the locker number on one side of the tag and the serial number of the key on the other side.
2. Call each student individually. Check to see that the correct locker and serial numbers are recorded on the tag. Place the key, properly tagged, into the manila envelope provided by the office and check off the student's name from your locker list.

3. If a student, for whatever reason, has not returned his or her locker key by the end of homeroom period on Tuesday, June 22, place the name of that student, the locker number and the serial number on a separate sheet along with your name and homeroom number and send that list to the office immediately. The office will handle collection of fines.
4. Return the manila key envelope with all tagged keys to the main office by the end of the day on Tuesday, June 22nd.

THANK YOU FOR YOUR COOPERATION.

. . .Procedures for the Distribution of

LOCKER KEY PROCEDURES

1. Issue one key for each student without charge. (Keys will be handled the same as textbooks.) If the key is lost during the year, $1.00 will be charged for a new key. If it is not returned at the end of the year, a $1.00 fine will be charged before the issuance of a report card.
2. Before issuing a key, record in DUPLICATE the locker number, serial number of the key, and the name of the student to whom it is issued. Keep one copy for your records and return the original to the main office.
3. Remove identification tags from issued keys.
4. Return all extra keys on the third day school is in session in the original envelope with your name and room number. PLEASE LEAVE IDENTIFICATION TAGS ON ALL KEYS RETURNED TO THE OFFICE.
5. If a student forgets or loses his key, he may have his locker opened by reporting to the hall locker duty teacher during homeroom period. At this time the student should remove all necessary material for the school day. Lockers WILL NOT be opened at any other time by the hall locker duty teacher. At the end of the day, the student may again have the locker opened at 3:00 p.m. by reporting to the main office at 2:10 p.m.

6. Students are to check on lost keys only through the homeroom teacher and not through the main office. If the key is located and returned to the office, it will be returned to the student via the homeroom teacher's mailbox.
7. Any key found not to be in working order should be so indicated by the locker number in the envelope when returning extra keys.

KINDERGARTEN (See Also: CLASS; CONFERENCE; SPECIAL EDUCATION; TEACHER AIDE; VOLUNTEERS)

. . .Kindergarten "Diploma"

ROUND RIDGE ELEMENTARY SCHOOL

____

has completed KINDERGARTEN and is ready for the First Grade

Date: __________________________ TEACHER: __________________

PRINCIPAL: __________________

. . .Notice to Parents

Dear Parents,

On ____________ , ____________ , 19 ________ , your child will be starting Kindergarten classes at our school. We hope that your child will find this a happy and enjoyable experience. We have taken the liberty of preparing this list of suggestions which have worked well in the past. We hope they will be helpful to you as well.

1. Come to school a little early and let your child explore the playground area. Show your child EXACTLY where you will be waiting after school. Repeat this several times.
2. When you are met at the door by your child's teacher, please remain cheerful and happy, say goodbye and leave promptly. It has been our experience that any tears disappear quickly as the day's activities begin.
3. At dismissal time, please wait outside the building at the spot you pointed out to your child earlier. The children will be brought to you and released only to you. (If someone else is to pick up your child, you must notify the school.)

4. Please remember that children are quick to pick up attitudes from adults. If you, personally, are enthusiastic, happy, and keep emphasizing how enjoyable school will be, your child will be also and will have no trouble adjusting to school.
5. This is a milestone in your child's life. Enjoy it with him.

We look forward to working with you in the coming school year.

. . .Parental Expectation Form

NAME OF PARENT (GUARDIAN): ______________________

ADDRESS: ______________________ TELEPHONE: ______________________

______________________ ZIP: ______________________

NAME OF CHILD: ______________________

IN WHAT SKILL(S) DO YOU FEEL YOUR CHILD NEEDS THE MOST HELP: ______

____

WHAT PROGRESS WOULD YOU LIKE TO SEE YOUR CHILD MAKE IN KINDERGARTEN: ______________________

____

____

WHAT IS YOUR BEST TIME FOR A CONFERENCE: ______________________

COULD YOU HELP SUPERVISE CLASS TRIPS AND ACTIVITIES: ____________

WOULD YOU BE AVAILABLE TO HELP IN CLASS WITH SUCH ACTIVITIES AS STORY-TELLING, SPECIAL ART PROJECTS, ETC.: ______________________

IF YES, WITH WHAT ACTIVITIES: ______________________

ANYTHING WE SHOULD KNOW ABOUT YOUR CHILD: ______________________

____

COMMENTS: ______________________

____

. . .Pre-entry Criteria Sheet

NAME OF CHILD: ______________________

DATE OF BIRTH: ______________________

PLEASE CHECK WHAT APPLIES:

( ) Toilet trained
( ) Feeds self
( ) Needs help feeding self
( ) Speaks understandably
( ) Seldom speaks
( ) Speaks in sentences

( ) Eats almost all foods
( ) Eats very few foods
( ) Has temper tantrums
( ) Teases other children
( ) Overactive
( ) Highly excitable
( ) Timid and/or shy
( ) Plays well with others
( ) Is 'picked on' by others
( ) Overly aggressive
( ) Does not speak (Explain on back.)
( ) Speech Impediment (Explain.)
( ) Initiates own actions
( ) Follows requests
( ) Cares for own property
( ) Is attentive
( ) Has many interests
( ) Few interests
( ) Has many fears
( ) Cries easily

MY CHILD NEEDS TO:

( ) Adjust to other children
( ) Become less active
( ) Become more active
( ) Become cooperative
( ) Relax
( ) Get interested in something
( ) Acquire manual/motor skills
( ) Become self-reliant
( ) Other: ____

____

COMMENTS: ____

____

____

. . .Progress Report (2 Forms)

(A) first form

NAME OF CHILD: ______________________ DATE: __________

KINDERGARTEN TEACHER: ______________________

SOCIAL ASPECTS: ______________________

____

PHYSICAL COORDINATION: ______________________

____

SKILL DEVELOPMENT: ______________________

____

READING AND MATH PROGRESS: ______________________

____

OUTSTANDING ACTIVITIES: ______________________

____

NEEDS IMPROVEMENT IN: ______________________

____

SPECIAL PROBLEMS: ____________________

____

COMMENTS: ____________________

____

TEACHER'S SIGNATURE: ____________________

PARENT'S SIGNATURE: ____________________

(B) second form

NAME OF CHILD: ____________________ DATE: __________

TEACHER: ____________________

REPORT FOR THE PERIOD FROM: __________ TO: __________

ITEM	EXCELLENT	GOOD	AVERAGE	POOR	IMPROVEMENT NEEDED
Recognizes letters					
Pronounces letters					
Names letters					
Recognizes numerals					
Counts					
Tells time					
Knows shapes & colors					
Knows home address					
Knows telephone No.					
Gets along with other children					
Cooperation					
General behavior					

Special Problems: ____________________

____

Overall Progress: ____________________

____

General Comments: ____________________

____

Teacher's Signature: ____________________

Parent's Signature: ____________________

L

LANGUAGE (See Also: BI-LINGUAL EDUCATION; EXCHANGE STUDENT)

. . .Foreign Language Night

Dear Parents,

On Thursday, April 29, 19XX, at 8:00 p.m., the Foreign Language Department will be holding its annual Foreign Language Night presentation. This event, which will be held in the cafeteria, involves students from the French, Spanish, and Russian classes of Rock Township High School presenting sketches, songs, and authentic folk dances—all in the various foreign languages. For your refreshment, authentic dishes representing many foreign lands will be served by our students.

This event gives our students an opportunity to practice the languages they have studied so hard to learn. It also is a very entertaining evening which many parents have praised highly in past years. All we need for its success is your attendance.

We look forward to meeting you.

Sincerely,
(Mrs.) M. Parone, Chairperson
Foreign Language Department

. . .Policy on the Appropriate Use of

We believe the old saying that "there is a time and place for everything." We especially apply this standard to the use of language by students in the school and classroom.

While certain language, whether it be termed 'vulgar' or 'obscene,' may be used with impunity in private conversations, we feel that such language is inappropriate for use in a public situation where individuals who are offended by such language are not at liberty to absent themselves from the situation.

Consequently, the use of vulgar, obscene, or profane language is expressly forbidden, and any student who shall use such language shall be subject to the disciplinary code of the school.

LEADERSHIP (See Also: CITIZENSHIP; CLUBS; EXTRA-CURRICULAR ACTIVITIES; NEGOTIATIONS; PROFILE SHEET; RECOMMENDATIONS)

. . .Guidelines for

LEADERSHIP

A LEADER is someone who:

ACCEPTS RESPONSIBILITY for his or her own actions and decisions.

INITIATES ACTIONS without being told for the good of the group.

MAKES DECISIONS logically and calmly, having weighed all the evidence.

STAYS CALM in the face of adversity or turmoil.

GETS OTHERS TO WORK because they want to work; not because they fear the consequences of not working.

GIVES ENCOURAGEMENT to others, spurring them to their best efforts.

GAINS RESPECT through his or her own actions, without demanding it.

IS KIND to all and tolerant of new and different ideas or opinions.

BE A LEADER!

. . .Student Leadership Evaluation Form

STUDENT'S NAME: ______________________________
GRADE: __________ HOMEROOM: ______________________
ACTIVITY: ______________________ DATE: __________
EVALUATOR: ______________________________
POST AND/OR POSITION OF STUDENT IN ACTIVITY: ______________
Please check the appropriate category:

QUALITY	FREQUENTLY	SOMETIMES	NEVER
INITIATES OWN ACTIONS			
ACCEPTS RESPONSIBILITY			
ADMITS MISTAKES			
RESPONSIVENESS TO OTHERS			
MAKES LOGICAL DECISIONS			
HANDLES PRESSURE WELL			
GAINS APPROVAL OF PEERS			
FOLLOWS THROUGH ON DECISIONS			
DISPLAYS CONSCIENTIOUS BEHAVIOR			

COMMENTS ON OVERALL PERFORMANCE: ______________________
____
____
RECOMMENDATIONS: ______________________________
____
SIGNATURE OF EVALUATOR: ______________________

LEARNING DISABILITIES

(See Also: ACCOUNTABILITY; CHILD STUDY TEAM; MAINSTREAMING; PERMANENT RECORDS; PSYCHOLOGICAL SERVICES; SPECIAL EDUCATION; TUTORS)

. . .Identification of

Name of Student: ______________________________
School: ______________________ Grade: __________
Date: __________ Evaluator: ______________________

PERSONAL AND HEALTH INFORMATION:

Date of Birth: ______________________ Sex: ( ) Male ( ) Female

Child living with: ( ) Both Parents ( ) One Parent ( ) Guardian(s)

Vision: __________ Hearing: ______________________________________

Health in General: ____

TEST INFORMATION:

Test Used: (1) ______________________ (2) ______________________

Results: (1) ______________________ (2) ______________________

Other: ____

ACHIEVEMENT RECORD:

Grades: ____

____

Tests: ____

____

Observation: ____

____

DIFFERENTIAL BETWEEN ABILITY AND ACHIEVEMENT:

( ) Reading Basics
( ) Comprehension
( ) Written Expression
( ) Oral Expression
( ) Mathematical Calculation
( ) Math Reasoning
( ) Listening Skills
( ) Logical Reasoning

Explain: ____

____

RECOMMENDATIONS: ____

____

____

____

SIGNATURE OF EVALUATOR: ______________________________________

TITLE: ______________________________________

. . .Referral for

TEACHER: ______________________________ DATE: __________

SCHOOL: ________________ GRADE AND/OR SUBJECT: ________

I have reason to believe that the following student may have a learning disability, and I hereby tender his/her name for evaluation:

Student: ____

Age: __________ Grade: ________________________________

Reason(s) why you believe this student may have a learning disability:

____

____

____

____

SIGNATURE OF TEACHER: __________________________

LESSON PLANS (See Also: CLASS; EMERGENCY; INSTRUCTION; OBSERVATION; STUDENT TEACHER; SUBSTITUTE TEACHER)

. . .Daily

Every teacher must prepare a written lesson plan for each class, sufficiently clear so that in a crisis another teacher can follow it. Each department has a lesson plan format which is to be used in the preparation of the plans. A copy of the lesson plan should be given to any administrator who observes a class.

Non-tenure teachers are to hand in lesson plans as indicated every Monday morning before school starts:

Activity Arts, Physical Education	- Mr. H. Johnson
English, Foreign Language, Social Studies	- Mrs. B. Harrington
Math, Science and Specials	- Mr. K. Warren

Tenure teachers will be notified via the Daily Bulletin when their lesson plans are due. They will turn them in as indicated above.

. . .Emergency Lesson Plan

By the end of the first week of school, teachers will be expected to provide the Department Chairperson with, and keep in current supply, at least one "Emergency Lesson Plan" to be used by substitute teachers in the event of unexpected absences. These plans should include the work to be done in each of your classes as well as seating charts, duty assignments (hall duty, bus duty, etc.), your entire daily schedule, location of supplies (extra textbooks, paper, etc.), and any other information needed by a substitute to carry on in your absence.

Please place these plans in a manila folder, identify on the tab with your last name, and submit them to the Chairperson of your Department.

LIBRARY (See Also: BOOKS; PASSES; VOLUNTEERS)

. . .Notice of Overdue Book/Materials

ROCK TOWNSHIP HIGH SCHOOL LIBRARY

Student: ____

Grade: ____________________ Homeroom: ________________

OVERDUE NOTICE

Book/Item: ____

Date Borrowed: ________________________ Today's Date: ______

No. of Days Overdue__________ at _______¢ per day.

Total Fine as of this date:________________________

Please report to the library immediately.

. . .Notice to Parents Concerning the Use of

Dear Parents,

Have you ever felt you'd like to:

Catch up on your reading?
Explore a new part of the world?
Learn a new skill or subject?
Start a hobby?

The Rock Township High School Library has books to fill your needs on all of these and much, much more. As a student at Rock Township High

School, your son or daughter has access to our facilities. As his or her parents, you are welcome to use them, as well. Please visit us at your convenience and examine our facilities. Should you find something that interests you (And we hope you will!), we shall be happy to let you borrow it.

Consider us as your source for reading and information—we like to be used!

Sincerely,
Karen Tennelly, Librarian
Rock Township High School

. . .Philosophy of

We believe that the school library exists for the use of the students in order to provide for their personal intellectual growth and to promote an interest in and an appreciation of the values of human achievement represented in the library's collection of material.

We believe in the free access of all students to the library facilities. We believe that these facilities should be structured to permit the greatest use by the greatest number of students. We believe that aid should be available to all students, and students should be taught to gain self-sufficiency in the use of library facilities.

. . .Soliciting Books for

Dear Parents,

BEFORE YOU THROW IT OUT—take a moment and consider these points:

Could those old books of yours be of interest or help to the students of Rock Township High School?

Do you have some back issues of magazines that teenagers might find interesting?

Do you have any photos, sketches, art reproductions, etc. that might be used by our students?

If the answer to any of these questions if 'yes,' we'd appreciate it if you could consider us. Instead of "throwing out" these materials, think about giving them to the school for use by our students in the library.

Please call me first at 234-5678, extension 7, and we can discuss any contribution you would care to make.

Thank you for your consideration.

Sincerely,
Karen Tennelly, Librarian
Rock Township High School

. . .Student Use of

To: ALL TEACHERS
From: K. TENNELLY, LIBRARIAN
Re: STUDENT USE OF THE LIBRARY

Students may be excused from either a class or a study hall to use the library provided that they have been issued a completed (name, time, subject, etc.) "Library Pass" by the teacher of the subject for which the library is to be used.

Please make arrangements with me in advance should you wish a group or a class of students to use the library at one time.

Please advise your students that substitute teachers are not permitted to send students to the library.

Thank you for your cooperation.

LOCKERS (See Also: HALL DUTY; KEYS; PASSES)

. . .Assignment of

LOCKERS

At the beginning of the school year, each student will be assigned an individual hall locker and will be issued a numbered key for it by the homeroom teacher. At the end of the school year, the student is to return the key or be charged one dollar Fines will also be assessed for willfully damaged keys.

Students are held responsible for the cleanliness of their lockers and are not to share them with other students.

To replace a key if it is lost, duplicate locker keys may be obtained from the office upon payment of $1.00. Should the original key be found later, the duplicate key may be returned for a refund of 50 cents—the remainder of the fine being charged for materials and labor.

. . .Locker List

LOCKER LIST

NAME OF TEACHER: ______________________________

Homeroom: ____________________ School Year: ____________

LOCKER KEY NUMBER	LOCKER NUMBER	ASSIGNED TO

. . .Locker Search Policy

The Board of Education acknowledges its respect for the privacy of the student attending the schools of this district, and provides each student with the use of a locker in which he or she may store clothing, school materials and other personal property. Although each student is responsible for locking the locker assigned to him or her against incursion by other students, all lockers are and shall remain the property of the Board of Education.

The Board also recognizes that a locker may from time to time be improperly used as a depository for substances or objects which are illegal or which constitute a threat to the health, safety and welfare of the occupants of the school buildings. The Superintendent, therefore, shall develop regulations for the inspection of student lockers that protect the school community from harm, cooperate with municipal or state authorities and ensure the rights of the student to whom the locker has been assigned.

Nothing in this policy or attendant regulations shall be construed to relieve school officials of their responsibility for the health, safety and educational welfare of the students in their care. Such officials shall retain the right to open and search school lockers with or without the knowledge or presence of the student or parent involved, but only when the circumstances are such that the protection of life and property demands such action.

Searches of a student's person, or his or her personal possessions, without a valid search warrant shall be prohibited unless the principal has a reasonable basis for believing that the student is concealing material the possession of which is prohibited by Federal, State, or Local Law.

. . .Policy on the Opening of

Students who forget to bring their locker keys to school may (within reason) arrange to have lockers opened either before school or after school. Students who wish to have their lockers opened in the morning are to:

1. Report directly to their homeroom teachers upon arrival at school.
2. Locate the locker duty teacher.
3. Remove from their lockers all that they will need during the course of the entire day.
4. Students who wish to have their lockers opened after school are to report to the office and remain so that proper arrangements can be made.

LUNCH (See Also: CAFETERIA; CLEANUP; WASTE)

. . .Duties of Supervisors

The supervision of the cafeteria during lunch periods is a full-time responsibility and a difficult one. Therefore, it is imperative that assigned teachers report to this duty on time.

While specific duties shall be assigned to individual teachers, it is the duty of ALL supervisors to see to the safety and well-being of the students in the lunch period. Moreover, supervisors shall be responsible for the maintenance in good condition of school property. Offending students are to be immediately removed from the situation and referred to the office for disciplinary action.

A properly functioning lunch period is only possible when ALL people cooperate.

. . .Lunch Schedules

To: ALL STUDENTS
Re: LUNCH PERIODS

There are five lunch periods at Rock Township High School. They are lettered A through E, and each period is held at a separate time. On your student schedule you will find a letter–A, B, C, D, or E–under the title "Lunch." This is the lunch period to which you are to report. Because of the large number of students attending each lunch period, students are expressly forbidden to attend any other period except the one assigned to them. Students are also expected to observe all the rules of cafeteria behavior as set down in the student handbook.

Following are the times of all lunch periods. Please see to it that you arrive promptly.

LUNCH "A"–10:53-11:23
LUNCH "B"–11:28-11:58
LUNCH "C"–12:03-12:33
LUNCH "D"–12:38-1:08
LUNCH "E"–1:13-1:43

If each student follows his or her schedule promptly and follows the rules set down in the handbook for cafeteria behavior, lunch period should be a pleasant time for everyone.

. . .Rules for Outside Lunches

When the weather permits, students may eat their lunches in the outside student lunch area located to the north of the school. This area, which was created by the Student Council, is for the use and enjoyment of all students at Rock Township High School. Because it is for the enjoyment of all, certain rules and regulations for its use are necessary.

LUNCH

1. All refuse is to be discarded in the trash cans provided for this purpose. These cans are emptied after each lunch period, so there will be sufficient room for the disposal of all waste.
2. Students are expected to clean up the table or area in which they have eaten. Remember that other students will be using the area after you. Provide them with a clean area.
3. Willful destruction of or damage to school property in this area is forbidden as it is throughout the school.
4. Smoking and/or the use of alcoholic beverages in this area are forbidden.
5. All the rules of the school apply.

This is your area. Let us all do our best to make it a pleasant place which may be enjoyed by all. Your cooperation is essential.

M

MAINSTREAMING (See Also: ACCOUNTABILITY; LEARNING DISABILITIES; PSYCHOLOGICAL SERVICES; SPECIAL EDUCATION; TUTORS; UNIT COORDINATION)

. . .Guide to Teachers

To: FACULTY
From: J. BENSON, PRINCIPAL
Re: MAINSTREAMED STUDENTS

In keeping with state mandates, a number of our Special Education and Handicapped students are being mainstreamed in our school. If one of these students is assigned to your class, you might find the following suggestions helpful:

1. Treat the student as you would any other member of your class. Do or say nothing that would single out or embarrass the student, but accept no behavior you would not accept from any other student.
2. In the case of some handicapped students it may be necessary to allow them to leave class a few minutes prior to the normal passing time. A separate sheet will be issued by the Nurse identifying these students.
3. As you would in any normal classroom, try to suit your academic work to your student's abilities. Mrs. Framton, Director of Special Services, will be happy to confer with you about any academic problems.
4. Understand that these students, no less than any others, are entitled to the best education you can give them. I know that you will do everything in your power to deal in a meaningful and effective manner with each and every one of your students.

. . .Philosophy of

We believe that every student in our school system is entitled both by law and by natural right to the best education we can offer. Toward that end, we believe that, wherever possible, all students should be a part of the normal school society, and that certainly no child should be set apart or excluded from that normal school society solely on the basis of a handicap.

Therefore, it is our policy that a thorough study shall be made of each child who is classified as handicapped or mentally retarded. This study shall be for the purpose of determining whether or not the child is capable of functioning in a normal school society and if such a placement would be to the benefit of the student. If, indeed, such placement would be beneficial, then such placement shall be made under the direction and supervision of the Department of Special Services.

MAP OF THE SCHOOL

(See Also: BUILDING; BULLETIN; BULLETIN BOARD; DISMISSAL PROCEDURES; FIRE DRILLS; HANDBOOK; OPEN HOUSE)

. . .Fire Exit Flow Diagram

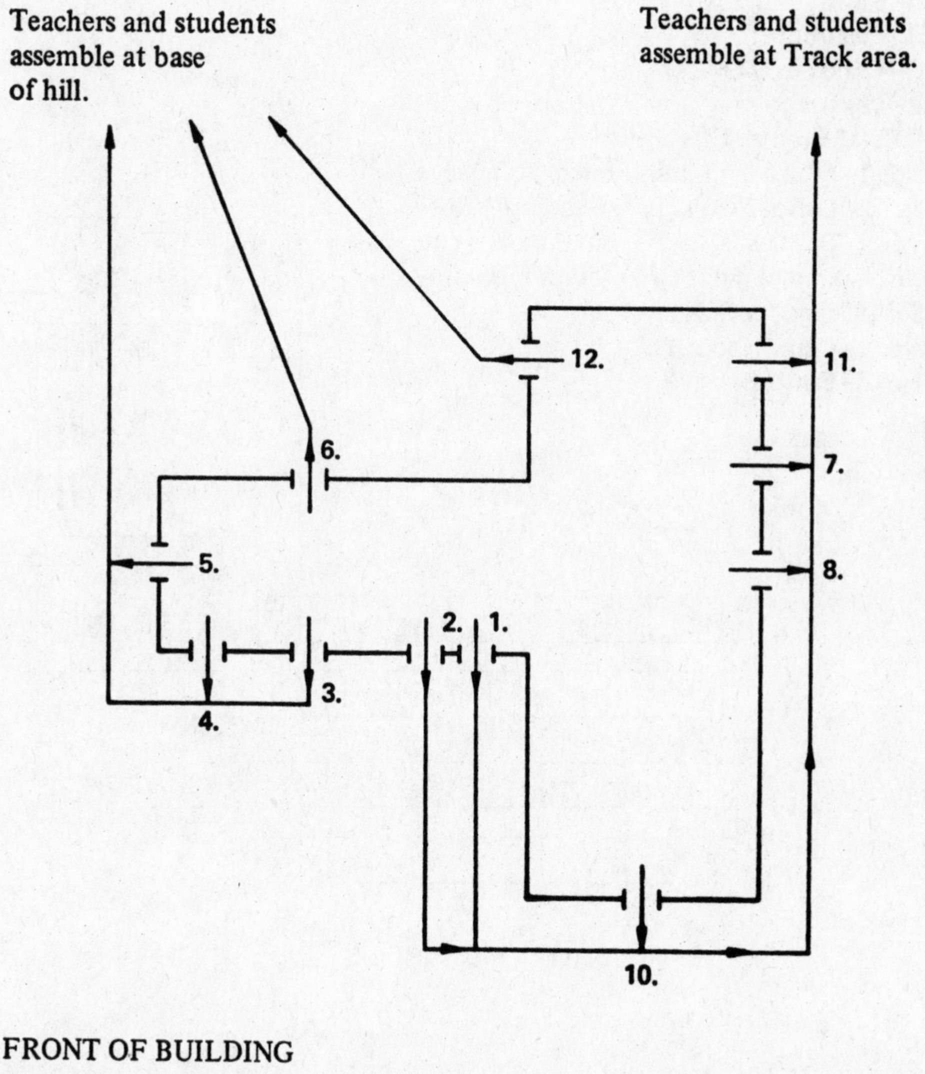

Above are indicated the lines of march away from the building in the event of a fire drill. Please check and remember your exit and its consequent line of march.

MAP OF THE SCHOOL

. . .Sample of School Map

KEY

A—Classroom
B—Storage for Art
C—Classroom
D—Office for A.V.A.
L—Lavatory
C.S.—Custodian Storage
No. 1—Office for Math, Foreign Language
No. 2—Office for English, Reading & Social Studies
No.3—Employment Orientation Program
Sci.—Office for Science
No. 4—Conf. Room 1
No. 5—Conf. Room 2

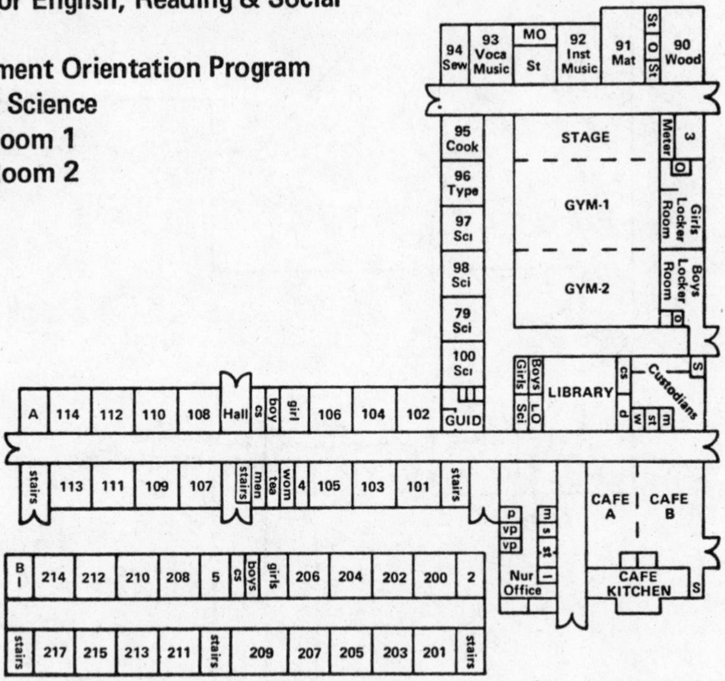

FRONT OF SCHOOL

MEDIA (See Also: NEWS COVERAGE; NEWSPAPER; NEWS RELEASES; PUBLIC RELATIONS)

. . .Guidelines for Dealing With

To: FACULTY
From: J. BENSON, PRINCIPAL
Re: MASS MEDIA

As most of you are aware, the local press and television station are taking a particular interest in Education of late. In particular, recent T.V. specials and articles in the local newspapers are concentrating on the quality of Education in our and surrounding school systems. Consequently, we may expect to be visited by various members of the media.

If you should be interviewed, may I suggest the following guidelines for your consideration:

1. Be honest. I, personally, am proud of our school and faculty. We have nothing to hide.
2. Tell the whole story. Certainly, we have problems and failures, but we also have outstanding successes. Make certain that the person who speaks to you is aware of the checks and balances within our system.
3. Don't make a PERSONAL grievance reflective of the school as a whole. All of us complain, I don't think we would be human if we didn't, but remember that we have procedures for handling grievances within our system. To air your grievances in the newspaper is not desirable.
4. This is your school; you have helped to make it the fine institution it is–BE PROUD OF IT!

I have every confidence that our school can stand every scrutiny. I know that you believe so, too.

. . .Information Sheet for Media Release

FOR IMMEDIATE RELEASE:

WHAT: ______________________________

____

____

WHEN: ______________________________

____

WHERE: ______________________________

____

WHO (People Involved): ______________________________

____

____

WHY: ______________________________

____

____

ANY OTHER PERTINENT INFORMATION: ______________________________

____

____

Date: ____________ Name of Contributor: ______________________________

Phone where you can be reached: Before 6 p.m. ______________________________

After 6 p.m. ______________________________

Signature of Contributor: ______________________________

MEDIATOR (See Also: BOARD OF EDUCATION; NEGOTIATIONS; REPRESENTATION)

. . .Providing Information for

Dear Mr. McConnel,

We have been informed of your appointment as mediator of the current impasse in negotiations between the Rock Township Board of Education and the Rock Township Education Association. We are delighted that you could see clear to help us.

As you are aware, our system will assume all of your expenses. If you will be kind enough to list them on the enclosed sheet, we will see to their prompt payment. We have reserved a room for you at The Howard Johnson Motor Inn, opposite the shopping center on Haskins Avenue. Please call me at 123-4567 when you arrive.

As you may be aware, the meeting will take place on Thursday, April 16, 19XX at 7:30 p.m. at the Office of the Board of Education, 123 Round Ridge Road. I shall be happy to arrange transportation for you.

I am enclosing a number of items such as school statistical breakdowns, salary schedules, and tax data. I hope you will find these helpful. Please feel free to call me should you require additional information or anything that may be of aid to you in the task that lies before you.

Thank you so much for your concern. We are grateful for your services.

Sincerely,
Thomas Smith,
Superintendent of Schools

. . .Request for the Services of

Dear Dr. Raleigh,

Pursuant to Section 18: 26-31 of the State Education Code, it is necessary that I inform you that a state of impasse exists between the Rock Township Board of Education and the Rock Township Education Association in professional negotiations. Consequently, I formally request that a mediator be appointed by the State Commissioner of Education.

I respectfully request your prompt attention to this matter. We shall make all arrangements for the mediator as soon as we receive further clarification from you.

Sincerely,
Thomas Smith,
Superintendent of Schools

MEDICAL

(See Also: DRUGS; EMERGENCY; HOSPITALIZATION; INQUIRIES; PSYCHOLOGICAL SERVICES; WORKING PAPERS; X-RAYS)

. . .Medical Excuse Form

SCHOOL:_______________________________ DATE:__________

STUDENT:____

GRADE:____________________ HOMEROOM:___________

THE ABOVE NAMED STUDENT IS EXCUSED FROM PHYSICAL EDUCATION FROM ______________ UNTIL ____________ , 19 ________.

REASON:____

CONFIRMED BY DR. _________________________________

STUDENT ASSIGNED TO: ______________________________

GUIDANCE COUNSELOR:______________________________

SIGNATURE OF SCHOOL NURSE:_________________________

OTHER INFORMATION: _______________________________

____

. . .Medication Form

SCHOOL:_______________________________ DATE:__________

STUDENT:____

DIAGNOSIS:____

MEDICATION: ______________________________________

DOCTOR IN CHARGE:_________________________________

DIRECTIONS FOR ADMINISTERING (e.g., one tablet, q.i.d., etc.):__________

____

SIGNATURE OF DOCTOR:__________________

SIGNATURE OF PARENT:__________________

. . .Request for Medical Information (2 forms)

(A) first form—for students

Dear Parents (Guardians),

We are always anxious to keep your child's health records up to date. This is particularly important in the case of an emergency. Could you take some time to help us? Please fill out the following form and have your child return it to his or her homeroom teacher.

Thank you for your cooperation.

NAME OF STUDENT: ______________________________ GRADE: __________

DISEASES OR ILLNESSES DURING THE PAST YEAR: ____________________

____

____

SERIOUS INJURIES, FRACTURES, OPERATIONS: ______________________

____

____

ADDITIONAL MEDICAL INFORMATION SINCE LAST UPDATE: ____________

____

____

SIGNATURE OF PARENT (GUARDIAN): ____________

(B) second form—for teacher candidate

NAME OF CANDIDATE: ____

ADDRESS OF CANDIDATE: ____

____ ZIP ___________

DATE OF PHYSICAL EXAMINATION: _________________________________

WEIGHT: ______________________ HEIGHT: ______________________

LUNGS: _______________________ HEART: _______________________

BLOOD PRESSURE: ______________ GENERAL CONDITION: __________

IS THE CANDIDATE CURRENTLY BEING TREATED? _____ IF YES, FOR WHAT: ____

____

( ) TINE TEST ( ) CHEST X-RAY DATE:______ RESULT:________

ANY CONDITION OR DEFECT WHICH WOULD PREVENT CANDIDATE FROM PERFORMANCE OF DUTIES?________IF YES, EXPLAIN:______________

____

CAN YOU RECOMMEND THIS CANDIDATE FOR EMPLOYMENT WHICH INVOLVES CLOSE CONTACT WITH SCHOOL-AGE CHILDREN: ____________

IF NO, EXPLAIN: ________________________________

____

NAME OF DOCTOR: ______________________________

ADDRESS: _____________________________________

______________________________ PHONE: __________

DATE:__________ SIGNATURE OF DOCTOR:______________

MEMO (See Also: CONFIRMATION; NOTE PADS; SUGGESTIONS; THANKS)

. . .Checklist Form

DATE:_________________________

TO:__________________________ FROM:__________________

( ) PLEASE SEND ME
( ) PLEASE REVIEW
( ) FOR YOUR APPROVAL
( ) PLEASE CIRCULATE
( ) FOR YOUR ACTION
( ) RETAIN FOR YOUR FILE
( ) LET'S DISCUSS
( ) PLEASE ADVISE
( ) PLEASE INITIAL AND RETURN
( ) PER YOUR REQUEST
( ) FOR YOUR INFORMATION
( ) MAY I HAVE YOUR OPINION?
( ) WOULD YOU PLEASE TAKE CARE OF THIS?
( ) OTHER (COMMENT):_______________________

____

____

. . .Short Message Form

TO:__________________________________ DATE:__________

FROM: J. Benson, Principal

RE:____

MESSAGE: ____

____

____

____

____

- -please detach and return- -

I have read your memo dated ____________________________

COMMENT: ____

____

____

Date: ______________________ Signature: ______________________

MINI-COURSE (See Also: COURSE OF STUDY; INSTRUCTION; NEW POLICY OR PROGRAM)

. . .Notice to Parents of

Dear Parents,

In the Spring, 19XX semester, the English Department of Rock Township High School shall be introducing Mini-Courses into the standard English Curriculum.

A "Mini-Course" is a course that lasts for one marking period only, rather than for a full year or semester. With these courses, we shall be able to offer a wide variety of courses on numerous subjects related to the English Curriculum, but not usually covered in any depth in regular classes. Such courses will include Introduction to Media, Poetry, Drama Techniques, Our Literary Heritage, Modern American Writers, Youth in Literature, and more.

It is hoped that these courses may help to open up a world of literary and English related activities to our students.

You will be receiving a list of the mini-courses offered, and we urge you to go over it with your son or daughter.

Sincerely,
K. Folsom, English Department
Rock Township High School

. . .Samples of Mini-Course Descriptions

E-14 INTRODUCTION TO MEDIA

The student is introduced to various forms of mass media used in the world today. A study is made of the ways in which people communicate on a mass basis. Various media are studied including newspapers, television, radio, and magazines. The various techniques of propaganda as used in the mass media are also studied.

E-20 MODERN AMERICAN WRITERS

The emergence of modern America is studied through the writings of the acknowledged masters of contemporary American literature. Students read and analyze works by Steinbeck, Hemingway, Fitzgerald, Faulkner, and others. Students come to appreciate the various stages of 20th century American History as reflected in the works of these authors.

MINORITIES

(See Also: ACCOUNTABILITY; BI-LINGUAL EDUCATION; EXCHANGE STUDENTS; PETITIONS; PUBLIC RELATIONS)

. . .Literature Concerning

MEMO

To: ALL DISTRICT LIBRARIANS
From: THOMAS SMITH, SUPERINTENDENT OF SCHOOLS
Re: MINORITY LITERATURE

America has been described as "A Nation of Immigrants." Certainly we can all agree with this, because we are all aware that it was the cooperative effort of people of ALL races, ALL religions, ALL nationalities that made our country great. Indeed, each group has contributed to America's growth and has a rich heritage to share with us.

Consequently, it is not only desirable, but essential that the libraries of our schools contain literature reflective of the efforts of all Americans, their contributions, and their heritages. We may be justly proud of the contributions made to our society by all its members, and we want our students to have ready access to information on each group.

We are directing, therefore, that all librarians take this into account when ordering materials and books for the library. It must be the effort of every librarian to provide an accurate and balanced reference source representing all Americans.

. . .Philosophy of Education Regarding

Education in a democracy is for everyone. The children in our schools are representative of a wide variety of ethnic, racial, and religious groups. These groups have all made a contribution to both the building of our nation and the "American way of life" as it has been termed. Consequently, in a democratic education the contributions, efforts, and cultures of all groups should be stressed and the students made aware of the contributions and cultures of all.

. . .Policy on Dealing with Prejudice

Prejudice exists. That is an unfortunate fact of life. Prejudice is detestable in society and unforgivable in an American classroom. Teachers are, of course, to take particular pains to rid every vestige of personal prejudice from themselves or their classrooms. Should an incident of prejudice occur in a classroom, teachers should not allow the incident to go by unnoticed. This would only lend a degree of passivity to the incident. Instead, the incident must be handled and every effort made to point out the unfairness and irrationality of prejudice and to insure that every effort be made to see that the incident NOT be repeated.

MONTHLY REPORTS

(See Also: ACCOUNTABILITY; NEWSLETTER; PERCENTAGE OF PROMOTION SHEETS; YEAR-END REPORT)

. . .Administrator's Form

SCHOOL:________________________________ DATE:__________

ADMINISTRATOR:____________________________________

REPORT FOR THE MONTH OF__________________ 19__________

AVERAGE DAILY ATTENDANCE:__________________________

MONTHLY REPORTS

NUMBER OF SUSPENSIONS: ________ NUMBER OF TRUANCIES: ________

NUMBER OF DISCIPLINARY REFERRALS TO ADMINISTRATIVE ACTION: ____

NUMBER OF PLACEMENTS IN ALTERNATE SCHOOL PROGRAM: ________

NUMBER OF NEW STUDENTS: ______ NUMBER OF STUDENTS LEFT: ______

PROBLEMS AND DIFFICULTIES: ________________________________

____

____

OUTSTANDING EVENTS OR ACTIVITIES: __________________________

____

____

COMMENTS: ____

____

____

SIGNATURE OF ADMINISTRATOR: ______________________________

. . .Of Tutoring

TEACHER: ______________________________ DATE: __________

NAME OF PUPIL BEING TUTORED: ____________________________

GRADE: ____________ SCHOOL: ____________________________

REASON FOR TUTORING: ____________________________________

IN WHAT SUBJECT(S): ______________________________________

THIS REPORT COVERS TUTORING FOR THE MONTH OF ________ , 19 ____

LIST DATES WHEN STUDENT WAS TUTORED: ____________________

____

____

TIME PER TUTORING SESSION: _______________________________

TOTAL TIME FOR THE MONTH: _______________________________

TEXTBOOK(S) USED: ____

____

PAGES COVERED IN TEXTBOOK(S): ____________________________

PLEASE DESCRIBE THE PROGRESS OF THE STUDENT: ______________

____

____

ANY PROBLEMS: ____

____

COMMENTS: ____

____

SIGNATURE OF TEACHER: ____

... .Teacher's Form

SCHOOL: ______________________________ DATE: __________

TEACHER: ____

SUBJECT(S): ____________________ GRADE(S): ____________________

ROOM(S) USED: ____

OUTSTANDING EVENTS OR ACTIVITIES: ______________________________

____

ANY CONDITION OF THE ROOM OR SCHOOL WHICH REQUIRES ATTENTION:

____

____

ANY STUDENT(S) WHO REQUIRE SPECIAL SERVICES: ____________________

____

SPECIAL PROBLEMS: ____

____

COMMENTS: ____

____

SIGNATURE OF TEACHER: ____

N

NATIONAL HONOR SOCIETY

(See Also: ACHIEVEMENT; AWARDS; CONGRATULATIONS; GIFTED STUDENTS; HONOR ROLL; PERMANENT RECORDS; SCHOLARSHIPS)

. . .Letter of Congratulations

(A) to parents

Dear Mr. and Mrs. Bennett,

On behalf of the entire faculty and staff of Rock Township High School may I extend our heartiest congratulations on your son Barry's election to the National Honor Society. This award reflects far more than mere academic achievement. Indeed, it is a testimony to Barry's high moral integrity, the constructive ideals he represents, and his outstanding school citizenship. He is, indeed, deserving of this honor.

In a very real sense, you share this honor with your son, for it is you who have provided the basis for the development of your son's character and the encouragement and backing that have made him such an outstanding student.

Again, we offer our congratulations and our best wishes for every success in Barry's future endeavors.

Sincerely,
J. Benson, Principal

(B) to students

Dear Barry,

Congratulations! Your election to the National Honor Society stands as a credit to yourself and our school. Over the past few years I have come to know you well, and I can think of no one more deserving of this honor. Indeed, you have exemplified the high standards of integrity, citizenship, and academic achievement that are the hallmark of the National Honor Society.

I want you to know that I am proud to have you in our school. May your future be bright and filled with the success you so richly deserve.

Sincerely,
J. Benson, Principal

. . .Media Announcement of

Barry Bennett, a junior at Rock Township High School, has been elected to the National Honor Society at the school according to Principal John Benson.

Bennett carries an "A" average, is president of the Junior Class, president of the Student Welfare League, a member of the Student Council, a member of the debating team, and plays first-string football at the school.

According to Rock Township High School Principal, John Benson, election to the National Honor Society is made on the basis of an evaluation of the student's academic record, moral integrity, and general school citizenship.

Barry Bennett will be inducted into the National Honor Society during a ceremony to be held later this month at the school.

NEGOTIATIONS

(See Also: ACCEPTANCE; BOARD OF EDUCATION; CONFERENCES; CONTRACT; FINANCIAL; HOSPITALIZATION; LEADERSHIP; MEDIATOR; REPRESENTATION; SALARY)

. . .Letter Suggesting Meeting Schedule

Dear Mr. Trumbull,

The Rock Township Board of Education would like to propose the following schedule of meetings for this year's negotiations for consideration by you and your negotiating team. Please inform us at your earliest convenience if this schedule is agreeable to you and your team.

1. Regular meetings shall be held on Wednesday evenings starting Wednesday, October 17, 19XX and continuing until the successful conclusion of negotiations.
2. Meetings will take place in the Board Room of the Board of Education Office, 123 Round Ridge Road, Rock Township.
3. Meetings shall begin promptly at 8:00 p.m. and conclude no later than 11:00 p.m.
4. Additional meetings and/or extension of meeting times may be scheduled by mutual consent of all parties.

We hope this schedule is agreeable to you. Please let us know your feelings as soon as possible.

Sincerely,
Jonathan B. Tanner, Secretary
Rock Township Board of Education

. . .Letter to Confirm Representation

Dear Mr. Trumbull,

Enclosed is a list of members of the Board of Education and representatives of the Superintendent of Schools. These people will constitute the Negotiations Team of the Rock Township Board of Education in negotiations for the school year 19XX-19XX. Mr. Thomas Harbinger has been designated as the Board's chief negotiator.

It is understood that while the negotiating team has been granted certain authority by the Board, the final contract proposal must be submitted to the entire Board of Education for ratification.

Sincerely,
Jonathan B. Tanner, Secretary
Rock Township Board of Education

. . .Memo on Record Keeping

To: ALL BOARD AND TEACHER NEGOTIATION TEAMS
From: THOMAS SMITH, SUPERINTENDENT OF SCHOOLS
Re: RECORD KEEPING DURING NEGOTIATIONS

The keeping of accurate records of all meetings is an essential developmental process. Nowhere is this more true than in the upcoming negotiations between the Rock Township Board of Education and the Rock Township Education Association. There must exist accurate records of negotiations in order that all parties may refer to them and receive pertinent and exact information.

Consequently, it is my suggestion that the first item of negotiations be the appointment of a secretary mutually agreeable to each party. I further suggest that the minutes of each meeting be reviewed by the chief negotiators for each party and signed by them as an indication that the minutes are accurate and truly reflect what has occurred at the meeting.

In this way, there should be no contention as to the representative nature of the records.

. . .Setting the Ground Rules for

Dear Mr. Trumbull,

We should like to propose to you and your negotiating team the following procedures for this year's negotiations.

1. The schedule of meetings shall be that suggested in the Board's letter of October 1, 19XX which has been approved without changes by the Rock Township Education Association.
2. Whenever possible, informal discussion shall obtain. In any case of disagreement, however, procedures from ROBERT'S RULES OF ORDER shall apply.
3. The Chairing of meetings shall alternate between the head negotiator for the Rock Township Board of Education and the Rock Township Education Association.
4. Visitors including, but not limited to, the principals of various schools in Rock Township may be present at negotiating sessions with the consent of both parties or at the specific request of the head negotiator of a party in order to testify to or clarify a point of negotiations. It is understood that these visitors shall take no part in direct negotiation procedures, but they shall act solely as observers or witnesses.
5. Expenses incurred during negotiations shall be equally divided between the Rock Township Board of Education and the Rock Township Education Association.

We hope that these procedures meet with the approval of your negotiating team. Please inform us as soon as possible of your decision.

Sincerely,
Jonathan B. Tanner, Secretary
Rock Township Board of Education

NEW POLICY OR PROGRAM

(See Also: IDEAS; IN-SERVICE; MINI-COURSES; PUBLIC RELATIONS)

. . .Explaining the Need for

MEMO

To: FACULTY
From: J. BENSON, PRINCIPAL
Re: FORMATION OF NEW PROGRAMS

Time has a nasty habit of creeping up on us. This is particularly true in light of current calls for relevance in today's education. Indeed, we must educate our students for a place in tomorrow's world.

Consequently, we must begin to take a close look at our course of study and ask ourselves if what is being taught is pertinent and relevant to education now–today. We must also ask ourselves if we are doing everything in our power to meet the needs of our community and our students who will be the citizens of tomorrow.

With this in mind, I am in the process of forming a committee to look into the revamping of our course of study and forming new programs that will meet tomorrow's needs. While I am well aware that something is not necessarily better just because it is new, I am also aware that just because something has been done in a certain way for years and years does not make it the *sine qua non* of progress.

I would appreciate your feedback on these ideas. I would also appreciate any volunteers to work on this committee. Active participation by the experts–you–will insure success.

. . .Soliciting Ideas for

MEMO

To: ALL STUDENTS AND FACULTY
From: J. BENSON, PRINCIPAL
Re: IDEAS FOR NEW COURSES

We are very proud of the course selections we offer at Rock Township High School. We feel that we offer our students a wide variety of choices throughout their years at our school.

In order to continue with this policy, we are in the process of examining our current course of study to see if there are places where the courses we presently offer might be revamped or new courses created.

This is where we could use your help. Do you have any suggestions? What courses should be revised? Should any be eliminated? What new courses would you like to see offered?

If you have any constructive thoughts on any or all of these questions, we would very much like to hear from you. There will be a special suggestion box located in the main office for the next two weeks. If you would write down your suggestions, sign the paper and place it in the box, you would be doing your school a great service. Signed suggestions will be answered.

We look forward to your suggestions.

NEWS COVERAGE (See Also: EDITORIAL; MEDIA; NEWSLETTER; NEWSPAPER; NEWS RELEASES; PUBLIC RELATIONS)

. . .Ground Rules for Reporters "On Campus"

Welcome to Rock Township High School–

We are certain that you are interested in getting a suitable story for your newspaper and following sound journalistic practices. We are also certain that you wish to go about your task without causing an undue disruption in the educational processes of the school. Toward that end, we have a few suggestions:

1. Please inform the main office of your presence in the building. This is required of all visitors to our school. We would also appreciate it if you would notify the main office when you are about to leave.
2. Students are not allowed to be removed from class without the permission of the main office.
3. Teachers are not to be disturbed during an assigned teaching period. Teachers are available during their professional periods; and a copy of any teacher's schedule is available from the main office.

4. We would ask you to remember that there are many sides to every issue. While we have no intention or desire to interfere with journalistic freedom, it is hoped that the ENTIRE story be presented, incorporating ALL points of view.

We hope that you will appreciate these suggestions and that your time at Rock Township High School will be profitable.

Sincerely,
J. Benson, Principal

. . .Soliciting News Coverage

(A) from a newspaper

Dear Editor,

We believe we have a newsworthy event about to occur which you may wish to cover in your newspaper.

On Saturday evening, November 15, 19XX, at 8:00 p.m. at Rock Township High School there will be an Alumni Dinner. This is an annual event at the school, but why should it command press coverage by your paper?

The answer is that several of our alumni have gone on to achieve a significant degree of success and public recognition. Among our alumni present on that evening will be Jennifer Adams McKee, first vice-president of the National Overland Bank, Sidney Callisher, director of Special Services for the Department of Justice of our state, Dr. Martin Baily, whose research into Genetics has received national recognition, and Mary Beth Downs, who you may be aware has a leading role in a current Broadway musical.

The presence of these and many other notables makes this an event worthy of coverage by your newspaper.

Should you wish any further information, please call me at 234-5678.

Sincerely,
J. Benson, Principal
Rock Township High School

(B) from radio or T.V.

Dear News Editor,

Having watched your television news shows for several years, I am well aware of the high quality of news coverage which your station represents. I am also aware that you make considerable effort to provide continuing coverage of newsworthy local events.

I believe that there is just such an event about to occur which would be worthy of your attention.

There is so much negative attention given to today's youth, would it not be refreshing to present a heartening story of youth involved in positive, selfless, constructive activity? Not only would this help to "balance out" the stories of teenage crime, but it would present a much more realistic appraisal of today's teenagers.

On Saturday morning, May 17, 19XX, from 11:00 a.m. to 2:00 p.m. at Rock Township High School a "carnival" will be held. This, in itself, is not unique, but the story behind it is rewarding and enlivening.

When one of our students suffered a tragic accident which left him a paraplegic, our students went to work to help him and his family. Through a number of strenuous, time-consuming, dedicated activities, the students of Rock Township High School have raised over $6,000.00 for their friend. The carnival is to be the culminating event.

On hand at the activity will be the young man and his family as well as all of the students who have worked so hard and so long. Also present will be State Senator Harlin James, who has taken a personal interest in our students' efforts.

I really feel that this activity is worthy of coverage by your television news staff. If I may provide any further information, please do not hesitate to call.

Sincerely,
J. Benson, Principal
Rock Township High School

NEWSLETTER (See Also: BULLETIN; EDITORIAL; INTRODUCTION; MONTHLY REPORTS; NEWS COVERAGE; NEWSPAPER; NEWS RELEASES; PUBLIC RELATIONS)

. . .Introduction to First Newsletter

(A) for parents and public

It is our hope that this newsletter for the parents of students at Rock Township High School will be the first of a continuing series at our school. It is the purpose of this publication to keep you up to date on the happenings in our school and to accurately represent to you exactly what is going on in the school. Too often, we have to depend on hearsay to determine what is happening. With the start of this newsletter, it is hoped that we can convey to you exact information that will be of interest and help to you.

It is our purpose to educate the students of Rock Township. If this newsletter can be of service to our student's parents and in this way aid in the academic and behavioral growth of our students, then we shall indeed feel gratified.

(B) in-house

Admittedly, we are a large school. With a growing enrollment and a staff of 72, communication often becomes a real problem. In the past, there have been legitimate complaints from teachers that they found out about an event or activity from a student rather than through administrative channels. This has occasioned the writing of this newsletter.

Hopefully, this newsletter, which I promise to get to you at least once a month, will help to keep you abreast of what is happening at our school both in the field of academic and administrative action and personally, with our colleagues and friends. If you have anything you might wish to include, I'd appreciate your suggestions.

It is my sincere wish that you will find these newsletters informative and enjoyable.

. . .Sample Page from a Newsletter

As this month begins, we are still awaiting the results of last month's statewide testing. We have been promised that those results will be in by the 15th. I'll let you know just as soon as I receive them.

The Curriculum Revision Committee reports that it is making real progress, and the Chairperson, Mr. Tomlinson, wanted me to thank you all for your many helpful suggestions.

** ** MAY DATEBOOK ** **

Tuesday, May 7	– Assembly–Band-Period 7–Auditorium
Thursday, May 9	– Failure Notices due in Guidance Office
Monday, May 13 Tuesday, May 14 – Wednesday, May 15–	Dr. Smith and evaluating team visits school for class observations.
Tuesday, May 21	– Faculty Meeting–3:15 p.m.–Library
Friday, May 24	– Assembly–Science Show–Periods 6 & 7–Auditorium
Monday, May 27	– Possible Failure for Year due in Guidance Office

** PERSONALITIES **

MR. HAROLD JENKINS of the English Department has just finished an article on teaching the gifted and talented which will appear in the State Education Association's magazine in the fall.

MISS JANET CUNNINGHAM of our Social Studies Department plans to be married on June 30. When she returns to us in September she will be Mrs. Robert Norris. Mr. and Mrs. Norris plan to honeymoon in the Bahamas.

MRS. JUDY WEBER of the Science Department, who left last month on Maternity Leave, will be returning to us in September. Mr. and Mrs. Weber are the parents of a son, Thomas James, born April 27 at 3:05 a.m.

MR. ALLAN BECKETT of the Social Studies Department will be receiving his Master's Degree in Pupil Personnel Services from Fairmont College on Sunday, June 2.

NEWSPAPER (See Also: BULLETIN; CLUBS; EDITORIAL; EXTRA-CURRICULAR ACTIVITIES; MEDIA; NEWS COVERAGE; NEWSLETTER; NEWS RELEASES; PUBLIC RELATIONS)

. . .Guidelines for the Use of Newspapers as Public Relations Vehicles

MEMO

To: ALL PRINCIPALS
From: JAMES NORRIS, DIRECTOR OF PUBLIC RELATIONS
Re: PUBLIC RELATIONS AND NEWSPAPERS

Recently, with a change in editorial policy at our local newspaper, we have been fortunate to receive increased coverage of school events. With this increased coverage, we have an excellent opportunity to present ourselves to the general public of Rock Township. While the majority of news releases have come and will continue to come from this office, Principals are increasingly being called upon by the local press to provide stories and articles of interest.

Consequently, I thought it might be of interest to you if I offered a few suggestions for your consideration:

1. EMPHASIZE THE POSITIVE. We have many outstanding students and activities in our schools. The public should be aware of this.
2. DON'T HIDE THE NEGATIVE. If something unfortunate has happened, do not try to cover it up. Present it honestly. State your opinion of the incident in a positive manner.
3. TELL THE WHOLE STORY. Make certain that you present all sides of an issue. If, for instance, 50 students stage a demonstration, be certain you mention that the other 500 students stayed in class and did not join them.
4. IF YOU ARE IN DOUBT, a phone call to this office will receive immediate attention.

Remember, we don't have to manufacture news. There are enough positive, energetic and fine activities going on in our schools to supply many news stories. Let's let the public know the good things that are going on in our schools.

. . .Philosophy of the School Newspaper

A school newspaper exists for the students of the school. While it cannot help but be reflective of the quality of life at a school and consequently serves as a public relations vehicle, it is primarily intended for the growth and entertainment and information of the school's students. Students who participate in the production of the school newspaper should learn the practices of good journalism. They should be involved in the actual production of the paper and through that involvement learn the intricacies of production and preparation. Students who receive the school newspaper should obtain from it accurate, unbiased and unprejudiced reporting, reflective of the events and activities that are so much a part of their school lives.

. . .Policy on Content of the School Newspaper

The school newspaper is a public vehicle intended for the students of the school and also intended to be reflective of school life. Consequently, the following guidelines for the content of the school newspaper are offered:

1. Language of an obscene, profane or vulgar nature is to be avoided at all times.
2. All reporting is to be accurate. Any story that appears in the paper must be checked for accuracy. This applies to all direct quotes as well as any description of policy or events.
3. Criticism is an editorial prerogative. News stories should be factual, without prejudice, bias or commentary.
4. Editorials should be positive in nature. Anyone can find fault. Any editorial of a critical nature should be accompanied by suggestions for positive improvement.
5. Personal invective has no place in any newspaper.
6. All sides of a story must be told. One-sided reporting must never be allowed.
7. News should be reflective of the efforts of our school and its students. The use of the names of *all* participants in an event or activity is encouraged.

NEWS RELEASES (See Also: EDITORIAL; INTRODUCTION; JOURNALS; MEDIA; NEWS COVERAGE; NEWSLETTER; NEWSPAPER; PUBLIC RELATIONS)

. . .Checklist for Newsworthiness

To the Faculty:

Is your story newsworthy?

Many teachers have stories concerning their classes or extra-curricular activities which they feel are worthy of release through our school system's Public Relations Office. Before YOU submit such a story, it would be appreciated if you could fill in the following checklist. If you can answer "Yes" to any seven questions, we would like to see it. If not, perhaps you might like to rethink it.

Thank you for your cooperation. This process will save us many hours of valuable time.

OFFICE OF PUBLIC RELATIONS

* * * * * * * * * * *

YES NO

( ) ( ) Does your story concern something that goes beyond the day-to-day operation of the school?

( ) ( ) Does your story emphasize positive interaction of students, students and faculty, or students and the community?

( ) ( ) Does your story emphasize positive aspects of school life?

( ) ( ) Does your story contain any unusual aspects which take it out of the realm of the mundane?

( ) ( ) Would anyone besides the parents of the students involved need or want to know about the story?

( ) ( ) Does the story have any humorous or heartwarming qualities?

( ) ( ) Have all the facts of the story been checked for accuracy?

( ) ( ) Does your story contain aspects with which a significant number of the general public could identify?

( ) ( ) Could you provide black-and-white photographs if needed?

. . .Model News Story

A group of students at Rock Township High School have been roaming the halls interrupting classes lately, and the faculty and administrators are delighted.

It began in the Social Studies class of teacher Mary Norris. "We were discussing the plight of the people in Costa Grande, who had been devastated by a hurricane followed by an eruption of a volcano," Mrs. Norris reported. "My class was shocked and moved by the suffering of these unfortunate people."

"We felt we had to do something," Tom Barron, a member of the class, recalls, "but we had no idea of how to go about it."

Mrs. Norris arranged for a visit by Mr. Frank Callerton, Associate Director of the American Relief Society. "I spoke to them of the urgent need for food, clothing, and medical supplies," stated Mr. Callerton, "and these great kids did the rest."

After that, Mrs. Norris and her students went into action. During each class period for the next week, students visited other classes in the school informing others of the desperate need of Costa Grande residents and asking for donations of food and clothing.

"They were marvelous," Mrs. Norris remembers. "The entire school reacted so well that we had a real problem of where to store the materials that were coming in."

"In all," reports Rock Township High School principal John Benson, "our students raised over seven thousand dollars worth of supplies. We are proud of them and their actions which bespeak the fine character of our students and community. They are a credit to the school and themselves."

The accumulated materials will be accepted by the American Relief Society at a school-wide assembly to be held next Monday morning at 10:00 a.m. at the school.

NON-RENEWAL OF CONTRACT (See Also: CONTRACT; REPRIMANDS; RIGHTS AND RESPONSIBILITIES)

. . .Of a Non-Tenured Teacher

Dear Mrs. Smith,

At the February 21, 19XX meeting of the Rock Township Board of Education it was determined that your teaching contract will not be renewed for the school year 19XX-19XX.

In accordance with the current contract between the Rock Township Board of Education and the Rock Township Education Association, you may, within thirty (30) days of this notification, request in writing from the Assistant Superintendent in charge of Personnel a written statement of reasons. Such statement shall be supplied within fifteen (15) days of receipt of such request.

You may also, within five (5) days of receipt of such statement, request and receive an interview with the Superintendent and following such interview, may request, within five (5) days, an informal appearance before the Board of Education. You may be represented by counsel or one individual of your choosing. You also have the right to present persons to the Board who will make statements on your behalf. Such persons shall be called into the meeting to address the Board one at a time and shall be excused from the meeting after making their statements.

Such informal appearance must be scheduled within thirty (30) calendar days of receipt of such request and the Board shall notify you, in writing, of its final determination within five (5) days following the informal appearance.

Sincerely,
James T. Shannon,
Assistant Superintendent

. . .Of a Tenured Teacher

Dear Mr. Jones,

It is with sincere regret that we must inform you that at the February 21, 19XX meeting of the Rock Township Board of Education it was determined that your teaching contract will not be renewed for the 19XX-19XX school year.

The reasons for this action are as follows:

1. During the period May 1, 19XX through February 15, 19XX, you were late to school an average of 55 minutes on 83 school days and late to your assigned classes an average of 7 minutes on no less than 194 occasions.
2. During the period May 1, 19XX through February 15, 19XX, you refused to prepare and/or submit lesson plans, emergency lesson plans, cumulative records, reports, and other written materials required by the main office.
3. During the period mentioned above, you appeared at school under the influence of alcohol to such an extent that you were unable to perform your professional duties on 21 separate occasions.
4. Classroom observations by qualified and certified supervisory personnel during the aforesaid period indicated several areas in which improvement was needed. Subsequent observations revealed no effort toward correction on your part and indicated a continuing decline in performance.
5. You were advised of the above situations in letters dated May 15, June 10, June 30, September 15, October 5, October 31, November 14, November 31, December 3, and December 17, 19XX and January 10, January 28, and February 14, 19XX. In each of these letters we advised you of the seriousness of the situation, advised you of possible consequences if these situations were not corrected and offered aid and direction in helping you overcome any difficulties which might be engendering these situations. None of these letters was answered.

You are advised that you are entitled to all the rights and procedures as outlined in Article 19 of the current contract between the Rock Township Board of Education and the Rock Township Education Association. It is the purpose and intent of the Rock Township Board of Education that due process be followed in all situations.

Please be advised that if it is your intent to appeal this decision of the Board of Education we must receive written notice of that intent within thirty (30) days of the receipt of this letter.

Sincerely,
James T. Shannon,
Assistant Superintendent

NOTE PADS (See Also: CONFIRMATION; MEMO; OPEN COMMUNICATIONS)

. . .Examples of Preprinted Note Pad Headings (3 Examples)

(A) first example

. . .for your consideration
from J. Benson. . .

(B) second example

A FIW WIRDS OF WIZDUM FROM J. Benson

(C) third example

Straight to you. . .

O

OBJECTIVES (See Also: CURRICULUM; GOALS; PHILOSOPHY; UNIT COORDINATION)

. . .Example of a Personal Teaching Objective

GOAL

It is my objective that each of my Media students becomes familiar with some ways in which some methods of propaganda are used in advertising.

PROCEDURES

My students will study ten commonly used methods of propaganda in order to learn the components of their construction.

My students will view the filmstrip "What's Going On Here?" in order to learn the effect propaganda can have on the general public.

My students will listen to the cassette recording "50 Old Time Radio Commercials" in order to examine ways in which propaganda has been used in advertising in the past.

My students will construct a "Propaganda Notebook" with clippings of actual advertisements from magazines and newspapers which illustrate the ten methods of propaganda they have studied in class in order to learn how prevalent propaganda is in today's advertising.

My students will conduct a round table discussion on how propaganda is used in television advertising in order to share insights into propaganda's use in the chief mass medium.

My students shall each construct an advertisement using one or more of the methods of propaganda studied in class in order to learn, first hand, the complexities involved in the use of the particular form of persuasion they chose.

OBJECTIVES

My students will demonstrate the ability to determine the particular method of propaganda used in an advertisement they have not previously seen.

EVALUATION

Evaluation shall be through observation, testing, class worksheets, the submission of a "Propaganda Notebook" and the presentation of an advertisement using one or more methods of propaganda.

. . .Examples of School-Wide Objectives

Rock Township High School will provide every student with the opportunity to:

Acquire a stock of basic information covering the principles of the physical, biological and social sciences, the historical record of human achievements and failures, and current social issues, including knowledge of the environment.

Acquire the knowledge, understanding and skills that permit his or her participation in a satisfying and responsible role in contemporary society.

Learn to enjoy the processes of learning, and to acquire the skills necessary for a lifetime of continuous learning and adaptation to change, and to use leisure time constructively.

Acquire basic skills in obtaining information, solving problems, thinking critically, and communicating effectively.

Acquire the ability to form satisfying and responsible relationships with a wide range of people, including those with social and cultural characteristics different from his or her own.

Acquire the ability and the desire to express himself or herself creatively in one or more of the arts, and to appreciate the esthetic expressions of other people.

Acquire the capacities for assuming satisfying and responsible roles in family life and society.

Acquire the knowledge, habits and attitudes that promote personal and public health and well being.

Become an effective and responsible contributor to the decision-making processes of the community, state, nation and world.

Develop an understanding of his or her own worth, abilities, limitations and potential.

OBSERVATION (See Also: ACCOUNTABILITY; EVALUATION; LESSON PLANS; STUDENT TEACHER; TEACHER AIDE; VOLUNTEERS)

. . .Of Behavioral Patterns

(A) anecdotal record

I observed Adam Brady on Monday, May 7, 19XX during his senior English class from 10:30 a.m. unti 11:15 a.m. It was Adam's first day back from a five-day out-of-school suspension.

Adam entered the room one minute after class had begun. The teacher said, "Adam, you're late; please see me after class." Adam answered, "Yeah," and walked slowly to his seat. Adam carried no books or supplies. A pencil was stuck behind his right ear. At his desk, he sat with his shoulders back, arms crossed, his left foot and leg out in the aisle. His eyes were on the window. He continued in this position while the teacher covered material relevant to the composition to be done that day in class. Paper was passed out. Adam received it from the boy in front of him, took none for himself, and tossed the paper over his head to the girl behind him. The paper scattered over the floor. Adam smiled and resumed his former position.

Some ten minutes later the class was working and Adam had not changed his position. The teacher went to Adam and spoke to him in a low voice. I could not hear what the teacher said, but Adam's answers were, "So what?" "Yeah." "Right," and "Yeah." The teacher left and Adam placed his head in his arms folded on his desk. He remained in this position for 17 minutes.

At the end of this time, he raised his head, stretched, yawned, took the pencil from behind his ear and began to write on the desk. Shortly thereafter the bell rang, and Adam left the room quickly, pushing a student out of his way.

COMMENT: This is the fifth observation of Adam Brady. His attitude and behavior have not changed throughout the period.

(B) social interaction observation report

SOCIAL INTERACTION OBSERVATION

STUDENT: ______________________ DATE: __________

CLASS OBSERVED: ______________________

TIME OBSERVED: FROM: ________ TO: ________

1. Number of Contacts with Teacher: __________
   - A. Contacts initiated by teacher: __________
   - B. Contacts initiated by subject: __________
2. Number of Contacts with Other Students: __________
   - A. Contacts initiated by other students: __________
   - B. Contacts initiated by subject: __________
3. With Whom Were Most Student Contacts Made: __________
   - A. How many contacts: __________
   - B. How many contacts initiated by student: __________
   - C. How many contacts initiated by subject: __________
4. Names of Students Surrounding Subject's Desk: __________

A. __________	E. __________
B. __________	F. __________
C. __________	G. __________
D. __________	H. __________

5. Nature of Subject-Initiated Contacts: __________
   ____
   ____
   ____
6. Observer's Comments: __________
   ____
   ____
   ____

SIGNATURE OF OBSERVER: __________

. . .Of Specific Areas (2 Forms)

(A) first form

OBSERVATION OF READING CLASS

TEACHER: ____________________ DATE: __________

SCHOOL: ____________________ GRADE: __________

ITEM	SATISFACTORY	UNSATISFACTORY
Display of Material Motivating Reading		
Teacher Motivation of Student Reading		
Provision for Individual differences		
Pupil Attention to Presented Activity		
Activities Developed From Reading		
Student Evidence of Growth in Reading A. Interpretation		
B. Comprehension		
C. Oral Reading		
D. Silent Reading		
E. Vocabulary		

OBSERVER'S COMMENTS: ____________________

TEACHER'S COMMENTS: ____________________

TEACHER'S SIGNATURE: ____________________

OBSERVER'S SIGNATURE: ____________________

OBSERVATION

(B) second form

OBSERVATION OF MATH PROGRAM

TEACHER: ______________________ DATE: __________

SCHOOL: ______________________ GRADE: __________

ITEM	SATISFACTORY	UNSATISFACTORY
Motivation for Math Activities		
Pupil Preparation for Math Activities		
Provision for Individual Differences		
Teacher Encouragement of Pupil Initiative		
Student Interest in Math Activity		
Student Evidence of Growth in Math A. Skills in Solving Problems		
B. Skills in Computation		
C. Skills in Reasoning		
D. Application to Life		

OBSERVER'S COMMENTS: ______________________

____

____

TEACHER'S COMMENTS: ______________________

____

____

TEACHER'S COMMENTS: ______________

OBSERVER'S COMMENTS: ______________

. . .Of Teachers

See EVALUATION. . .Of Teachers
Three forms for Teacher Observation/Evaluation are listed there.

OPEN COMMUNICATIONS (See Also: NOTE PADS; PUBLIC RELATIONS; SUGGESTIONS; THANKS)

. . .Administrator's Message to Staff and Students

MEMO

To: ALL FACULTY AND STUDENTS
From: J. BENSON, PRINCIPAL
Re: COMMUNICATIONS

I honestly believe that it is only through talking honestly to each other that people achieve an open, truthful relationship in which they may work productively for the good of all.

Hopefully, we can establish, right here at Rock Township High School, just such an atmosphere of open communication. I ask you not to hide your concerns. My office will always be open to every member of our school, and I invite your comments. I stand ready to discuss all points of view.

Remember, this is your school, and you have a stake in its future. Let us keep our communications open and work together for our school's ultimate good.

. . .School Policy Statement to Parents

Dear Parents,

I have just issued a memo to the faculty and students of Rock Township High School stating my belief that open communications among all levels are essential for the peak functioning of our school. I have invited everyone at the school to share their concerns, ideas and suggestions with me. I have stated that my office is open to them at all times.

I would like you to know that these same sentiments are extended to you, the parents of our students. This school belongs to you as much as to your children. You have their best interests at heart and want what is best for them. Consequently, I would be anxious to share your thoughts.

Please feel free to contact me at any time.

Sincerely,
J. Benson, Principal

OPEN HOUSE

(See Also: ADULT EDUCATION; ALUMNI; BACK-TO-SCHOOL NIGHT; MAP OF THE SCHOOL; PUBLIC RELATIONS)

. . .Handout to Those Attending

WELCOME TO ROCK TOWNSHIP HIGH SCHOOL

We are very pleased that you could visit us. We hope that you will enjoy your stay and will want to come again. The school is open to you, and we hope that you will take this opportunity to observe our facilities and the process of continuing education going on in our school.

When visiting classes, we ask that you take seats in the rear of the room. Not only will this afford you observation of the entire class, but the students will be less distracted by your presence, and you will get an accurate picture of a classroom session.

Should you wish a student guide to aid you in your tour, please ask in the main office, and a member of the Student Council will be happy to assist you.

For your convenience, a bell schedule for change of classes is attached. The Main Office will gladly answer any questions.

This is your school. Enjoy your stay.

J. Benson, Principal

. . .Message to Parents About

Dear Parents,

We would be very pleased if you would accept an invitation.

On Wednesday, November 14, 19XX, Rock Township High School will be holding an Open House for all members of the community from 9:00 a.m. until 3:00 p.m. The entire school will be open for visitation and observation. Visitors may attend class, inspect our facilities, join in activities and even eat with the students in the cafeteria if they wish. Visitors may travel freely through the school or, if they wish, a student guide will be assigned to aid them. The main office will, of course, be open for any inquiries or questions.

This day provides an excellent opportunity for parents to observe the place where their children spend such a great part of their lives.

We sincerely hope that you will be able to come and spend some time with us. We look forward to meeting you.

Sincerely,

J. Benson, Principal

. . .Message to Teachers About

MEMO

To: FACULTY
From: J. BENSON, PRINCIPAL
Re: OPEN HOUSE

On Wednesday, November 14, 19XX from 9:00 a.m. to 3:00 p.m. we will be holding an Open House at our school. All members of the community will be invited to visit our school and observe our facilities and classes. I know we will all want to make this day an enjoyable one for our visitors, and toward that end. I'd like to offer some suggestions:

1. Provide directions where needed. If visitors are unaccompanied by a student guide, be prepared to direct them to their destinations. Assign one of your students to help if necessary.
2. Include visitors in your class. If you are giving a quiz, let them take it as well. Ask their opinion, if possible. Make it clear that you welcome their participation.
3. Do not discuss an individual student. It would be unfair to hold up your classes for discussion with a parent. I know you wish to be courteous, so suggest to such a parent that you set up a conference at a convenient time.
4. Be yourself. I AM VERY PROUD OF THE QUALITY OF EDUCATION IN OUR SCHOOL. We have no need to "show off." Conduct your normal classes, and I know that our visitors will be as impressed as I am.

I am certain that, with your help, this will be a profitable and enjoyable day for all.

OPENING PROCEDURES

(See Also: ASSEMBLIES; ATTENDANCE; P.T.A.; SCHEDULE)

. . .For an Assembly

In response to many suggestions on improving assembly procedures, the following practices shall be implemented for all future assemblies:

1. Teachers will hold classes in rooms until called to the auditorium over the PA System.
2. When a class is seated, the teacher in charge will send a message via student to Mr. Harrington, vice-principal, that the class has arrived. Such a message would read, "Mr. Jones' class is seated."
3. Mr. Harrington will be located at the foot of the stage and will check off names until full attendance is completed.
4. At that point, Mr. Harrington will cue the band, and they will play our school song.
5. Immediately upon completion of the school song, teachers will have their students rise, and the National Anthem will be played.
6. Upon completion of the National Anthem, the assembly will begin.
7. Please familiarize your students with these procedures and provide active supervision at the assembly.
8. It is hoped that by the implementation of these procedures all assemblies may begin promptly and without undue "interruptions" such as classes entering late or the need to "quiet down" the audience.

. . .For the School Year

OPENING DAY GENERAL INFORMATION

1. Students having a seven-period day will begin to arrive at school starting at approximately 7:55 a.m. Those students will report to their homerooms to find out where their first period class is scheduled. (See Item 4.)

2. The rest of the students will begin to arrive at school at approximately 8:45 a.m.
3. Large, clearly visible signs for each grade will be positioned just outside the entrances. Hopefully, these will channel and direct the incoming student traffic.
4. All students are to obtain their homeroom numbers from alphabetically arranged master lists which will be posted as follows:

   Grade 10–Second floor hall at the head of the center stairs.

   Grade 11–Just inside the entrance for Grade 11 students.

   Grade 12–On the bulletin board outside the main office.
5. Homeroom Period will be from 8:57 a.m. until approximately 10:10 a.m.
6. The bell system will be disconnected until after the extended homeroom period.
7. The time between 10:10 a.m. and 10:44 a.m. will be divided into two segments of approximately twelve minutes each for Periods Two and Three. Three minutes for passing will be provided, and classes will begin and end on voice instructions given over our public address system.
8. Beginning with Period Four (10:44 a.m.) the bell system will be connected, and we will thereafter proceed as per the regular schedule with Periods Four, Five, Six and Seven.

. . .Of a School Day

OPENING EXERCISES

1. The school day shall begin with the recital of the "Pledge of Allegiance" followed by the playing of the National Anthem.
2. The homeroom teacher shall see to it that the Flag is saluted in the room.
3. Following the National Anthem, attendance is to be taken, and the Student Council Homeroom Representative will read the Daily Bulletin.
4. Should a pupil refuse to participate in the saluting of the Flag because of religious scruples, he or she is not required to do so, but he or she must be quiet and respectful during the ritual.

P

PARENTS (See Also: COMPLAINTS; COUNSELING; DISCIPLINE; HANDBOOK; P.T.A.; RIGHTS AND RESPONSIBILITIES; SPECIAL EDUCATION; SUSPENSION; THANKS; TUTORS; VOLUNTEERS; ZONING)

. . .Introduction to Handbook For

INTRODUCTION

We are most happy to be able to send you this *Handbook For Parents*. All too often the home and the school are looked upon as two functioning entities separated by a student. Sadly, this is quite often true. It is with the hope of bridging this gap that this handbook was prepared.

Within these pages you will find the rules of our school, an explanation of the services we offer and our expectations for the education of your child. You will also find specific directions for implementing any of the procedures necessary for your involvement in our school. We hope you will find this information useful.

We look forward to serving you and your children throughout the coming year. If we may be of service, please contact us at the numbers you will find within this, your *Handbook For Parents*.

. . .Invitation to Parents

Dear Parents of Ninth Grade Students,

You are cordially invited to hear about your child's secondary education.

On Thursday, May 15, 19XX, from 8:00 p.m. until 10:00 p.m. at the Rock Township High School Auditorium, Mrs. Janet Talmann, 10th Grade Guidance Counselor, will discuss what will happen to your child when he or she enters Rock Township High School. She will cover the 10th Grade Curriculum, sports activities, and extra-curricular programs. She will also answer any questions parents may have.

I shall be there, and I look forward to meeting you.

Sincerely,
J. Benson, Principal
Rock Township High School

. . .Progress Report to Parents

PROGRESS REPORT

In my opinion ______________________ has been doing approximately as well as he is able to do and has been showing a proper attitude in his work for the week ending (date) __________.

Period	Subject	Teacher's Signature	REMARKS: If the teacher cannot conscentiously sign the above statement, please state the reason.
1			
2			
3			
4			
5			
6			
7			
HR			

Homeroom Teacher's Signature: ______________________

Students should present these forms with name, date and subjects properly filled and ready for the teacher's signature each Friday.

* *

I have examined the above form for the week ending Friday, __________

Parents's Signature: ______________________

I understand that the student is fully responsible for:

1. Presenting these forms to the teachers on Friday during his or her class periods.
2. Bringing these forms to me, properly filled out, to me every Friday evening.
3. Returning these forms to the Guidance Office on Monday morning.

Parent's Signature: ______________________

. . .Response to a Complaining Parent

Dear Mrs. Fisher,

I am in receipt of your letter of January 17, 19XX in which you express your concern that the teachers in our school are not assigning homework. Specifically, you state your amazement that your son, William, never has any assigned work to do at home because, as he reported to you, no work was ever assigned by his teachers.

I want to thank you for your concern in bringing this matter to my attention. I personally investigated by seeing the teachers involved, interviewing several students who have the same schedule as your son, and talking to William.

I must report to you that homework is assigned in all of your son's classes. The students I saw reported an average hour per night of assigned homework. Earlier today, when I saw William, he was able to tell me the homework he had been assigned over the past week. William's teachers further report that his assigned work has not been forthcoming.

I have informed William that I will be contacting you. If we may be of any help to you in solving this problem, please feel free to contact us at any time.

Again, thank you for your interest in our school.

Sincerely,
J. Benson, Principal

. . .Soliciting Parental Aid

To the Parents of Hill Middle School Bus Students:

I am writing in reference to a problem which has persisted relating to the transportation of your son or daughter. I am not sure if they have related to you some of the bus incidents we have had to face during the past five months. If not, I would like to take this opportunity to enumerate some of them.

There have been incidents of snowballs thrown at the bus and on the bus, at the driver,vandalism including cut and burnt seats, snowballs thrown at other buses after arriving at their bus stops in the afternoon, obscene writing on seats, smoking and improper language directed at the driver, and objects being thrown from the bus. As you can see, all this brings me serious concern as to the safety and welfare of your son or daughter.

Because of the seriousness of this matter, I solicit your help in discussing this with your son or daughter.

Please feel free to contact the school at 873-9006 if you have any questions. Thank you for your cooperation in this matter.

Sincerely,
Harold James,
Principal

PASSES (See Also: ABSENCE; CONFIRMATION; CUTTING; HALL DUTY; LIBRARY; LOCKERS)

. . .All-Purpose Pass

Please excuse the following student. This student is to report to:
________________________________.

NAME:____________________ DAY: ______ PERIOD:________

TEACHER REQUESTING STUDENT: ________________

. . .Classroom Pass

HALL PASS

Date: ____________________________

Time: ____________________________

Student:___________________________

Reason for Excuse (please initial):

______ 1. Main Office
______ 2. Nurse's Office
______ 3. Library
______ 4. Room # ____
______ 5. Lavatory
______ 6. Excused Lateness by Teacher
______ 7. Other (explain): ____________

Teacher:__________________ Rm:_______

PERCENTAGE OF PROMOTION SHEETS

(See Also: ACCOUNTABILITY; EXAMINATIONS; GRADUATION; MONTHLY REPORTS; PERMANENT RECORDS; YEAR-END REPORT)

. . .For a Teacher

PERCENTAGE PROMOTION REPORT

TEACHER: ____________________

DEPARTMENT: ____________________

SUBJECT	# STUDENTS	# PASSED	# FAILED	# INCOMPLETE	% PASSED

THIS FORM IS TO BE COMPLETED BY THE TEACHER AND SUBMITTED TO THE DEPARTMENT CHAIRPERSON NO LATER THAN TUESDAY, JUNE 21, 19XX.

. . .For the School

PERCENTAGE PROMOTION REPORT

SCHOOL: ____

FOR THE SCHOOL YEAR 19 _____ -19 _______

GRADE 10

SUBJECT	# STUDENTS	# PASSED	# FAILED	# INCOMPLETE	% PASSED

GRADE 11

GRADE 12

TOTAL BY GRADE

GRADE	# STUDENTS	# PASSED	# FAILED	# INCOMPLETE	% PASSED
10					
11					
12					
School					

Signature of Administrator: ______________________

Title: ______________________

PERMANENT RECORDS

(See Also: ADDRESS; GRADES; GRADUATION; GUIDANCE; HONOR ROLL; IDENTIFICATION; LEARNING DISABILITIES; NATIONAL HONOR SOCIETY; PERCENTAGE OF PROMOTION SHEETS)

. . .Of Faculty

(A) address cards

Date ______________

Name (Mr.; Mrs.; Miss; Ms.): ______________________

Present Address: ______________________

______________________ Zip ______________

Telephone: ______________________

Permanent Address: ______________________

______________________ Zip ______________

Telephone: ______________________

Person to Notify in Event of Emergency:

Name: ______________________ Telephone: ______________

Relationship: ______________________

(B) assignment record

ASSIGNMENT RECORD

NAME:________________________________ page_____ of______

DEGREE(S):____________________________________

CERTIFICATION:________________________________

DATE FIRST EMPLOYED:__________________________

DATE OF TERMINATION:__________________________

DATES		SCHOOL	DESCRIPTION OF DUTIES
From	To		(Include Grade Level and Subject(s) taught)

(C) guidelines for review of personal file

Every employee of Rock Township has the right to review his or her personal file which is kept in the Central Administration Building. The following are guidelines for such a review:

1. Review of a personal file shall be by appointment only. Such an appointment should be made at least 24 hours in advance.
2. An employee has the right to be accompanied by a person or persons of his or her choosing. The names of such person or persons must be registered at the time of review.
3. An employee has the right to make copies of material in his or her personal file, but no material may be removed from the file without specific written permission of the Board of Education.
4. A member of the Board of Education or a person or persons designated by the Board may be present during the time of review.
5. An employee has the right to make written comments on any material in his or her personal file. These written comments

shall be attached to the material commented upon and become a permanent part of the employee's personal file.

6. An employee may review his or her personal file twice in any one calendar year.

. . .Of Students

(A) academic record card

Student's Name: ______________________________

Student's Address: ______________________________

____________________ Zip __________

Parent or Guardian: ________________ Telephone: __________

Date Entered School System: ____________ Date Left: __________

GRADE ________ School Year 19 ___ -19___

SUBJECT	GRADES					TEACHER
	1	2	3	4	Final	
English						
Phys. Ed.						

Extra-Curricular Activities, Awards, Etc.

____

____

(B) notice of right to review

Dear Parents,

As parents of a student in the Rock Township School System, you have the legal right to review the permanent record folder of your child. This folder contains the academic and social record of your child's progress in the school system. It is kept on file in your child's school.

PERMANENT RECORDS

You have the right to review this folder in person either alone or in the company of a person or persons of your choosing including legal counsel. You may make copies of any material in the file, but no material may be removed from the file without specific permission of the Board of Education.

If you have any questions regarding this procedure, please call the Central Administration Building at 123-4567 or your child's school.

Sincerely,
Thomas Helms,
Assistant Superintendent of Schools

(C) parental release form

Student's Name:____________________________ Grade: __________

Student's Date of Birth:____________ School:____________________

I hereby authorize the Rock Township Board of Education to release copies of permitted records checked below to:

____

____

____

( ) Observations and ratings by professional staff members acting within their sphere of competency.

( ) Samples of pupil work.

( ) Information obtained from professionally acceptable standard instruments of measurement such as inventories, aptitude tests, vocational preference inventories, achievement tests, standardized intelligence tests, PSAT, ACT, and SAT scores.

( ) Authenticated information provided to a parent or adult pupil concerning achievements and other school activities which the pupil wants to make a part of his or her records.

( ) Verified reports of serious or recurrent behavior patterns.

( ) Extracurricular activities and achievements.

( ) Rank in class and academic honors earned.

( ) Other: ____________________________________

Signature of Parent/Guardian
or Adult Student: __________________________

Address: ____________________

____

Relationship to Student: ____________________

Date: ____________________

(D) request for

SCHOOL: ____________________ DATE: __________

ADDRESS: ____________________

____

Dear Sir:

RE: ____________________ D.O.B.: __________

ADDRESS: ____________________

____

Please forward all mandated records for the above-named student who has enrolled in the __________ grade of the Rock Township Public Schools.
In addition, we would appreciate receiving copies of all permitted records as per the parent release below.

Thank you for your prompt attention to this matter.

DIRECTOR OF GUIDANCE: ____________________

- -

Please check the appropriate response:

I ( ) DO ( ) DO NOT authorize the release of all permitted records of the above-named student to the Rock Township Public Schools:

SIGNATURE OF PARENT/GUARDIAN OR ADULT STUDENT: __________

ADDRESS: ____________________

____

RELATIONSHIP TO STUDENT: ____________________

DATE: ____________________

PERMISSION SLIPS (See Also: FIELD TRIPS; PASSES)

. . .Example of (Long Form)

From time to time the class will go on various walking field trips within the town. This form is to get your approval for all such trips. Separate forms will be sent home for any long distance trips.

PERMISSION SLIPS

I hereby give my permission for my son/daughter, ______________________, to accompany the class on various local walking field trips during the school year. All trips will be under the direction of a teacher.

Parent's Signature: ______________________

. . .Example of (Specific Form)

I hereby give permission for my son/daughter, ______________________, to go on a class trip to ______________________

on (date) ______________________

Time of Leaving School: ______________ Time of Return: ______________

Means of Transportation: ______________ Cost per Student: ______________

I understand that the trip will be under the supervision of a teacher.

I hereby relieve the Rock Township Public School System of all responsibility beyond that of normal supervision.

Signature of Parent or Guardian: ______________________

. . .Policy Statement on

It shall be the policy of the Rock Township Board of Education that every student going on a school-sponsored trip of any nature provide his or her teacher or person in charge of the trip with a form signed by his or her parents granting permission for the student to participate in the trip.

This permission form should contain the destination of the trip, the times (approximate) of leaving and return to school, the cost per child (if any), and must contain the statement, "I HEREBY RELIEVE THE ROCK TOWNSHIP SCHOOL SYSTEM OF ALL RESPONSIBILITY BEYOND THAT OF NORMAL SUPERVISION."

These permission forms should be completely collected at least one day prior to the trip and must be turned in to the principal prior to leaving on the day of the trip. No student is to be allowed on any trip without such a permission form, and no teacher is to take any student who has not provided such a form.

PETITIONS (See Also: COMPLAINTS; DEMONSTRATIONS; INQUIRIES; ISSUES; MINORITIES; RIGHTS AND RESPONSIBILITIES; VOTING)

. . .Answer to

Dear Mrs. Farrell,

I am in possession of a petition containing 473 signatures of parents of students at Rock Township High School requesting the reinstatement of the Saturday Morning Intra-mural Sports Program.

As you may be aware, that program was cut from our current school year's activities when the Board of Education mandated certain cuts in expenditures due to the failure of passage of the school budget. Please believe me that it was a difficult decision to make. The program was a popular one and had many beneficial aspects which it pained me to lose. I really can appreciate your point of view.

I shall advise the Superintendent and the Board of Education of your petition. In the meantime, I invite you and any other interested and concerned parents to call upon me at your convenience. Perhaps we may discuss alternate avenues toward the solution of this problem.

Please call me and arrange for a meeting. I look forward to meeting you.

Sincerely,
J. Benson, Principal

. . .Informing Others of the Existence of

Dear Dr. Smith,

Recently I received a petition (a copy of which is enclosed) requesting the reinstatement of an intra-mural program of sports activities which was one of the activities cut due to recent budgetary difficulties.

I have invited the parent leaders to discuss the matter with me. Since the petition was signed by 473 parents, it seems likely that they shall be extremely concerned. Indeed, as I discussed with you previously, this was a very popular program, and we anticipated reactions to the cut.

I wonder if there might not be a way of getting this program going again. Perhaps we might investigate the legality of using parental volunteers for reinstating the program on a partial basis.

Please keep me informed of your wishes in this matter. I shall let you know the results of my first meeting with the parents involved.

Sincerely,
John Benson

. . .Publishing Solutions to

TO ALL PARENTS:

It gives me great pleasure to inform you that the Saturday Morning Intra-mural Sports Program, which had been cut from this year's activities at our school, has been reinstated and will begin operation on Saturday, October 21, 19XX at 8:00 a.m.

As you are aware, budgetary cuts necessitated the removal of the program. Thanks to Mrs. Edna Farrell and over 470 concerned parents, however, we were able to find a way to reinstate the program. Thanks to these concerned parents and the cooperation of our Board of Education, we were able to hire one full-time activities director and run the rest of the program with parents who have volunteered their invaluable time and energies.

Thank you all for your time and effort in helping return this valuable program to our students.

With sincere thanks,
J. Benson, Principal

PHILOSOPHY (See Also: ACCOUNTABILITY; CURRICULUM; GOALS; IDEAS; OBJECTIVES; RIGHTS AND RESPONSIBILITIES)

. . .Of a School System

We believe that each child is endowed with his or her own individual capacities and characteristics, and that our schools, to the best of our abilities, should provide each child with the kind of education best fitted to him or her as an individual. We know that the needs of children are similar, but not identical, and we try to adapt our program to this knowledge.

As a child becomes older and more mature, we try to provide him or her with the opportunities to make choices for himself or herself, as we believe that the making of wise choices is a necessary part of living in a democracy. We try to avoid asking youngsters to make choices too difficult for their level of development and maturity.

We believe a spirit of free inquiry is essential to education in a democracy. To establish the climate essential for freedom, teachers and administrators need to follow book selection practices calculated to provide a wide variety of reading experiences.

. . .Of Education

We believe that a public school system anywhere in the United States of America exists to serve all the children of all the people as best it can. From the age of five to twenty each child has the right to attend the public schools. From the age of six to sixteen each child is compelled by law to be enrolled in school.

We believe, therefore, that those involved in education must make every effort to meet the needs of all students in granting them the fullest possible educational opportunities.

POLICE AND JUVENILE AUTHORITIES

(See Also: DRINKING OF ALCOHOLIC BEVERAGES ON SCHOOL GROUNDS; DRUGS; EMERGENCY; VANDALISM)

. . .Guidelines for Police Contact

The following offenses are cause for assignment to ASP, suspension or expulsion, and may also constitute juvenile or adult offenses. The Police will be contacted where prudent:

1. The use of, the sale of, the distribution of, the possession of, or being under the influence of narcotics, dangerous drugs, controlled dangerous substances or alcoholic beverages.
2. Destruction of, or defacing property.
3. Extortion/Shakedown.
4. Stealing/Theft.
5. Forgery.

6. Threatening or attacking other students and/or school personnel.
7. Malicious damage to school personnel's property.
8. Carrying a dangerous and/or offensive weapon.
9. Willful and continued disobedience.
10. Disruptive conduct.
11. Vulgarity or profanity.
12. The use of tobacco anywhere on school property.
13. Gambling.
14. Unauthorized parking or use of a student's vehicle during school hours.
15. Leaving school without permission during the school day.
16. Failure to report to office with discipline slip.

. . .Request Form for Coverage of a Function

REQUEST FOR POLICE COVERAGE

(This form is to be submitted to the Rock Township Police Department at least one week prior to the event at which you require police coverage. It is understood that the police officer shall be compensated at the hourly rate established by the Township Committee.)

SCHOOL: ____________________

LOCATION (Address): ____________________ PHONE: ____________

____

DATE OF COVERAGE: ____________________

FOR WHAT FUNCTION: ____________________

NATURE OF FUNCTION (Please describe what will be happening.): ____________

____

DUTIES OF OFFICER AT FUNCTION (Please specify—Transporting funds, crowd control, supervision, etc.): ____________________

____

NUMBER OF OFFICERS REQUIRED: ____________________

PERSON IN CHARGE OF FUNCTION: ____________________

TO WHOM SHALL OFFICER REPORT: ____________________

SIGNATURE OF PERSON MAKING REQUEST: ____________________

DATE OF REQUEST: ____________________

PROFESSIONAL ASSOCIATIONS

(See Also: CONVENTION; INQUIRIES; QUALITY; RETIREMENT)

. . .Memo on Membership in

To: FACULTY
From: J. BENSON, PRINCIPAL
Re: MEMBERSHIP IN PROFESSIONAL ASSOCIATIONS

Mr. Joseph Leighton of our Science Department has been appointed Faculty Representative for the current school year. Besides the tasks of that office, he will be responsible for handling membership in professional organizations.

It is my hope that when Mr. Leighton sees you regarding membership, you will want to join ALL the associations from the local to the national. We live in a world that is constantly changing, where new ideas and new methods are being developed every day. Especially in Education must we strive toward relevance and innovative methods to meet the needs of today's students. There is no better way to share, express and learn about these concerns than in joining with your fellow educators throughout the state and nation. Moreover, these organizations have worked in the past and will continue to work in the future for the betterment of educators and education.

I sincerely urge that you consider joining all professional associations.

. . .Seeking Information from

Dear Mr. Harrison,

I am currently enrolled in a doctoral program at Fairmont University. As part of my doctoral thesis, I would like to include some statistics on the rise in membership in your association in relationship to the rise in the number of teachers over the period from 1961-1970.

Perhaps you might be able to help me. If at all possible, I would like your membership figures for that time period. Also, I believe that you possess the figures on the number of actively employed teachers during each year of that time period. I would appreciate those as well. Moreover, any comments which you might care to make would be most beneficial to me.

I shall, of course, be happy to supply any costs attendant to my request, and due credit will be given in the final thesis.

I sincerely hope that you will be able to grant my request. I look forward to hearing from you in the near future.

Yours sincerely,
Joseph T. Leighton

PROFILE SHEET

(See Also: INTRODUCTION; LEADERSHIP; PUBLIC RELATIONS; RECOMMENDATION)

. . .For an Administrator

NAME ____

ADMINISTRATIVE POSITIONS HELD (Include position, school, and date): ______

____

EDUCATIONAL BACKGROUND (Institution, degree, date): ______________

____

NON-ADMINISTRATIVE EDUCATIONAL EXPERIENCE: ______________

____

WORK EXPERIENCE OUTSIDE EDUCATION: ______________________

____

COMMUNITY SERVICE: ______________________________

____

CLUBS, GROUPS, ORGANIZATIONS, ACTIVITIES: ______________

____

HOBBIES AND INTERESTS: ____________________________

____

PUBLICATIONS: ____________________________________

____

AWARDS AND HONORS: ______________________________

____

OUTSTANDING CHARACTERISTICS: ______________________

____

. . .For a Teacher

NAME ______________________________

TEACHING EXPERIENCE (Position, school, and date): ______________

____

EDUCATIONAL BACKGROUND (Institution, degree, and date): ______________

____

WORK EXPERIENCE OUTSIDE EDUCATION: ______________

____

EXTRA-CURRICULAR ACTIVITIES SPONSORED: ______________

____

COMMUNITY-RELATED SERVICE: ______________

____

PROFESSIONAL AND RECREATIONAL CLUBS AND ORGANIZATIONS: ______

____

AWARDS, HONORS, PUBLICATIONS: ______________

____

AREAS OF PERSONAL INTEREST: ______________

____

NOTEWORTHY CHARACTERISTICS: ______________

____

PSYCHOLOGICAL SERVICES

(See Also: CHILD STUDY TEAM; LEARNING DISABILITIES; MAINSTREAMING; MEDICAL; REFERRAL; SPECIAL EDUCATION)

. . .Notice to Parents of Referral to

Dear ______________________,

Our aim within the Rock Township School System is to provide every child with the best education possible. Consequently, we try to take all steps necessary for insuring that each child is performing at his or her maximum capabilities. This is why we are notifying you.

Your son/daughter, ______________, a ____________ grade student at ______________________ School, has been referred to our

Child Study Team for psychological evaluation. The reason(s) for this referral follow: ______________________________

____

The member of the Child Study Team in charge of your child's case is: ______________________. He or she may be reached at ______________. You may direct all inquiries to this person who will be glad to answer any questions you may have.

We sincerely hope that we may be of service to you and your child.

Sincerely,
Barbara H. Yarrow, Co-ordinator
Child Study Team

. . .Referral Form for

REFERRAL FOR PSYCHOLOGICAL EVALUATION

STUDENT: ______________________ GRADE: __________

SCHOOL: ______________________________

PERSONAL DATA:

DATE OF BIRTH: ______________ PLACE OF BIRTH: ______________

HEIGHT: ______________ WEIGHT: ______________

CHILD'S DOCTOR: ______________ PHONE: ______________

PARENTS: ( ) both living–together ( ) both living–divorced or separated

( ) __________ deceased ( ) guardians ( ) step parent(s)

ADDRESS: ______________ HOME PHONE: ______________

______________ ZIP ______________

REASON FOR REFERRAL (Include all observed characteristic and actions which prompted referral): ______________________________

____

____

ACTION PRIOR TO REFERRAL (Describe previous actions, disciplinary and academic, and the relative degree of success of each): ______________________________

____

____

PERSON MAKING REFERRAL: ______________________________

POSITION OF PERSON MAKING REFERRAL: ______________________________

SIGNATURE: ______________________________

DATE: ______________________________

P.T.A. (See Also: OPENING PROCEDURES; PARENTS; PUBLIC RELATIONS; TEACHER AIDE; THANKS; VOLUNTEERS)

. . .Administrator's Message in PTA Bulletin

To the Members of the Rock Township High School PTA:

I am happy to be able to include this personal message in the first PTA Bulletin of the school year. In the past, the PTA has served the students of our school in an exemplary manner, and I am certain that this year will be no different. The energy, enthusiasm, and concern evidenced by the members of our Parent-Teacher Association are welcome and beneficial adjuncts to Rock Township High School and our children's education.

I look forward to this year and the positive involvement of the Rock Township High School PTA.

J. Benson, Principal

. . .Soliciting Participation in

Dear Parents,

The Rock Township High School PTA invites you to become a member for the 19XX-19XX school year. Let us strive for 100% membership. The money from your dues is used for the benefit of your children.

Dues are $1.00 per year per person. Please indicate below the names of the people joining and the amount remitted. This tear-off sheet should then be returned by your child to his or her homeroom teacher whether or not you wish to join.

Yours sincerely,
Ellen Narnel,
Membership Chairperson

------------------------TEAR-OFF HERE------------------------

NAME OF STUDENT (1)________________ GRADE ___ H.R. ___
(2)________________ GRADE ___ H.R. ___

I ( ) DO ( ) DO NOT wish to join. NAME: ________________
ADDRESS: ________________________________
PHONE: ________________ AMOUNT ENCLOSED: $ ________

Our special activities are only as successful as our parent participation. Please indicate areas in which you would be willing to help this year.

( ) Tutoring Math
( ) Tutoring Reading
( ) Tutoring Grammar
( ) Nurse's Office Aide
( ) Dance Chaperone
( ) Student Clubs
( ) Teacher Aide
( ) Typing
( ) Reading Aide
( ) Refreshments
( ) Homeroom Telephone List
( ) Special Projects
( ) Other: ____

. . .Soliciting the Aid of

Dear Mrs. Anderelli,

The Parent-Teacher Association of Rock Township High School has been so helpful in the past, that I feel a real sense of ease and comfort in asking you and your organization for help.

Very shortly, we shall be starting a school-wide testing program for a period of three days. Since all students will be involved in the testing, the students we normally rely on for office aides, Guidance aides, and general communication aides will not be available to us.

I wonder if it would be possible for some of our PTA members to help out by assuming those duties on the days of the testing? It would not only be a tremendous help to us, but it would insure the smooth functioning of the school during the testing program.

I would appreciate it if you could call or drop in for a visit. I shall give you all the particulars at that time.

Thank you in advance for your help.

Yours sincerely,
J. Benson

PUBLICATION

(See Also: CONGRATULATIONS; ISSUES; JOURNALS; NEWS RELEASES; PUBLIC RELATIONS)

. . .Letter of Congratulations on

Dear Pete,

Congratulations! I just finished reading a copy of your book, EXPANDING THE SCIENCE CURRICULUM. It is, in my opinion, one of the finest works of its type that I have ever read. You are to be congratulated on your insight, ingenuity, and fine method of presentation that make your book not only readable and entertaining, but highly informative and thought provoking as well.

I consider myself and the student body of Rock Township High School extremely fortunate to have you as a member of the faculty.

Again, congratulations and best wishes for every success in this and all your future endeavors.

Best regards,
John Benson

. . .Notice to Newspapers of

FOR IMMEDIATE RELEASE:

Peter J. Connors, Chairperson of the Science Department at Rock Township High School, is the author of a new book on methods of teaching science. Entitled EXPANDING THE SCIENCE CURRICULUM, the book examines new and innovative ways of teaching science on the secondary level.

The book is published by Parker Publishing Company, a division of Prentice-Hall, Inc. It has been selected as a feature selection of the Educator's Book Club.

Mr. Connors has been a science teacher at Rock Township for nine years. He has served as Department Chairperson for the past five years. Although this is Mr. Connors first book, he has written several articles which have appeared in educational journals, has done public relations work for the Rock Township school system, and is involved in public relations work for the Rock Township Education Association.

PUBLIC RELATIONS

(See Also: BULLETIN; DEMONSTRATIONS; EDITORIAL; EXTRA-CURRICULAR ACTIVITIES; INTRODUCTION; JOURNALS; MEDIA; MINORITIES; NEW POLICY OR PROGRAM; NEWS COVERAGE; NEWSLETTER; NEWSPAPER; NEWS RELEASES; OPEN COMMUNICATIONS; OPEN HOUSE; PROFILE SHEET; P.T.A.; PUBLICATION; THANKS; VOLUNTEERS; VOTING)

. . .Guidelines for Administrators

To: ALL ADMINISTRATORS
From: WILLIAM SMITH, SUPERINTENDENT
Re: PUBLIC RELATIONS AND OUR SCHOOLS

Public relations serve a useful purpose in today's society on all levels. We in education as well should take advantage of public relations methods in informing the public of what is going on in our schools and presenting our side of what is going on in education. An informed public cannot help but be well-disposed toward our school system when they are aware of the fine activities and outstanding education that are taking place.

As an administrator, you are the singular person most aware of what is happening in your building. Let's make certain that we inform the public of all that is going on.

Is there a new program? A class doing something special? A teacher or administrator who has distinguished himself or herself in some way? A student who has some unusual or outstanding characteristics, abilities or accomplishments? An activity that would be of interest to the community? A speaker invited to the school who might be of special interest? All of these and more are fit topics for public relations releases.

Please take some time to compile these releases and send them to this office. Make certain you identify the school and the person issuing the release. It would also be appreciated if you would check the spelling of all names used in an article.

It is up to you to keep the public informed. I have confidence that you will do the job completely and efficiently.

. . .Guidelines for Teachers

To: FACULTY
From: J. BENSON, PRINCIPAL
Re: PUBLIC RELATIONS

I have been informed by the Superintendent that we should become aware of public relations in regard to the community we serve. "An informed public," Dr. Smith stated, "cannot help but be well-disposed toward our school system when they are aware of the fine activities and outstanding education that are taking place." I think we can all agree with that statement.

Are you doing something with your class that might be of public interest? Do you sponsor an extra-curricular activity that is engaged in a special project? Do you have a student who is in some way "special?" What about you? Will you be receiving a graduate degree? Published anything lately? Doing some unusual public service?

These are just some ideas, and I am certain you can think of many more. Don't let potential stories go by unnoticed.

Mr. Peter Connors of the Science Department has agreed to act as public relations coordinator for our school. If you have any ideas for public relations releases, please see Pete as soon as possible.

I know that you will cooperate as you have in the past, and I am certain that our school will be brought forward in the best possible light.

Q

QUALITY (See Also: ACCOUNTABILITY; ACHIEVEMENT; APPRECIATION; INSTRUCTION; PROFESSIONAL ASSOCIATION; TEACHER AIDE; THANKS; VENDORS; YEAR-END REPORT)

. . .Letter on Quality of Instruction

An Open Letter to the Faculty:

I have just completed classroom observations of the entire faculty, and I would like to share a thought with you.

If faced with a choice between a ten-pound hunk of quartz and a one-carat diamond, very few of us would choose the former. Yet all too often we are tempted to go after quantity at the expense of quality. We want bigger, more expensive programs, more equipment, more, more, more.

During my observations I was struck by the thought that in regard to quantity, we are doing as much as possible under our budget to bring the greatest possible educational opportunities to our students, but much more impressive was the quality of instruction going on in this building.

You are to be congratulated on the quality of your teaching. Your concern, dedication, and expertise were manifested in the interesting, dynamic, and thorough classes I had the pleasure to witness during my observations.

I am proud of you all, and I would gladly and confidently compare the quality of instruction in this school with any in the nation.

What a pleasure it is to be the principal of this school!

Sincerely,
J. Benson, Principal

. . .Letter on Quality of Performance

Dear Mr. Sandler,

As Chief Custodian of Rock Township High School please accept my thanks for the fine job which you and your staff are doing. The fine quality of your work is reflected throughout the school. The hallways, the classrooms, the grounds, and the school as a whole are in marvelous condition due to your unceasing efforts. Moreover, I have received a number of compliments from the faculty on the fine job you are doing and the prompt and courteous manner in which requests are handled.

Please convey to your staff my appreciation for their fine performance, and a personal 'thank you' to you for all you have done.

Sincerely,
J. Benson, Principal

R

READING (See Also: CLASS; CURRICULUM; SPECIAL EDUCATION; SUMMER SCHOOL; TUTORS)

. . .Form for Reviewing Reading Program

School: ______________________ For the Year 19___-19___

Director of Reading Program: ______________________

Number of Students Involved in Program: ______________________

How Many From Each Grade:

GRADE	NUMBER OF STUDENTS
______	______________
______	______________
______	______________
______	______________

Instruments of Measurement: ______________________

____

Number of Students Showing Significant Improvement (Attach Copies of Supportive Evidence): ______________________

Number of Teachers Making Referrals to Program: ______________________

Materials Used in Program: ______________________

____

____

Methods of Instruction: ______________________

____

____

____

Comments of Program Director: ______________________

____

____

. . .Letter to Parents on Reading Program

Dear Parents,

Ask anyone who has ever built a bookcase, fixed a car, or repaired a faulty light socket, and he will tell you – in order to do the job, you must have the proper tools.

In a very real sense, the "job" of our children is learning. They must learn now in order to prepare themselves to take an active, functioning place in adult society. A chief "tool" in that learning process is the ability to read. Without the tool of reading, our children are cut off from the printed word, one of the main sources of learning. To a child who cannot read, learning is as frustrating as trying to cut a log in half without a saw.

Fortunately, we can do something to help such a child. Our school has a full program of reading instruction. Our aim is to help the child who is reading below grade level or who may have special problems with the reading process.

Students may be referred to the reading program by teachers, through the results of standardized tests, or a parent may request an evaluation of a child's reading ability.

If you have any questions, please feel free to call the school.

Sincerely,

Robin G. Lee, Director
Reading Program

. . .Reading Progress Report

Progress Report of:________________________________ Grade: ________

Date of Report: ______________________ Date Entered Program:________

Diagnostic Instrument:____

Grade Level of Reading on Entering Program: ___________________________

Areas of Improvement: ____

____

Areas in Which Improvement Is Needed:_____________________________

____

Recommendations for Improvement:________________________________

____

Comments: ____

____

Signature of Program Director: ____________________

RECOMMENDATION

(See Also: LEADERSHIP; PROFILE SHEET; WORK-STUDY PROGRAM)

. . .Of an Administrator

Dear Dr. Smith,

It is my pleasure to recommend to your attention Mr. John H. Benson who is a candidate for the principalship of the high school in your district.

I have known Mr. Benson in a professional capacity for five years. During that time he has served as Vice Principal of our High School. His administrative record has been outstanding, and he has proven himself capable and efficient.

Mr. Benson has the ability to relate effectively to students, faculty, parents, and fellow administrators. He accepts responsibility readily and carries out his duties with efficiency and dispatch. He seems to have the ability to sense the needs and feelings of others and make others feel that they are a contributing part of the whole picture. In the field of community relations, especially, Mr. Benson was able to bring about positive community involvement that had been absent before his positive approaches brought results.

In short, Mr. Benson has proven himself to be an outstanding administrator, and one you would do well to consider seriously for the position.

If you have any further questions, I should be happy to discuss them with you.

Sincerely,

Victor L. Carlinson, Superintendent
Calleville School District

. . .Of a Student

Dear Sir:

I am quite happy to recommend Jason Banner for admittance to your college in September of 19XX. As principal of Rock Township High School, it has been my pleasure to be associated with Jason for the past three years. Since you are in possession of his records, you are already aware of his outstanding academic record. I am also in a position, however, to be aware of Jason's record of personality development and community involvement.

Whether as an elected officer of the Student Council, Editor of the Yearbook, Editor of the school newspaper, or organizer of a myriad of school activities, Jason has always been a responsible, enthusiastic, and competent young man, anxious to help, of high moral principles, and one with the unique ability to admit his mistakes and learn from them.

Perhaps it is an indication of his personality and proficiency that he is respected and popular with faculty and students alike.

I am happy to recommend Jason Banner to your institution without qualification.

Sincerely,

J. Benson, Principal

. . .Of a Teacher

Dear Sir:

It has been my privilege to know Mrs. Barbara Klaniff for a period of approximately seven years. In that time I have known her both in her professional capacity and in various social situations.

It is my observation that as a teacher she is a true professional, performing her duties with the utmost efficiency and ability. She is innovative and dynamic in the classroom, infusing her students with tremendous motivation and instilling in them an appetite for the joys of learning. She aids without reprimand, corrects without disparagement, and teaches by example and deed as well as textbook fact. She is extremely popular with faculty and students, who seek out her advice and counsel. This she gives without reservation, unselfishly and without condescension.

Socially, I know Mrs. Klaniff to be a person of moral principle, grace and polish, and someone who can handle the amenities of any situation. She is bright, inquisitive, and multi-talented. She has a gentle and delightful sense of humor which stands her in good stead with her old friends as well as people she has just met.

It is without reservation that I recommend Mrs. Barbara Klaniff to your attention.

Yours sincerely,

J. Benson, Principal
Rock Township High School

REFERENCES (See Also: CERTIFICATION; WORK-STUDY PROGRAM)

. . .Reference Checklist

REFERENCE CHECKLIST

Have the references of the candidate been checked for:

( ) Authenticity ( ) Accuracy

Additional Comments From Sources Checked: ______________________________

____

____

Comments on Candidate's References: ______________________________

____

____

Signature of Person Checking References: ______________________________

. . .Request for Confirmation of

Dear ____________________,

Recently ______________________________ applied for the position of ______________________________ in our school system and has given your name as a reference.

We are in the process of evaluating the candidate's application, and as you are one of the candidate's named references, we would appreciate your comments.

We are particularly interested in any comments you might have concerning the candidate's teaching abilities, personality and ability to relate to students and faculty, and any other comments you might care to make in helping us arrive at a decision.

We appreciate your time and effort. A stamped, addressed envelope has been enclosed for your convenience.

Yours sincerely,

. . .Request for References

Dear Dr. Carlinson,

I am writing to you because I wish to personally inform you that I have applied for the position of High School Principal in the Rock Township School System. As you are aware, I am currently serving as vice-principal of Calleville High School. My application reflects no dissatisfaction with that position. I think you know that I find my duties and my colleagues interesting and challenging. I feel, however, that I must take this opportunity to try to further my career as well as enlarge the scope of my responsibilities and administrative knowledge.

I am hoping that you may be kind enough to supply me with a reference for the position. I hope that I have performed my duties as vice-principal in such a manner that you may comment upon my abilities. I would certainly appreciate any comments you might care to make.

With your permission, then, I shall indicate you as a reference on my application.

Thank you for any and all considerations.

Sincerely,

J. Benson, Vice-Principal
Calleville High School

REFERRAL

(See Also: CHILD STUDY TEAM; COUNSELING; CUTTING; DETENTION; DISCIPLINE; DRINKING OF ALCOHOLIC BEVERAGES ON SCHOOL GROUNDS; DRUGS; PSYCHOLOGICAL SERVICES; SPECIAL EDUCATION)

. . .All Purpose Form for

NAME OF PERSON MAKING REFERRAL: ____________________

SCHOOL: ____________________ DATE: __________

PERSON BEING REFERRED: ____________________

GRADE: __________ AGE: ___ DATE OF BIRTH: __________

REFERRAL

HOME ADDRESS: ____

______________________________________ ZIP: ______________

REFERRAL TO WHAT PROGRAM OR AGENCY: ______________________

REASON FOR REFERRAL: ______________________________________

____

____

WHAT HAVE YOU TRIED PRIOR TO MAKING THIS REFERRAL? ________

____

____

WHY DO YOU FEEL THAT REFERRAL TO THIS PROGRAM OR AGENCY WILL BE BENEFICIAL TO THE PERSON BEING REFERRED? ____________

____

____

YOUR SIGNATURE: ______________________

POSITION: ______________________

. . .Letter of Referral to an Outside Agency

Dear Dr. Kinnon,

In the past your Center for Childhood Psychiatric Services has been of invaluable help for us in identifying the particular needs and areas of concern in certain of our students. Therefore, we feel reassured in referring another student to you.

You will find the particulars of her case in the enclosed copies of reports, forms, and school referrals. We are quite anxious to hear your evaluation of this student and your recommendations for future action.

Your report may be sent directly to me at the Central Administration Building, 123 Crescent Drive.

If I may be of any service to you in your evaluation, please do not hesitate to call.

Thank you for your attention to this matter.

Sincerely,

Jennifer T. Rastner, Director
Child Study Team

REJECTION (See Also: COMPLAINTS; REPRIMANDS; VENDORS)

. . .Of a Candidate for a Position

Dear Mr. Gilden,

Thank you for applying for a position in the Rock Township School System. It is gratifying to know of your interest in us. As you may be aware, there were a great many applications for the position, and we regret if there was a delay in getting back to you.

We regret to inform you that the position has been filled. With so many applicants with such fine qualifications, the choice was a difficult one, indeed.

Unless you request otherwise, your application will be kept on file for the next two calendar years. Should a vacancy in your field occur, we will notify you.

Again, thank you for your application.

Yours truly,

Harold Betner,
Assistant Superintendent

. . .Of an Idea or Suggestion

Dear Mr. Hildebrand,

Thank you so much for sharing your idea on the restructuring of the school lunch program with me. It is obvious that a great deal of thought went into it, and your intentions of saving time and trouble for those involved are also obvious and greatly appreciated.

It is with sincere regret, therefore, that I must answer that your idea cannot be implemented at the present time. The rescheduling you suggest would necessitate the need for two additional classrooms during periods four and five to house those sections which your plan would reschedule.

You may not be aware of it, but *all* classrooms are already in use at that time. There simply is no room available, and I am certain that you will agree that overcrowding is not an acceptable answer.

Let me thank you again for your suggestion, and if further discussion might prove profitable, please feel free to contact me at any time.

Yours sincerely,

J. Benson

REPORT CARDS (See Also: EVALUATION; EXAMINATION; FAILURE; GRADES; GUIDANCE; PERMANENT RECORDS; SUMMER SCHOOL)

. . .Policy Statement On

It shall be the policy of the Rock Township School System that every pupil enrolled in the system shall receive an evaluation of his or her progress four times each school year. Such evaluation shall be in writing, indicating the pupil's progress during the preceding 45 school days. This written report shall be signed by the pupil's parent or legal guardian and returned to the school following the first three marking periods.

In addition to these written reports of progress, elementary schools shall hold parental conferences twice a year, in the fall and spring, during which a child's progress may be discussed by the teacher and the child's parents or guardians.

. . .Procedures For

To: FACULTY
From: GUIDANCE OFFICE
Re: PROCEDURES FOR REPORT CARDS

Report cards will be distributed to students on Friday, November 29. The following procedures for the marking and distribution of report cards shall be in effect:

A. The first marking period ends on Friday, November 15.

B. Beginning Monday, November 18, Office Copies of the report cards will be available in the Guidance Office. Teachers are to enter their students' marks on these Office Copies no later than the end of the school day on Thursday, November 28.

C. On Friday, November 29, report cards will be issued to students during homeroom period. Homeroom teachers are responsible for filling in the appropriate information on the report card for each student in their homerooms.

D. During the day, students will carry the report cards to all classes where teachers will mark the student for the appropriate subject, including grades for work habits and social attitudes.

E. Students will take the report cards home at the end of the school day. These report cards are to be signed by a parent or legal guardian and returned to the homeroom teacher no later than Wednesday, December 4. Homeroom teachers shall retain these signed report cards for future use.

F. A copy of the teacher's Marks Report Sheet is due in the Guidance Office at the end of the school day on Friday, November 29.

G. First Marking Period – September 5-November 15 – 45 days.

H. Teachers are reminded that any remarks made on the report cards should be consonant with good public relations practices.

. . .Sample Report Cards (2 forms)

(A) first form – all subjects

ROCK VIEW ELEMENTARY SCHOOL

19____-19____

PROGRESS REPORT OF ________________________________

GRADE __________ HOMEROOM ________ TEACHER ____________

Subject	Marking Period 1	2	3	4	Final Avg.	Comment

WORK HABITS: 1. 2. 3. 4.

CITIZENSHIP: 1. 2. 3. 4.

EXPLANATION OF GRADING

A – Superior	Work Habits & Citizenship:	1 – Outstanding
B+ – Excellent		2 – Satisfactory
B – Very Good		3 – Needs Improvement
C+ – Good		4 – Improvement Noted
C – Satisfactory		5 – Parent Conference Requested
D – Poor But Passing		
F – Failing		

SIGNATURE OF PARENT OR GUARDIAN

MARKING PERIOD ONE: ______________________________

MARKING PERIOD TWO: ______________________________

MARKING PERIOD THREE: ______________________________

(B) second form – individual subject

ROCK TOWNSHIP HIGH SCHOOL

19 ___-19___

STUDENT: ____________________ HOMEROOM ____________

GRADE ____________ SUBJECT ______________________

TEACHER ______________________________

MARKING PERIOD	GRADE	WORK HABITS	SOCIAL ATTITUDES	TEACHER'S INITIALS
1.	______	______	______	______
2.	______	______	______	______
3.	______	______	______	______
4.	______	______	______	______
FINAL	______			

COMMENTS:

MARKING PERIOD ONE:

MARKING PERIOD TWO:

MARKING PERIOD THREE:

REPRESENTATION (See Also: ATTENDANCE; CONFIRMATION; IDENTIFICATION; MEDIATOR; NEGOTIATIONS; STUDENT COUNCIL; VOTING)

. . .Letter Suggesting

(A) in a committee

Dear Mrs. Tanner,

Thank you so much for accepting the position of chairperson of the Liaison Committee. I have the greatest confidence in your leadership abilities, and I know you will do an outstanding job.

When you are forming your committee, I would suggest that you include at least two representatives from each department. These may include department chairpersons if you think it appropriate. This, I feel, would make for a committee of a reasonable size which would be representative of the entire faculty. I also believe that service on this committee should be on a voluntary basis.

You are, of course, at liberty to form your committee in any manner you choose. I look forward to working with you in the near future. Please inform me when you are ready for the first meeting, and we can arrange a schedule.

Yours sincerely,

J. Benson, Principal

REPRESENTATION

(B) in negotiations

Dear Mr. Bryant,

The enclosed list of members of the Rock Township Board of Education, legal counsel and the Superintendent of Schools shall constitute the Board's negotiating team for the 19XX-19XX negotiations.

We look forward to receiving a list of representatives of the Rock Township Education Association Negotiating Team at your earliest convenience. At such time we will contact you to arrange for a mutually convenient time for our first meeting.

Sincerely,

Louis T. Hardly, Secretary
Rock Township Board of Education

. . .Representation Checklist

REPRESENTATIVE CHECKLIST

Representative	Date of Meeting								
FOR THE BOARD:	11/27	12/9	12/18	1/7	1/14	1/21	1/28	2/4	2/11
FOR THE R.T.E.A.									

REPRIMANDS (See Also: BEHAVIOR; COMPLAINTS; DISCIPLINE; NONRENEWAL OF CONTRACT; REJECTION; SECRETARY; SUSPENSION)

. . .To a Faculty Member

(A) for a minor infraction

Dear Mr. Hyers,

I regret having to bring to your attention certain recent events, but I feel that the situation warrants it. On Monday, Wednesday and Thursday of last week you were over half an hour late to school. This resulted in your missing your homeroom assignment and necessitated having one of your colleagues cover your assignment. Nor is this the first time this year that something of this nature has happened.

I am certain that you will wish to remedy this situation immediately. If there is any way in which I may help, I shall be happy to do so. Please feel free to contact me at any time.

Sincerely,

J. Benson, Principal

(B) for a serious infraction

Dear Mr. Smith,

I sincerely regret having to write this letter. For the good of our school and the profession of Education, however, I feel that it is necessary to bring to your attention a most serious matter.

On Thursday, October 21, 19XX, during Period One of the school day, it was brought to my attention that you had been brought to the Nurse's Office by one of your colleagues. When I visited you there, it was readily apparent that you were heavily under the influence of alcohol. In fact, you were indisposed to such a degree that you had to be driven home.

I am certain that you must realize how serious something of this nature is. It was only through the concern and good graces of your colleagues that you were saved from an embarrassing situation in front of your classes.

Your personal life is, of course, your own. When it interferes with your professional duties, however, it becomes the concern of every educator.

This is the second time in two years that such an incident has occurred. It must not, and it shall not happen again.

A copy of this letter is being sent to the Superintendent to be placed in your personnel file. If an incident of this nature should again occur, we will have no recourse but to recommend to the Board of Education your immediate dismissal.

We sincerely regret the necessity of this action. If there is any way in which we may help you overcome this problem, we stand ready to offer any assistance you may require. Please feel free to seek our aid at any time.

Sincerely,

J. Benson, Principal

. . . To a Student

(A) for a minor infraction

Dear Robert,

On Tuesday, November 17, you were referred to the main office for running in the hallways to such an extent that another student was knocked down and narrowly escaped serious injury.

I sincerely urge you to consider fully the consequences of your actions in the future. Part of maturity is learning to consider the rights, safety and feelings of others. Had the other student been injured as a result of your impetuous actions, you would have been faced with a situation with serious consequences.

I know that you will understand the purpose of this letter, and make every effort to see that the situation does not occur again. I am sending a copy of this letter to your parents, and I look forward to contacting you for happier reasons in the future.

Sincerely,

J. Benson, Principal

(B) for a serious infraction

Dear Adam,

I find it necessary to write to you about a most serious matter. On Wednesday, January 18, you were referred to my office for striking another student with a window pole. The student required emergency treatment and stitches.

This is not the first incident of this nature in which you have been involved. In fact, during your two years at Rock Township High School you have been referred to the office for fighting or hitting other students no less than sixteen times. This is a most serious record, and one which must be dealt with starting immediately.

Society will not tolerate belligerent behavior of this nature, and neither will we. A student in our school is expected to display a mature and cooperative attitude. This you have not manifested. If you wish to remain a student in our school, you must manifest a drastic and immediate change in your attitude and behavior.

You are currently on a nine-day suspension. When you return to school, I personally expect that an incident of this nature will not occur again. Indeed, it must not. If it does, the very next incident will necessitate a recommendation to the Board of Education for your immediate expulsion from our school system.

Let me reiterate, we will not tolerate any displays of overtly aggressive, belligerent or anti-social behavior. Such behavior will be dealt with swiftly and to the fullest extent of the powers of the Board of Education.

A copy of this letter is being sent to your parents and the Superintendent of Schools.

Sincerely,

J. Benson, Principal

RESIGNATION (See Also: ACCEPTANCE; RETIREMENT; THANKS)

. . .Acceptance with Regret

Dear Mrs. Kramer,

I am in possession of your letter of resignation, which I accept with sincere regret.

RESIGNATION

I am happy for your husband's promotion and wish him every success in the future. May the days ahead bring you happiness. My only regret is that it necessitates your moving to another state. You are an educator of sensitivity, insight and ability, and we shall be sorry to lose your services.

Thank you for your years of service to our district. I am sincere in saying that it has been a pleasure and honor working with you. When you are settled in your new location, I hope you will consider returning to teaching. Wherever you are, I know you will be a benefit to your students and community. Please do not hesitate to use my name as a reference.

Again, best wishes for every happiness and success in the future.

With best wishes,

Thomas Smith, Superintendent

. . .Example of a Letter of

Dear Dr. Smith,

Please be advised that it is my intention to resign my position as a teacher in the Rock Township School System at the end of the current academic year.

Please know that I have enjoyed my seven years of teaching in Rock Township, and I have the highest personal regard and respect for my colleagues and the entire educational staff of this system.

I am leaving only because my husband has received a considerable promotion in his job which necessitates our moving to another state. Indeed, I know I shall miss my colleagues and my students. I shall also miss working with people the caliber of yourself and the other members of the professional staff.

Thank you for all you have done for me in the past, and know that I shall always remember my days in Rock Township.

Very truly yours,

(Mrs.) Gloria Kramer

RETENTION (See Also: CHILD STUDY TEAM; EXAMINATIONS; FAILURE; SPECIAL EDUCATION; SUMMER SCHOOL; YEAR-END REPORT)

. . .Form for Review of

STUDENT PROMOTION REFERRAL FORM

A. BACKGROUND

Student: ______________________ Teacher: ______________________

Grade: ______________________ Date of Birth: ____________________

Previous Retentions: ____________________ School Year: ______________________

B. STUDENT PROGRESS:

Subjects: Grades: Final Avg.: Citizenship: Work Habits:

C. REASONS FOR QUESTIONING PROMOTION:

D. PARENT COMMENTS:

E. TEACHER COMMENTS:

F. COMMENTS OF TEAM:

G. ADMINISTRATIVE DISPOSITION AND REASONS:

. . .Letter to Parents on

Dear Mr. and Mrs. Halstrom,

Please be informed that your son, David, currently a second grade student in Rock View Elementary School, will be retained in the second grade for the next school year.

We have taken this action after conferences with you and David's teacher as well as an in-depth study of David's needs. We feel that it is in David's best interests to be retained at this time, particularly in light of the fact that David still needs to master reading and writing fundamentals which are essential to his continuing education.

It is our sincere hope that this will be a beneficial experience for David and help build a firm foundation for his future education.

Thank you for your understanding and cooperation.

Sincerely,

William Sanderson, Principal

RETIREMENT (See Also: PROFESSIONAL ASSOCIATION; RESIGNATION; THANKS)

. . .Form for

RETIREMENT APPLICATION

NAME:________________________ SOCIAL SECURITY NO.______________

SCHOOL:__________________________ POSITION:____________________

AGE:______________________ DATE OF BIRTH:_______________________

NO. OF YEARS TEACHING:__________ DATE FIRST EMPLOYED: __________

YEARS IN TOWNSHIP: ________ DATE FIRST EMPLOYED IN TWP: _________

STATE EDUCATION ASSOCIATION MEMBERSHIP NUMBER:_______________

PENSION AND ANNUITY FUND NUMBER:______________________________

CURRENT SALARY:________________ EMPLOYEE NO.:________________

TEACHING EXPERIENCE (List positions held in chronological order, addresses of schools, and dates of employment.):

____

____

____

____

PERSONAL INFORMATION:

ADDRESS:________________________ TELEPHONE:________________

____________________________________ ZIP:_______________

WHEN DO YOU WISH TO RETIRE:_________________________________

. . .Letter to Retiree

Dear Mr. Sloan,

I have been advised that you will be retiring at the end of the current school year. May I be the first to wish you a happy and peaceful retirement. It is my sincere hope that the years ahead will be a time of joy and accomplishment for you.

Over the years I have worked with you, it has been my honor and pleasure to get to know you both professionally and on a personal basis. On both accounts, I hold you in the highest esteem. Indeed, you are not only an outstanding human being, but the epitome of the professional educator.

I know that the faculty and students will miss you, as will I. You have left behind you a rich legacy of competence and affection, the memory of which shall stand us in good stead in the years to come.

Again, best wishes on your retirement, and please remember to visit us frequently.

Sincerely,

J. Benson, Principal

RIGHTS AND RESPONSIBILITIES

(See Also: ACCOUNTABILITY; CITIZENSHIP; ISSUES; NON-RENEWAL OF CONTRACT; PARENTS; PETITIONS; PHILOSOPHY)

. . .General Statement Concerning

As citizens of the United States, we are privileged as are very few people in this world to have certain rights guaranteed to us by our Constitution. These rights help to insure the quality of our lives as well as our personal freedom. Nor are these rights restricted to any class or group of people above any others. These safeguards of our liberty are guaranteed to all.

We must also be mindful that with these rights come responsibilities Not only are we all responsible for our own actions, but we have the responsibility of considering the rights of others as well. Indeed, when the rights of one individual conflict with the rights of another, it is through the consideration of all concerned parties that an amicable solution may be attained.

Let us all be mindful of the rights we possess as citizens and the responsibilities that accompany them.

. . .Statement of Parent's Rights

Dear Parents,

Under the law you have a number of rights regarding the education of your child. The following is a brief explanation of these rights in order that you may be fully informed when making decisions concerning the education of your children:

A. YOU MAY REVIEW EVALUATION TESTS AND PROCEDURES

It is your right to examine fully and question any and all tests used in the educational placement of your child as well as any procedures used in these placements.

B. YOU MAY BE ADVISED OF THE RESULTS OF ALL EVALUATIONS

It is your right to see the results of all testing and evaluation in which your child is involved.

C. YOU MAY REVIEW ALL SCHOOL RECORDS

It is your right to examine any and all school records which relate to your child. You may make copies of any material which pertains to your child, and should you consider any material in your child's file to be misrepresentative or inaccurate, you may petition to have that material removed.

D. YOU MAY DENY OR GIVE ACCESS TO YOUR CHILD'S RECORDS

It is your right to deny access to your child's records to anyone other than educational personnel. Indeed, you must be notified in writing and your signature obtained before anyone other than those specifically designated by the district may see your child's records.

E. YOU MAY REQUEST AND BE GIVEN A HEARING

It is your right to request a hearing with educational authorities should you disagree with the evaluation, placement or disposition of special incidents involving your child. The procedures for requesting such a hearing are available from the Central Administration Office at any time.

If you have any questions concerning these rights and their application to you or your children, please feel free to contact the Central Administration Office for clarification.

Yours sincerely,

A. Richard Tucker,
Assistant Superintendent

S

SALARY (See Also: FINANCIAL; NEGOTIATIONS; RETIREMENT)

. . .Addendum to

It is the policy of the Board of Education that teachers will be paid on the basis of training and experience, irrespective of the grade level or subject area.

All teachers entering the system are to be recommended by the Superintendent and are to be placed by him in their proper category according to their training and on the proper salary step according to their experience.

To receive the salary appropriate to the degree, it shall be necessary that a teacher possesses that degree. Equivalency of credits will not be recognized as a substitute for a degree.

. . .Deduction from

TEACHER: ____

SCHOOL: ________________________________ DATE: __________

Dear ______________________,

A deduction of $ ____________________ will be made from your next salary check. We have listed below the reason(s) for this deduction:

If you should wish further clarification or if you should wish to contest this decision, please call the Salary Office at 123-4567 as soon as possible.

Sincerely,

. . .Example of Salary Guide

SALARY GUIDE

19XX-19XX

Year	BA	BA+10	BA+20	BA+30	MA	MA+10	MA+20	MA+30	Doctorate
1.	10,000	10,200	10,400	10,600	10,800	11,000	11,200	11,400	11,600
2.	10,200	10,400	10,600	10,800	11,000	11,200	11,400	11,600	11,800
3.	10,400	10,600	10,800	11,000	11,200	11,400	11,600	11,800	12,000
4.	10,600	10,800	11,000	11,200	11,400	11,600	11,800	12,000	12,200
5.	10,800	11,000	11,200	11,400	11,600	11,800	12,000	12,200	12,400
*6.	11,000	11,200	11,400	11,600	11,800	12,000	12,200	12,400	12,600
7.	11,200	11,400	11,600	11,800	12,000	12,200	12,400	12,600	12,800
8.	11,400	11,600	11,800	12,000	12,200	12,400	12,600	12,800	13,000
*9.	11,600	11,800	12,000	12,200	12,400	12,600	12,800	13,000	13,200
10.	11,800	12,000	12,200	12,400	12,600	12,800	13,000	13,200	13,400

*Longevity increment, add $250.00

SCHEDULE

(See Also: BULLETIN BOARD; HANDBOOK; IN-SERVICE; OPENING PROCEDURES)

. . .Bell Schedule

Teacher's Bell . . . . 7:55 a.m.
Warning Bell 8:06
1st Period Begins. 8:10
End of 1st Period 8:54
Homeroom Period Begins 8:58
Homeroom Period Ends 9:08
2nd Period Begins 9:12
End of 2nd Period. 9:56
3rd Period Begins 10:00
End of 3rd Period 10:44
4th Period Begins 10:48
    Lunch A Begins. 10:48
    End of Lunch A 11:09
    Lunch B Begins. 11:13
    End of Lunch B. 11:34
End of 4th Period 11:34

5th Period Begins	11:38
Lunch C Begins	11:38
End of Lunch C	11:59
Lunch D Begins	12:03 p.m.
End of Lunch D	12:24
Lunch E Begins	12:28
End of Lunch E	12:49
End of 5th Period	12:49
6th Period Begins	12:53
End of 6th Period	1:37
7th Period Begins	1:41
End of 7th Period	2:25
Activity Period Begins	2:30
Teacher's Bell	2:40
End of Activity Period	3:15
Late Buses Leave	3:20

. . .Notification of Change in

SCHEDULE CHANGE

NAME:____________________ GRADE:________

HOMEROOM:____________ EFFECTIVE DATE:________

OLD SCHEDULE					NEW SCHEDULE				
Per.	Subject	Room	Teacher	Initial	Per.	Subject	Room	Teacher	Initial
1									
HR									
2									
3									
4									
5									
6									
7									

TO THE STUDENT: All schedule changes must be initialed by the teacher involved. When this form is complete, it is to be returned to the Guidance Office.

. . .Student Schedule Form

COURSE SELECTION

NAME: ____
Last, First Middle Initial

ADDRESS: ______________________________ PHONE: ______________

______________________________ ZIP: ______________

I wish to have a SIX / SEVEN period day. (Circle One)

REQUIRED: 1. Physical Education
2. English

ELECTIVE: 3. ____________________
4. ____________________
5. ____________________
6. ____________________
7. ____________________

STUDENT SIGNATURE: ____________________________

PARENT SIGNATURE: ____________________________

The completed schedule is to be handed in to your English teacher no later than Wednesday, March 22, 19XX.

. . .Teacher Schedule Form (2 Forms)

(A) first form

Dear ______________________________ ,

Below is a copy of your schedule for the 19XX-19XX school year. If we are forced to make any class changes, you will be notified on or before the second week in August.

J. Benson, Principal

Code:
- L.P. — Lunch Patrol
- CAFE. — 2nd a.m. bus arrival supervision in Cafeteria
- HALL/ KEYS — Hall supervision and key duty
- HALL — Hall duty
- OFFICE — Specific duties will be assigned

SCHEDULE

L — Lunch (teacher)
P — Professional period
CL-I — Cluster I planning period
CL-II — Cluster II planning period

1	H.R.	2	3	4 a b	5 c d e	6	7

(B) second form

19XX-19XX

TEACHER SCHEDULE

TEACHER: ______________________________

SCHOOL: ______________________________

____

PERIOD	ASSIGNMENT	ROOM NUMBER
1.		
2.		
3.		
4.		
5.		
6.		
7.		

Homeroom Assignment: ______________

Duty Assignment: ______________

SCHOLARSHIPS (See Also: AWARDS; FINANCIAL; GIFTED STUDENTS; GRADES; NATIONAL HONOR SOCIETY)

. . .Announcing Availability of

To: ALL SENIORS
From: J. BENSON, PRINCIPAL
RE: COLLEGE SCHOLARSHIPS

Please be informed that there are two college scholarships available exclusively to Seniors at Rock Township High School.

The first is a five-thousand-dollar scholarship presented by the Rock Township Education Association. It is awarded on the basis of a competitive examination which will be held on Saturday, March 30, at 10:00 a.m. in the cafeteria. While there is no fee for taking this examination, Seniors must register for it at the main office prior to that date.

The second is a four-thousand-dollar scholarship presented by the Rock Township Art League to a senior student who intends to pursue a career in the arts. It is awarded on the basis of evaluation of an art portfolio. Interested students should see Mrs. Wilson for details.

I sincerely hope that many of you will wish to try for these valuable scholarships.

. . .Letter on Awarding of

Dear Miss Jarret,

Congratulations! This letter is to inform you that you have been chosen as this year's winner of the Rock Township Art League Scholarship. Your outstanding performances in "Dames At Sea," "Kismet" and "The Glass Menagerie" have shown this committee not only your great versatility as an actress, but also the high degree of dedication and integrity which you bring to each of your roles.

Your extensive participation in community theater also came to our favorable attention: the stunning costumes you designed and executed for 'Elsa' in "The Sound of Music," 'Dolly' in "Hello, Dolly" and for "Anita' and 'Maria' in "West Side Story." All of them showed your masterful grasp of theatrical style and sensibility.

It is our deepest wish that you use the $4,000.00 Rock Township Art League Scholarship in your continuing study of the performing arts.

Congratulations and best wishes for what we are certain will be a very promising theatrical career.

Sincerely,

Joan Sullivan Atwater,
President of Scholarship Fund,
Rock Township Art League

SECRETARY (See Also: APPRECIATION; CLERICAL SERVICES; REPRIMANDS; SUPPLIES)

. . .Dismissal of

Dear Ms. Gerald,

We regret the necessity of informing you that your employment by the Rock Township Board of Education as a secretary will be terminated at the end of the working day on Friday, April 16, 19XX.

During your four months of employment, we have found it necessary to send you letters of reprimand on nine separate occasions. We have brought to your attention your continued lateness, the general poor quality of work processed through your desk, the loss by you of three very important letters which occasioned serious consequences through your lack of delivery, your taking of Board property for your personal use, and much more. In our last letter we advised you that a repeat of any of these actions would necessitate reappraisal of your employment by the Board.

To date no improvement has manifested itself, and recently, you were responsible for losing important budget forms which will mean that necessary supplies will be drastically delayed. Moreover, you refused to admit the mistake which further added to the delay until responsibility was definitely established.

Therefore, we feel that the action of the Board is more than warranted. You will receive your final paycheck in the mail on Friday, April 23, 19XX.

Sincerely,

R. Allen Kempfort,
Assistant Superintendent

. . .Note of Appreciation to

Dear Mrs. Goldman,

Now that the school year is almost over, I'd like you to know how much I appreciate the myriad ways in which you have helped me during the past months.

I speak not only for your excellence in secretarial matters, but of all those ways in which you go above and beyond your duties. Your foresight, diligence and concern are not only appreciated, they are essential to me.

Thank you again for your help. It is a pleasure working with you.

Cordially,

J. Benson, Principal

SEPTEMBER (See Also: CALENDAR; OPENING PROCEDURES; SUMMER SCHOOL)

. . .Letter to Faculty on

Dear Faculty Member,

Welcome back! I sincerely hope that your summer was a happy and restful one, and that you are looking forward to the year ahead. I know that I am happy to see you back, and I have every hope for the success of the coming year.

The month of September is a hectic one for us all. There seems so much to do. Indeed, it is in September that we lay the basis for the months to come. I know that we will all make an effort to start off the year in a firm but positive manner. This school plays a major part in all of our lives, so let us make it a pleasant, efficient and harmonious place to work and learn.

I have a feeling that this is going to be our best year ever, and I am happy to be working with you.

Sincerely,

J. Benson, Principal

. . .Schedule for the Month of

SCHEDULE FOR THE MONTH OF SEPTEMBER, 19XX

Friday, September 1, 19XX	Professional day for teachers; full faculty meeting 1:00 p.m. in cafeteria.
Monday, September 4	Labor Day – no school
Tuesday, September 5	Professional day for teachers; Departmental Meetings (see schedule)
Wednesday, September 6	School begins at the regular time
Wednesday, September 13	Attendance and enrollment sheets due in Guidance Office
Friday, September 15	Last day for students to change courses
Tuesday, September 19	English Department meeting – 2:30 in Room 105
Thursday, September 21	Social Studies Department meeting – 2:30 in Room 207 Fine Arts meeting – 2:30 in Room 211 Math Department meeting – 2:30 in Room 98
Monday, September 25	Full Faculty meeting – 2:35 in the cafeteria
Wednesday, September 27	Phys. Ed. Meeting – 2:30 in library
Friday, September 29	Monthly report sheets due in Main Office by end of teacher's day

SIGN-IN SHEETS (See Also: ABSENCE; CONFIRMATION; SUBSTITUTE TEACHER)

. . .Checklist Form

SIGN-IN SHEET FOR THE MONTH OF

September

Date

TEACHER	6	7	8	11	12	13	14	15	18	19	20	21	22	25	26	27	28	29						

. . .Policy on

The teachers in each building are provided with time sheets in the office of that building. The newly agreed-upon system as negotiated between the Board of Education and the R.T.E.A. requires merely the placing of a check mark and the teacher's initials in the appropriate box after the name of the teacher and on the appropriate date. When the agreed-upon time for signing in each building has come and passed, this time sheet will be withdrawn by the principal or his representative, and a different time sheet provided which will require the signature of the employee and his time of arrival.

Time sheets shall be checked by the principals of the buildings and turned into the administration office at the conclusion of each month. Should a principal observe habitual tardiness on the part of a teacher in his or her building, this problem should be attacked via a principal-teacher conference. Should such a conference between principal and teacher be unsuccessful, the matter should be reported to the office of the Superintendent. If habitual tardiness is not then curbed, salary deduction may be ordered by the Superintendent.

SMOKING (See Also: BEHAVIOR; DISCIPLINE; DRUGS; SUSPENSION)

. . .Letter on Violation

Dear Mr. and Mrs. Razner,

This is to inform you that on Monday, November 2, 19XX, at approximately 9:30 a.m. your son, Robert, was referred to this office for smoking in the second floor boys' lavatory.

As you may be aware, it is the policy of the Board of Education that students are not allowed to smoke on school grounds. The Board has set an automatic suspension of three days as the penalty for the violation of this rule.

Consequently, your son is suspended from school on November 2, 3, and 4, 19XX. He may return to regular classes on Thursday, November 5, 19XX. It is sincerely hoped that in the future Robert will appreciate and cooperate with the rules established for the successful operation of the school.

Thank you for your cooperation.

Sincerely,

Howard A. Kelly,
Vice-Principal

. . .Policy Statement on

It shall be the policy of the Board of Education that no student may smoke anywhere on school grounds. Violation of this policy shall result in a three-day suspension of the student or students involved.

Smoking by district employees is not permitted in any classroom, hallway or instructional area when school is in session or students are present. Smoking is permitted during the school day in designated areas only.

SPECIAL EDUCATION

(See Also: ACCOUNTABILITY; CHILD STUDY TEAM; EVALUATION; KINDERGARTEN; LEARNING DISABILITIES; MAINSTREAMING; PARENTS; PSYCHOLOGICAL SERVICES; READING; REFERRAL; RETENTION; TUTORS; UNIT COORDINATION)

. . .Consent for Placement in

STUDENT: ______________________________ DATE: __________

The above-named student has been classified in the following areas:

( ) MENTALLY RETARDED ( ) LEARNING DISABILITIES

( ) EMOTIONALLY DISTURBED ( ) SPEECH HANDICAPPED

( ) VISUAL IMPAIRMENT ( ) HEARING IMPAIRED

( ) PHYSICALLY HANDICAPPED

SIGNATURE OF ADMINISTRATOR: ______________________________

* * * * * * * * * * * * * * * * * * * *

DATE: ____________________

I, as the parent or guardian, hereby

( ) give ( ) do not give

my consent for the placement of ______________________________

in the special education classes of the district.

SIGNATURE OF PARENT OR GUARDIAN: ____________________

ADDRESS: ______________________________

______________________________ ZIP: __________

. . .Evaluation Form for Student

STUDENT: ______________________________ DATE: __________

ADDRESS: ____________________ TELEPHONE: __________

______________________________ ZIP: __________

NAME OF PARENT OR GUARDIAN: ____________________

TEACHER: ____________________ SCHOOL: ____________________

REASON FOR REFERRAL: ________________________________

____

PERSON MAKING REFERRAL: ____________________________

SPECIFIC PROBLEMS OF STUDENT IN CLASSROOM: ____________

____

STEPS TAKEN TO REMEDY PROBLEMS AND RESULTS: __________

____

RESULTS OF PARENTAL CONTACTS: ______________________

____

GENERAL COMMENTS: ________________________________

____

Please attach pertinent health information.

. . .Letter to Parents on Due Process

Dear Parents of Special Education Students,

In a recent letter we informed you of your legal rights regarding the placement and education of your child. One of those rights was the right to request a hearing if you should disagree with the classification and/or placement of your child.

You should be aware that, if you request such a hearing, you have certain rights during that hearing. You have the right to:

A. be represented by legal counsel;

B. request a closed hearing;

C. request the presence of school personnel;

D. cross-examine all witnesses;

E. present your own witnesses;

F. request and obtain a record of the hearing;

G. determine whether the child should be present; and

H. obtain an independent evaluation.

Moreover, interpretation for the deaf and/or translation into languages other than English shall be provided.

We hope that this information shall be beneficial to you should you require it.

Sincerely,

Maria Adams Hartmen, Director
Office of Special Education

. . .Letter to Parents on Progress

Dear ______________________,

It is most important that the school and the home work together for the good of the child. Particularly in the field of special education, a firm relationship between parent and teacher can be a tremendous benefit.

Consequently, it is our purpose to keep the home informed of the progress of the child enrolled in our special education program. We have set up a meeting for this purpose as follows:

DATE:_________________________ TIME: ______________

PLACE: ____

If you cannot make this meeting, please call the Office of Special Education at 123-4567, Ext. 7, and we will arrange a time that is more convenient for all concerned.

Looking forward to meeting you, I remain

Very truly yours,

. . .Letter to Parents on Testing

(A) obtaining permission

Dear ______________________,

In a previous letter we informed you that your child had been referred to this office for evaluation and possible placement in our special education program. We further explained the reasons for the referral and your legal rights in this matter.

We are ready to begin our evaluation. The following is a list of the tests and/or procedures we intend to employ and the purpose for each:

Test or Procedure	Purpose
______________________	______________________
______________________	______________________
______________________	______________________
______________________	______________________

We wish to obtain your permission in order that we may proceed with the testing procedures outlined above. We feel this is in the best interest of your child, as we are anxious to provide your child with the best possible education in the light of his or her needs.

If you will please fill out the form below and return it to me, we will proceed with the evaluation and inform you of the results before any action is taken.

Yours sincerely,

Maria Adams Hartmen, Director
Office of Special Education

- -

I have received notification of the referral of my child, ____________ , to the Office of Special Education for evaluation and possible placement. I have been advised of the reason(s) for this referral and my legal rights in this matter. I, hereby,

(Check those items which apply.)

( ) grant permission for the evaluation described above.

( ) request a conference to discuss the referral and evaluation

( ) request further clarification of my rights.

SIGNATURE OF PARENT OR GUARDIAN: ____________________

DATE OF SIGNATURE: ____________________

(B) reporting results

Dear ______________________ ,

Recently, we informed you that your child, ____________________ , had been referred to this office for evaluation and possible placement in our special education program. At that time we informed you of the reason(s) for this referral and your legal rights in this matter. Later, we obtained written permission from you to conduct an evaluation of your child.

That evaluation has been completed with the following results:

Test or Procedure	Results
____________________	____________________
____________________	____________________
____________________	____________________
____________________	____________________

On the basis of this evaluation, we recommend the following:

____

____

____

If you wish further information on these recommendations or if you disagree with it, please call me at 123-4567, Ext. 7, and we shall be happy to arrange for a mutually convenient conference.

Thank you so much for your cooperation in this matter.

Yours sincerely,
Maria Adams Hartmen, Director
Office of Special Education

. . .Policy on Compliance with

(A) federal laws

It is the policy of the Board of Education that there shall be established a program within the District to meaningfully meet and deal with the needs of every handicapped child within the District. Such a program shall include procedures for referral, screening, evaluation and placement as well as provisions for the housing of the program, training and transportation of these pupils. The plan shall also be in complete compliance with any and all existing federal, state and local laws.

The Board further proclaims that it shall be the intent and purpose of the Board to provide the fullest possible education to every child within its jurisdiction in relation to the child's individual needs and requirements.

(B) state laws

The Rock Township School District has established a comprehensive program of special education for those students who have difficulty with the regular curriculum and education program. Child study teams made up of psychologists, social workers and learning disability teachers are responsible for the proper placement of students in special education programs.

All child study team procedures are in accordance with the rules and regulations of the State Board of Education.

The various special education classes within the district are staffed by certified personnel. When the needs of the child require special educational facilities not available in the district, the Board of Education has the responsibility to place the child in an out-of-district facility on a tuition basis.

SPORTS (See Also: AWARDS; EXTRA-CURRICULAR ACTIVITIES; PUBLIC RELATIONS; THANKS)

. . .Certificate of Participation in

ROCK TOWNSHIP HIGH SCHOOL

This is to certify

that

____

has successfully participated in the Rock Township High School Sports Program, specifically –

____

____

presented this ______________ day of ______________, 19___

__________________, Principal __________________, Coach

. . .Invitation to "Sports Night"

Dear Parents,

The fall sports season at Rock Township High School has finally come to an end. We can all be justly proud of the fine records of our teams and the degree of enthusiasm, sportsmanship and dedication evidenced by the team members.

On the evening of Thursday, November 14, 19XX at 8:00 p.m. in the school cafeteria we will be holding our annual "Sports Night." At that time we will be honoring your sons and daughters who have participated so well in our sports program. The awards will be many and the speeches short.

We need only one thing to make the evening a total success – you. Please try to be there and join us in saying thanks to our athletes who have given so much of themselves for our school.

Sincerely,

Coach J. Murphy, Football
Coach A. Henry, Boys' Track
Coach T. Manering, Girls' Track
Coach B. Thompson, Soccer
Coach H. McKee, Cross Country
Coach K. Lessler, Intramurals
Coach B. Waters, Cheerleaders

. . .Letter of Requirements for Participation

Dear Parents,

For your information we have prepared the following guidelines for all students who intend to participate in organized sports acitivities at our school.

A. Students and their parents are expected to read the rules pertaining to his or her sport and return a form stating that the parent and student have read the rules and understand their responsibility.

B. A student dropping out of a sport has the obligation to confer with the coach prior to leaving the team. He or she may not, during the same season, leave one team for another without both coaches being in agreement. The student also may not participate in a new season until his or her participation in the preceeding season is officially completed.

C. A student must attend classes on days when practice or games are scheduled unless the student has been given an excuse to be absent from a school administrator. Illness shall be reported to the school office and coach by telephone.

D. A student suspended from school or enrolled in the Alternate School Program (ASP) may not participate in any athletic contest until the suspension is lifted.

E. A student must observe all training rules set down by the coach. Repeated offenses against rules pertaining to the use of drugs, alcohol and tobacco will result in a student being dismissed from the sport.

F. Attendance at all practice sessions is obligatory unless the student has a valid excuse for his or her absence.

G. Coaches are to set the standards and example for student conduct during practice sessions, while traveling to away contests, in the locker room, on the bench and on the playing fields.

H. Since transportation to and from games is provided by the Board of Education, students may not use their own transportation to any contests. If a student wishes to return home from a contest other than by bus, he or she must present written authorization from his or her parent or guardian.

It is our hope that these regulations will be of service to you in understanding the functioning of our sports program.

Sincerely,

William Moone, Head Coach

. . .Permission Form for Participation in

I hereby grant permission for my son/daughter, ______________________________,
to participate in the sports activity ______________________________.

I further grant permission for a physical examination of my son/daughter. I have read the rules and regulations of the sport and understand them and the responsibilities of myself and my son/daughter.

I relieve the school of all responsibility beyond that of normal supervision.

SIGNATURE OF PARENT: ______________________________

DATE: ______________________________

STUDENT COUNCIL (See Also: APPRECIATION; REPRESENTATION; SUGGESTIONS; THANKS)

. . .Delineation of Purpose of

The Rock Township High School Student Council is organized on the basis of homeroom representatives headed by five students called the executive board (Student Council Officers) and are advised by a faculty member. All students are given an equal chance to be a homeroom representative, and elections are held late in the year for Student Council offices. Any student can submit ideas to the Student Council Executive Board or the Administration.

Participation in Student Council activities provides each student with an opportunity to offer valuable service to the school and to develop those characteristics of leadership so vital to our American way of life.

. . .Letter of Appreciation to Faculty Advisor

Dear Mrs. Burnes,

As the school year draws to a close, I have been thinking of the many fine activities that have taken place which have been sponsored by our Student Council. Not only have these activities been highly successful and enjoyable, but the growth in maturity and civic consciousness of the Student Council members has been manifest.

I feel that a large share of the credit for that growth must go to you. Your fine personal example, combined with your dedication and unselfish devotion to the highest ideals of the educational profession, has been a vital, driving force in molding an outstanding Student Council that has literally become a training ground for future leaders.

My deepest thanks and appreciation for your fine efforts.

Sincerely,

J. Benson, Principal

. . .Letter of Appreciation to Members of

Dear Jim,

As this current school year draws to a close, I would like to express to you my thanks for your participation in the Student Council this year and my appreciation for your services to our school.

As a member of the Student Council you have the satisfaction of knowing that you have served your fellow students by formulating policies and arranging activities that have benefited the entire school.

Again, my thanks and my appreciation for a job well done.

Sincerely,

J. Benson, Principal

. . .Nominating Petition

ROCK TOWNSHIP HIGH SCHOOL
STUDENT COUNCIL

NOMINATING PETITION FOR HOMEROOM REPRESENTATIVES

TO THE STUDENT: This form is to be completed by each of your teachers for his or her approval and returned to your homeroom teacher no later than FRIDAY, SEPTEMBER 30, 19XX.

_______________ (Name of Student) _____ (H.R.) _______________ (H.R. Teacher)

To Teachers: Please check the appropriate place, indicate any comments and initial. When making your decision, please keep in mind the following: Positive Leadership, Citizenship, Punctuality, Etc.

Teacher	Initial	Subject	Yes	No	Comment

STUDENT COUNCIL ADVISOR: _______________

ASSISTANT PRINCIPAL: _______________

STUDENT INFORMATION

(See Also: ADDRESS; EVALUATION; GUIDANCE; MAINSTREAMING; PUBLIC RELATIONS; ZONING)

. . .Release of Confidential Information

To the Rock Township Board of Education:

I herewith authorize you to release to the party or parties named below any and all information contained in the school records of:

STUDENT: _______________

ADDRESS: _______________

_______________ ZIP: _______________

TELEPHONE: ______________________ DATE OF BIRTH: ____________

NAME OF PARENT OR GUARDIAN: ______________________________

Please release this information to:

NAME: ____

ADDRESS: ____

____

ATTENTION OF: _______________________________________

I understand that this form grants you permission to release confidential information in the records of the above-named student.

SIGNATURE OF PARENT OR GUARDIAN: ______________________________

DATE OF SIGNATURE: ______________________________

. . .Student Information Sheet

STUDENT DATA SHEET

NAME: ____

(Last) (First) (Middle)

ADDRESS: ____

____

TELEPHONE: __________________________ DATE OF BIRTH: ____________

PARENT OR GUARDIAN: ____

(Last) (First) (Middle)

If Federal Employee, please give location: ______________________________

STUDENT TEACHER (See Also: ACCEPTANCE; CLASS; EVALUATION; INSTRUCTION; LESSON PLANS; OBSERVATION)

. . .Cooperating Teacher's Acceptance Form

Dear ________________________ ,

I agree to accept the following student for an education practicum in my classes. I further agree to aid in the evaluation of this student and to discuss his progress with his mentor.

STUDENT TEACHER

NAME OF STUDENT TEACHER: ______________________________

COLLEGE OR INSTITUTION: ______________________________

NAME OF STUDENT'S MENTOR: ______________________________

PRACTICUM BEGINNING DATE: ______________________________

PRACTICUM ENDING DATE: ______________________________

SIGNATURE OF COOPERATING TEACHER: ______________________________

DATE: ______________________________

. . .Evaluation Sheet

STUDENT TEACHER: ______________________________

THIS IS MY __________ EVALUATION. DATE: ______________________________

AREAS IN WHICH IMPROVEMENT HAS BEEN NOTED: ______________________________

____

____

AREAS IN WHICH IMPROVEMENT IS NEEDED: ______________________________

____

____

OVERALL PROGRESS TO DATE: ______________________________

____

____

SPECIAL AREAS OF PRAISE OR CONCERN: ______________________________

____

____

GENERAL COMMENTS: ______________________________

____

____

SIGNATURE OF COOPERATING TEACHER: ______________________________

. . .Guidelines for

The steady increase in the number of young men and young women who come to the Rock Township Public Schools to do their student teaching and the high importance of the experience itself necessitate the following memorandum which will set forth some basic operational suggestions for a school district policy.

The student teaching experience serves as the culmination of the future teacher's college preparatory program. The goal of the school district is to provide an environment which will encourage the maximum growth of the teacher candidate. All activities of the school relative to student teaching must be implemented only after a thorough consideration of the effect on its primary objective, that of guaranteeing the best possible education for the children of the district.

Additionally, the responsibilities and rights of the cooperating teacher should be considered in the organization of the student teaching program.

It is not the intent of the school district to dictate the teacher education program of the preparatory institutions. Rather, the district is attempting to work with the college in the fulfilling of the responsibility for teacher preparation.

. . .Observation Form

STUDENT TEACHER: ____________________

DATE OF OBSERVATION: __________ OBSERVATION NUMBER: ________

NATURE OF CLASS: ____________________

TIME OF DAY: __________ NUMBER OF CHILDREN: ________

ITEM	GOOD	SATISFACTORY	NEEDS IMPROVEMENT
Control of Class			
Teaching of Concepts			
Teaching of Facts			
Provision for Individual Differences			
Sense of Humor			
Rapport with Class			
Handling of Problems			
Clarity of Presentation			

OBSERVER'S COMMENTS:

STUDENT TEACHER'S COMMENTS:

OBSERVER'S SIGNATURE: ____________________

STUDENT TEACHER'S SIGNATURE: ____________________

SUBSTITUTE TEACHER (See Also: CLASS; INSTRUCTION; LESSON PLANS; SIGN-IN SHEETS; TEACHER AIDE)

. .Checklist for Information Packet

SUBSTITUTE PACKET CHECKLIST

NAME OF SUBSTITUTE: ______________________________

SUBSTITUTING FOR: ______________________________

MATERIALS ENCLOSED:

( ) Teacher Schedule
( ) Map of School
( ) Hall Passes
( ) Substitute Report Form
( ) Discipline Referral Sheets
( ) Substitute Guidelines Sheet

. . .Obtaining a Substitute

When a teacher finds it necessary to be absent from school, he or she must inform the proper person of this upcoming absence during the following times:

1. Between 6:00 p.m. and 9:00 p.m. the evening before the day of the intended absence. (No telephone call is ever to be made to the person in charge of getting substitutes between 9:00 p.m. and 6:00 a.m. of the following day.)
2. Between 6:00 a.m. and 7:00 a.m. on the morning of the day when a teacher will be absent.
3. At these times your message will be taken and recorded on a Code-A-Phone.
4. The proper number to call is *339-6640*.
5. When calling, you will give your name, department, the reason for absence, the anticipated length of your absence, and your parking assignment number.

NAME–DEPARTMENT–REASON FOR ABSENCE
LENGTH OF ABSENCE–PARKING NO.

If the staff member's absence is to extend for more than one day, and that fact was not reported with the initial call, the staff member may report the fact that he or she will be out a second day to the secretary of the school during the first day's absence. The secretary can then reserve the services of the same substitute for the second day of absence and the absences thereafter before the substitute leaves the building. The school secretary should pass on this fact to the person who acquires substitutes.

. . .Substitute Report Form

SUBSTITUTE REPORT TO THE TEACHER

Date(s) of Work: ______________________________

Teacher's Name: ______________________________

Substitute's Name: ______________________________

	Old Assignments Collected	Current Assignments Collected	Pages of Classwork Completed	Names of Disruptive Students
Per. 1				
Per. 2				
Per. 3				
Per. 4				
Per. 5				
Per. 6				
Per. 7				

Comments:

____

Please leave all work collected, this form, and any other materials in the department office prior to leaving the building. Thank you.

. . .Teacher Evaluation of Substitute Form

TEACHER REPORT ON SUBSTITUTE

Date(s) of Absence: ______________________________

Teacher's Name: ______________________________

Substitute's Name: ______________________________

Period Subject

Period Subject

Period Subject

Period Subject

Period Subject

Were the lesson plans followed? ( ) YES ( ) NO

Was the classwork completed as assigned? ( ) YES ( ) NO

Did you find the condition of your room satisfactory? ( ) YES ( ) NO

Did the substitute leave a report for you? ( ) YES ( ) NO

Were you pleased with the work of the substitute? ( ) YES ( ) NO

COMMENT:

Please turn in this form to the main office by the end of the day on which you return to school.

SUGGESTIONS (See Also: COMPLAINTS; IDEAS; IN-SERVICE; ISSUES; MEMO; OPEN COMMUNICATIONS; STUDENT COUNCIL)

. . .Faculty Suggestion Form

NAME: ______________________________

DEPARTMENT: ______________________ DATE: __________

SUGGESTION FOR IMPROVEMENT

The following suggestion is for the improvement of our school within the limits of financial and legal responsibility and within the boundaries of practicality:

____

. . .Student Suggestion Form

SUGGESTION FORM

NAME:____ DATE:____________

HOMEROOM:_________ H.R. TEACHER: ___________ GRADE:___________

I think that the following suggestion would really help our school:

____

SUMMER SCHOOL

(See Also: APPLICATION; FAILURE; INSTRUCTION; READING; REPORT CARDS; RETENTION; SEPTEMBER; TEXTBOOKS; TUTORS)

. . .Application for Teaching in

APPLICATION FOR SUMMER SCHOOL EMPLOYMENT

NAME:____ DATE:____________

ADDRESS:____________________________ TELEPHONE:_______________

____________________________________ ZIP:_______________

CERTIFICATION:____

CURRENT EMPLOYER:____

CURRENT DUTIES:____

DATE AVAILABLE:____

SUBJECT AND GRADE LEVEL PREFERENCE:__________________________

REFERENCE (Please give the name and address of someone who is currently familiar with your professional abilities.):

____

____

NUMBER OF YEARS EMPLOYED AS TEACHER:_________________________

COMMENTS:____

____

SUMMER SCHOOL

. . .Report to Teacher on

Dear Teacher,

This is to inform you of the progress of a student currently in your classes. This student has attended the Rock Township Summer School Program. A brief summary of that experience is indicated below for your information:

STUDENT: ____

REASON FOR SUMMER SCHOOL ATTENDANCE: ______________

COURSE(S) TAKEN:

SUBJECT	TEACHER	FINAL GRADE
____________	____________	____________
____________	____________	____________
____________	____________	____________

This information is for your benefit in dealing with the student. It should be considered confidential.

Sincerely,

Howard Mason, Coordinator
Summer School Program

. . .Student Report Form

SUMMER SCHOOL PROGRESS REPORT

STUDENT: ____

NAME OF COURSE: ____

TEACHER: ______________________________ DATE: ___________

FINAL GRADE: _______ WORK HABITS: ________ CITIZENSHIP: ________

COMMENT:

____

SUPPLIES (See Also: CLERICAL SERVICES; EQUIPMENT; SECRETARY; TEXTBOOKS; WASTE)

. . .Budget Form for

BUDGET FORM FOR GENERAL SUPPLIES

NAME:______________________________ ROOM:__________

DIRECTIONS: Include all instructional supplies except audio-visual, paper, and desk-top items. These items are to be included on separate forms by the subject co-ordinator. A supply item is usually expendable and usually costs under $25.00 per item. Examples include work books, prepared ditto masters, mini-course and gym supplies.

AMOUNT	ITEM	QUANTITY	UNIT COST
		GRAND TOTAL	

. . .Inventory of Supply Room Memo

To: MS. HARRIET DONNER
From: J. BENSON, PRINCIPAL
Re: SUPPLY ROOM INVENTORY

We are starting the budget process in our school this week. I would like you to be ready for a complete supply room inventory by October First. As usual, we will assign two teacher aides and four seniors from the business and commercial department.

We need, of course, the amount on hand of each item and the amount used since last year's inventory. I realize that general supplies constitute a relatively small share of our total budget. Strangely enough, it is an item which seems to be most closely scrutinized each year. It is particularly embarrassing in the final budget review to have large amounts of any item still on hand as the fiscal year comes to an end. Try to substitute paper that is in great supply for requests for another, less plentiful paper.

I'm certain that you will do a great job, as usual. Thank you.

. . .Requisition of

SUPPLY REQUISITION FORM

NAME: ______________________________ DATE: ____________

HOMEROOM: ____________________ DEPARTMENT: ____________

I hereby request that the following supplies be sent to my room:

QUANTITY	ITEM (Give supply numbers where applicable.)

This is my ______ request of the current school year.

. . .Supply Issue Receipt

GENERAL SUPPLY ROOM

Item #: ______________________ Date: ______________

Description: ______________________________

Amount Requested: ______________________________

Amount Delivered: ______________________________

Comment: ______________________________

Teacher's Signature: ______________________ Dept.: __________

SUSPENSION (See Also: ASP; BEHAVIOR; DRUGS; PARENTS; REPRIMANDS; SMOKING; VANDALISM)

. . .Follow-Up to Enlist Parental Aid

Dear Mr. and Mrs. Brady,

As you are aware, your son, Adam, is currently on suspension from Rock Township High School for an incident in which he struck another student with a window pole, injuring the other student. As you are also aware, this is only one of a number of incidents involving violence in which Adam has participated.

Soon, Adam will be returning to school, and we are most anxious that an incident of this nature does not again occur. We are deeply concerned for Adam's future, as we are certain you must be. Therefore, we are anxious to cooperate with you for Adam's ultimate benefit.

We would like to invite you to come to school and arrange for a conference with myself and Adam's Guidance Counselor. It is not our intent to dwell on the past, but rather to formulate a program of positive involvement and improvement for Adam's future school career.

Won't you please contact us, and let us see if we can work together for the good of your son.

Yours sincerely,

J. Benson, Principal

. . .Letter on Lengthy Suspension

Dear Mr. and Mrs. Andersen,

We regret to inform you that your daughter, Kelli, is herewith suspended from school for a period of fifteen days. We have taken this action in accordance with the disciplinary policy established by the Rock Township Board of Education.

On Wednesday, February 17, 19XX, your daughter was referred to my office for selling marijuana to other students. The sale was witnessed by two teachers, further attested to by the student who purchased the marijuana, several packets of the substance were in your daughter's hands when the teachers interrupted the incident, and Kelli has admitted this and several other sales.

We are certain that you realize how extremely serious this situation is. This is not only a violation of school rules but of civil and federal law as well.

The reporting of this incident to the civil authorities is the prerogative of the Board of Education. A meeting will be held in my office on Tuesday, February 23, 19XX at 10:00 a.m. Present at that meeting will be the Assistant Superintendent of Schools, the legal council of the Board of Education, a representative of the Board, and myself. You are most seriously urged to attend this meeting for a disposition will be made at that time as to the further handling of your daughter's case. For your information, a statement of your legal rights in this matter has been enclosed.

We are most anxious to arrange an equitable solution to this most serious problem. I shall look forward to seeing you on the 23rd. Meanwhile, should you have any questions, please do not hesitate to call.

Sincerely,

J. Benson, Principal

. . .Policy on Due Process

The Board deems the suspension of a student to be a very serious penalty that should be imposed for disciplinary reasons only when the student has materially and substantially interfered with the maintenance of good order in the school, or it is necessary to protect the student's physical or emotional safety and well-being.

The principal shall have the power to suspend students for good cause. Such action shall be reported to the Superintendent within one day of the suspension.

Before any student is suspended for ten (10) school days or less, he or she shall be provided the following:

A. Oral or written notice of the charges against him, and if he or she denies them, an explanation of the basis of the charges made, and an opportunity to present his or her side of the story.

B. The exact number of days the suspension will last.

There need be no delay between the time of notice of the charges is given and the time of the hearing.

Before any student is suspended for more than ten (10) school days or expelled from school by the Board of Education, he or she shall be provided:

A. A written notice of the charges made against him or her.

B. A preliminary hearing at which time he or she will be presented with an explanation of the basis of the charges made.

C. An opportunity to present his or her side of the story.

A full hearing shall be scheduled before the Board of Education as soon as practicable, but no later than ten (10) school days following the preliminary hearing. This hearing shall be held in closed session, but the Board's decision shall be rendered at an open meeting. At the time of the full hearing, the student shall be permitted to be represented by counsel, confront and cross-examine the witnesses supporting the charge made against him or her and to call his or her own witnesses to verify his or her version of the incident. The Board may base its decision on a report of a hearing, but only after both parties have had an opportunity to review that report and comment thereon.

Expulsion may be effected only upon order of the Board. The Superintendent is required to provide an alternative program of education suited to the special needs of each child less than 16 years of age who constitutes a threat to the good order of the educational community or to himself or herself while in school. The method of placement in such a program and the continuous review of that placement shall comply with all state laws and regulations for special education.

At the start of each school year, the Board of Education, students, and parents shall be furnished a list of punishable infractions and the penalty set for the first and all subsequent violations. Those who violate the printed rules shall be subject to the penalty specified therein. The Superintendent is charged with the responsibility of developing rules and regulations to implement this policy.

The Superintendent shall report all suspensions to the Board at each regular meeting, and he shall provide a brief description of each case in which he was required to render a decision. Whenever possible, the Board shall protect the identity of students.

. . .Report to Central Office on

To: DR. THOMAS SMITH, SUPERINTENDENT
From: J. BENSON, PRINCIPAL, ROCK TOWNSHIP HIGH SCHOOL
Re: STUDENT SUSPENSION

Please be advised that on Wednesday, February 17, 19XX, I suspended from school for a period of fifteen (15) school days a student named KELLI ANDERSEN, currently enrolled as a junior at the school.

I took this action in accordance with Board of Education policy when it was determined that the student had been selling marijuana to other students. A preliminary hearing was held at that time, and the student was presented with written notice of the charges, an explanation of the basis of the charges made, and an opportunity to present her side of the story. At that time the student admitted this and other sales.

If you will be kind enough to inform me as to your wishes concerning the time and place of the formal hearing, I shall notify the student's parents, appraise them of the situation, and enclose material explaining their rights in this matter.

SYMPATHY (See Also: MEDICAL; RESIGNATION)

. . .Letter on the Death of

(A) an administrator

Dear Mrs. Sumner,

I feel I cannot adequately express my sympathy on the passing of your husband. George and I worked together for many years, and it was my honor to count him among my friends. He was a man of exceptional warmth and wisdom, and his loss leaves a void that will not be readily filled.

I knew George as an outstanding administrator, a man whose natural abilities of leadership inspired and enlivened those under his purview to their finest achievements. He was universally liked by the teachers throughout the township as well as by his fellow administrators. Moreover, he earned the respect of all who came in contact with him.

I wish you would do me a favor. Please contact me and tell me what I can do at this time. Please believe that it will be my honor to render whatever assistance I may.

Again, my sincere condolences.

Sincerely,

Thomas Smith, Superintendent

(B) a student

Dear Mr. and Mrs. Gennert,

All of us here at Rock Township High School, faculty and students alike, were shocked and overcome with grief at the untimely passing of your son, Robert. Bob, as he was known to us, was a student of whom we all thought highly; a boy to whom we pointed with pride as a student at our school.

Various members of the faculty who had Bob in class or knew him through his various activities have spoken to me and asked me to convey their sense of loss and their deepest sympathies. This I do and add my own. Bob shall be missed by us all.

We are sincere in offering any help we can give in this time of crisis. Do not hesitate to call upon us if we may be of service.

With deepest sympathy,

J. Benson, Principal

(C) a teacher

Dear Mrs. Franklin,

How saddened we were to hear of Greg's passing. I know I speak for the entire faculty as well as myself when I tell you that his death has left a very real void which can never be entirely filled. The student body, the faculty and I cannot help but sense this to our abiding sorrow.

Our only consolation is the knowledge that we were privileged to know and work with Greg over the years. During that time we came to know him as a person of intelligence and integrity, always anxious to help, whose life and career were an inspiration to us all.

We also take comfort in the fact that a part of him will continue to live, reflected in the lives of the students he has instructed and guided. As a teacher, he gave of himself (perhaps the greatest gift of all), and those students who were fortunate enough to fall under his tutelage will carry his ideals, his knowledge, and his moral principles into the world, and the world cannot help but be a better place for it.

Our hearts are with you at this most difficult of times.

With deepest sympathy,
John Benson, Principal

. . .Letter upon Serious Illness or Accident

Dear Bob,

I was just informed of your emergency trip to the hospital and your need for surgery. I am sorry to hear of it, but I know that you are in good hands, and I am certain that your recovery will be complete. Please rest assured that you are in our thoughts and prayers.

Please take all the time you need for a complete recovery. We are in touch with Joan, and I know you'll be receiving many visitors just as soon as you are well enough to enjoy our company.

Right now, your main concern should be getting well. Following that, we expect to see you back here. You are a most valuable member of our school; an exemplary member of the educational profession. We need you, and we want you back healthy and ready for hard work. Besides, I'm selfish – I don't know how long the school will be able to function without you.

In the meantime, if there is anything you want or anything we can do for you, I hope you know that all you have to do is ask.

Please, get well soon.

With best wishes,

John Benson

. . .Letter upon Tragedy in a Family

Dear Bill and Carol,

You have our deepest sympathy. The loss of a child is certainly one of life's greatest tragedies. When we heard of Ginger's passing, our hearts went out to you. There are no words which seem appropriate, but please know that we join you in your grief.

Know also that we are here, and anything we can do, we will do gladly. Please call upon us and let us know what we can do to help.

Our sincere and deepest sympathies to you in this time of loss and sorrow.

With deepest sympathy,

John Benson

T

TARDINESS (See Also: ABSENCE; CUTTING; DETENTION)

. . .Form for Reporting

TEACHER:____

ROOM:________________________________ DATE:__________

TARDY STUDENTS

PERIOD ONE

____

PERIOD TWO

____

PERIOD THREE

____

PERIOD FOUR

____

PERIOD FIVE

____

PERIOD SIX

____

PERIOD SEVEN

____

TARDINESS

. . .Notice to Parents

Date: ______________________________

Dear ________________________,

This is to inform you that your son/daughter, ________________________,
was late for school on ________________________________. **This is the**
________________ **time that he/she has been late this year. Let us make every effort to impress upon him/her the importance of getting to school on time. Please sign this form and return it to me.**

TEACHER: ________________________

PARENT: ________________________

. . .Policy on

The following shall be the policy and procedures for handling lateness to class by students:

1. Students who arrive late to class should be challenged and asked for a written pass.
2. In the absence of a written pass, the student must be admitted to the class. He or she is not permitted to be sent to the office or to any teacher to obtain such a pass.
3. Teacher action for lateness is imperative (e.g.: reduction of citizenship grade, parent conference, detention, are some of the possibilities which are left up to the discretion of each teacher).
4. Teachers are requested not to detain students after class or permit students to remain with them for part or all of a period to which they are not assigned without *prior approval by the teacher to whom the student is assigned.*

TEACHER AIDE

(See Also: ADULT EDUCATION; CLASS; INSTRUCTION; KINDERGARTEN; OBSERVATION; P.T.A.; QUALITY; SUBSTITUTE TEACHER; TUTORS)

. . .Guidelines for Selection

Teacher Aides play a valuable role in the educational process. In many cases they are an essential part of the process. Consequently, before considering the qualifications of a potential Teacher Aide, it is important that the candidate possess certain personal characteristics:

A. THE PERSON MUST LIKE CHILDREN.

B. THE PERSON MUST FEEL THAT THE POSITION IS AN IMPORTANT ONE.

C. THE PERSON MUST HAVE THE ABILITY TO WORK WITH MANY KINDS OF PEOPLE IN A VARIETY OF SITUATIONS.

D. THE PERSON MUST BE ABLE TO ACCEPT RESPONSIBILITY.

E. THE PERSON MUST EVIDENCE A DEDICATION TO THE IDEALS OF EDUCATION.

F. THE PERSON MUST BE RELIABLE AND OF GOOD CHARACTER.

. . .Report from

For the Period ______________________ to ______________________, 19___

Students Tutored and in What Subjects: ______________________

____

____

Assignments Completed: ______________________________

____

____

Total Hours in Classroom: ______________________________

Total Hours Other Than Classroom: ______________________

Total Hours for Period: ______________________________

Conditions That Should Be Brought to Attention of Teacher: __________

____

____

TEACHER AIDE

Comments: ____
____
____

SIGNATURE OF TEACHER AIDE: ______________________
DATE: ______________________

. . .Report on

Teacher Aide: ____

Teacher: ______________________________ Date: __________

Report for the Period from ______________ to ______________, 19____

HAS AIDE PERFORMED ALL ASSIGNED DUTIES? ( ) YES ( ) NO

HAS AIDE SUPPLIED WRITTEN REPORT? ( ) YES ( ) NO

HAS SERVICE BEEN SATISFACTORY? ( ) YES ( ) NO

If 'NO,' Explain: ____
____

Comments: ____
____
____

SIGNATURE OF TEACHER: ______________________

. . .Request for

REQUEST FOR TEACHER AIDE

TEACHER: ______________________________ ROOM: __________

GRADE OR SUBJECT: ______________________ DATE: __________

I hereby request the assistance of a teacher aide:

TIME NEEDED (Be specific—what periods; time of day; etc.):

IN WHAT SUBJECT(S):

WHAT DAY(S) OF THE WEEK:

DUTIES (What exactly would you expect the teacher aide to ao?):
____

TELEPHONE (See Also: HANDBOOK; PASSES)

. . .Telephone Conversation Report Form

REPORT ON TELEPHONE CONVERSATION

Date of Conversation: ____________ Time of Day: ____________

Phone Call Was From ____________ to ____________

Reason for Call: ____________

____

Summary of Conversation: ____________

____

____

____

Comments: ____________

____

____

SIGNATURE: ____________

DATE OF REPORT: ____________

TIME OF REPORT: ____________

. . .Telephone Usage Form

ROCK TOWNSHIP HIGH SCHOOL
TELEPHONE USAGE REPORT

for the week from ____________ to ____________, 19 ___

DATE	TEACHER	# CALLED	REASON*	TIME & CHARGES**

* REASON – personal, school business, parent contact, etc.

** TIME & CHARGES – if a toll call.

The faculty is reminded that the expense of all toll calls for personal reasons must be borne by the individual

. .Usage Policy

(A) for students

There are two pay telephones for student use after school; one in the main hall and one near the door to the main office. In the morning before school and during the day, students who have urgent reasons for using the telephone are to obtain permission from their teachers and be excused from class in the regular manner.

Unless an emergency exists, students are requested to avoid asking for permission to use the office phone.

(B) for teachers

Teachers are not to use the school phone except for school business for incoming or outgoing calls (except in cases of emergency). Two pay phones are available for personal calls. Calls to parents should be made *privately* in the Guidance Office.

TEXTBOOKS (See Also: EQUIPMENT; SUMMER SCHOOL; SUPPLIES)

. . .Budget Form for Textbooks

NAME:____ ROOM:____________

DIRECTIONS: Include all student books other than library books. An inventory of books on hand by *type*, not title, must be included.

TOTAL COST	Title or Program	Grade(s)	Quantity	Unit Cost	Total on Hand
	Total This Page				
	Total All Pages				

. . .Distribution Form

TEXTBOOK DISTRIBUTION

For the period from ____________________ to ____________________, 19 ___

Department: ____________________ Chairperson: ____________________

Title of Text	No. of Copies	Sent to	Date Sent	Date Returned

Signature of Department Chairperson: ____________________

Date: ____________________

. . .Financial Obligation Notice (for students)

TEXTBOOK FINANCIAL OBLIGATION AS OF ____________________, 19___

____________________ ____________ ________ $____________

(NAME OF STUDENT) (GRADE) (H.R.) (AMOUNT OWED)

FOR: ____

(REASON: BOOK DAMAGE, LOSS, LIBRARY FINE, ETC.)

____

(NAME OF TEACHER)

. . .Form for Suggesting New Textbooks

TEXTBOOK SUGGESTION FORM

NAME (of person making suggestion): ____________________

DEPARTMENT OR GRADE: ____________________

This form is to be used to suggest a new textbook for use in the school. This suggestion is then to be submitted to the Textbook Review Committee. You will be notified of the disposition of your request.

TEXTBOOKS

TITLE & AUTHOR:

PUBLISHER:

SUBJECT AREA OF BOOK:

WHAT BOOK(S) WOULD THIS REPLACE:

COST PER UNIT:

BRIEFLY DESCRIBE CONTENT:

WHERE MAY A SAMPLE COPY BE OBTAINED:

BRIEFLY EXPLAIN WHY THIS NEW BOOK SHOULD
BE INTRODUCED INTO THE CURRICULUM:

. . .Requisition Form

TEXTBOOK REQUISITION FOR THE SCHOOL YEAR 19 ___-19___

SCHOOL:______________________ PRINCIPAL:______________
PUBLISHER & ADDRESS: ______________________________

____

Grade	Title of Book	Author	Copyright Date	List Price	No. to be Ordered	Total Cost	Department Number

THANKS

(See Also: ACHIEVEMENT; APPRECIATION; MEMO; OPEN COMMUNICATIONS; PARENTS; P.T.A.; PUBLIC RELATIONS; QUALITY; RESIGNATION; RETIREMENT; SPORTS; STUDENT COUNCIL; VOLUNTEERS)

. . .To an Administrator

Dear Dr. Carlson,

Please allow me to express my gratitude for your support of my candidacy for the position of assistant superintendent of schools. Naturally, I would be overjoyed to accept the position, but even if it is not offered to me, I shall always remember your kindness, your intercession on my behalf, and your most generous and gratifying letter of support.

You may rest assured that if I do obtain the position, I shall do everything in my power to justify your faith in me, as I shall continue to perform my present administrative duties to the best of my abilities and to your expectations should the Board select another candidate.

My heartfelt thanks for everything you have done.

Sincerely,
A. Kitteridge

. . .To Parents

Dear Mrs. Payson,

You constantly amaze me. Just when I think you have done all that it is possible to expect for our school, you go and do even more, and I find myself thanking you all over again.

The way in which you organized and ran the benefit bazaar was nothing short of marvelous. Your enthusiasm, vigor and boundless energy were an example to us all, and the funds raised through this activity will benefit all our students.

I hope you realize how much you are appreciated around here and how thankful I am to have you as a friend and a tireless worker for our school.

Sincerely,
J. Benson, Principal

THANKS

. . .To Students.

To: ALL STUDENTS
From: J. BENSON, PRINCIPAL
Re: THANK YOU

Only a few days remain of the present school year. At this time it is fitting that we think back on the time that has passed; that we recall those incidents which have made this a memorable year in our lives.

This is true for me no less than you, and when I remember the good times and the bad, the work and the play, the setbacks and the accomplishments, I keep coming back to you, the students of this school. In the final analysis, it is the student body that makes a school what it is, and you have made it an outstanding school, a place which is exciting to be in and of which we may all be justly proud. For your cooperation and your efforts, I am deeply grateful.

Have a wonderful summer and thank you for making this such a wonderful year.

. . .To Teachers

To: ALL TEACHERS
From: J. BENSON, PRINCIPAL
Re: I'M THANKFUL –

I'M THANKFUL – for the fine year which is about to end; for the high quality of education which has taken place; for a dedicated and professional faculty . . .

I'M THANKFUL – for having the chance to work with you; for your cooperation; for all the extra effort you have put into making this school such a wonderful place to be . . .

I'M THANKFUL – for knowing you; for the way you have made me feel at ease; for knowing that you are there and that I can always depend on you . . .

I'M THANKFUL – for YOU, the faculty, and I offer you my deepest gratitude . . .

HAVE A GREAT SUMMER!!!

TUTORS (See Also: ASP; REFERAL)

. . .Announcement of Openings

To: ALL TEACHERS IN ROCK TOWNSHIP
From: ANSON KITTERIDGE, ASSISTANT SUPERINTENDENT
Re: TUTORING

Please be advised that there are a number of openings currently available for tutors. Openings are in the following areas:

ELEMENTARY – all subjects.

SECONDARY – English, all levels; Social Studies, junior and senior levels; Math, in Calculus, Solid Geometry and Trigonometry; Science, in Chemistry and Physics.

Applications for tutoring positions will be accepted at the Central Administration Office through Friday, October 7, 19XX. Qualifications include proper certification and experience in a particular subject area. Compensation will be on the basis set forth in the master contract between the Board of Education and the Rock Township Education Association.

. . .Application for a Tutoring Position

NAME: ______________________________ DATE: __________
ADDRESS: ________________________ TELEPHONE: __________
________________________________ ZIP: __________
Date of Employment in Rock Township: ______________________
Current Teaching Assignment: ______________________
Nature of Teaching Certificate: ______________________
Earliest Time of Day Available: ______________________
Will You Tutor on Saturday or Sunday: ______________________
Subject(s) in Which You Are Qualified to Teach: ______________________
Experience in Subject(s): ______________________
Any Conditions You Require for Tutoring: ______________________
____

. .Report to Parents on Tutoring

Dear ______________________________,

I have tutored ____________________ for the period from ____________________ to ______________________, 19___ in the subject(s) ______________________ ____.

In that time, we covered the following material:

Book(s) and Pages Covered: ____
____
____

I observed the following about your child's progress:

____
____
____
____

Sincerely,

____

. . .Report to the Central Office on

MONTH: ____________________________________, 19 ___
PUPIL: __________________________ SCHOOL: ____________ GRADE: ________
ADDRESS: ____
INSTRUCTOR: ___________________________ SUBJECT(S): ______________________

EACH AREA BELOW SHOULD BE COMPLETED IN DETAIL:

SUBJECT: (Reading, arithmetic, etc. – page numbers and skills being worked on, etc.)

TEACHER'S PROCEDURES: (Teacher-made materials, methods and techniques used and which work best with student, tests given and items of interest)

STUDENT'S PROGRESS: (Academic progress, attitude and physical condition)

FURTHER RECOMMENDATIONS:

GRADE FOR MONTH:

TERMINATION: (Date of return to regular class, or moved, or date when instruction terminated, reason for, etc.)

SIGNATURE OF INSTRUCTOR: ____________________

DATE: ____________________

. . .Request for

Rock Township Board of Education:

I hereby request that my son/daughter/ward, ____________________,
be tutored in the subject(s) of ____________________.
Signature of Parent or Guardian: ____________________

– – – – – – – – – – – PLEASE FILL OUT COMPLETELY – – – – – – – – – – –

NAME OF STUDENT: ______________ TELEPHONE: ______________
ADDRESS: ____________________
____________________ ZIP: __________
SCHOOL ATTENDED: ____________________ GRADE: ______
SUBJECT(S) DESIRED: ____________________
REASON FOR REQUEST: ____________________
____

APPROXIMATE LENGTH OF CHILD'S ABSENCE FROM SCHOOL: __________

SIGNATURE OF PARENT OR GUARDIAN: ____________________

DATE OF REQUEST: ____________________

U

UNIT COORDINATION (See Also: ACCOUNTABILITY; CHAIRPERSONS; CHILD STUDY TEAM; CURRICULUM; GUIDANCE; MAINSTREAMING; OBJECTIVES; PSYCHOLOGICAL SERVICES; SPECIAL EDUCATION)

. . .Example of (for a child study unit)

The child study team of a local school district has the responsibility of examining, classifying, and recommending special education programs for pupils considered to be handicapped or needing special help. Guidelines are provided by the State Department of Education to determine what constitutes a local child study unit for the purposes of diagnosing learning handicaps and recommending educational programs. A basic child study unit in our state consists of a school psychologist, a school social worker, a learning disabilities specialist and appropriate medical personnel. The child study team may also include such professionals as medical specialists, the school nurse, the school administrator, reading and guidance personnel, speech correctionists and classroom teachers.

How does a child needing help come to the attention of the child study unit? Children who fail to make an adequate school adjustment emotionally, socially, or academically may come to the attention of the team in one of several different ways. Parents themselves may ask the superintendent of schools, the principal, or the director of special services to consider their child's special needs either before or after he or she enters school. Or, the child may be brought to the attention of the team by the regular classroom teacher, the school principal, the guidance counselor or the school nurse.

Once a referral is made, the Child Study Unit then obtains as much information as possible regarding the child through testing, observation, and conferences with the school staff and parents. Information from other sources may also be requested by the unit or submitted by the parents. In some instances the school district may obtain information from ophthalmologists, otologists, audiologists, neurologists and other specialists.

After reviewing their findings on the child, the members of the unit then consider the educational alternatives which can be offered. These include the placement of the child in a special class in the home school district, or in another school district, or in a program operated by a State Agency as a State College or State School. If none of these are available, the Board of Education may consider a suitable private non-sectarian program. Placement of children in such private facilities by school districts must be approved by the County Supervisor of Child Study and the Department of Education.

If none of the above alternatives are available, arrangements may be made for the child to receive individual instruction at home or at school. Any handicapped child in a regular or special class who needs supplementary instruction, such as auditory training, speech correction, or instruction in Braille, may also receive it as part of his or her school program.

Upon completion of the case study, the child study team reports its recommendations to the local superintendent of schools who, in turn, makes the educational placement with full consideration given to the report of the examiners.

Another aspect of the child study unit is its role in educational planning and curriculum development. Often, when the child study team participates in educational planning, it can propose ways in which the curriculum can be developed to promote academic gain, proper mental health, and the prevention of emotional disturbances. The unit should also seek ways to provide opportunities for enrichment of superior students as well as to provide help for slower students. Often the team works closely with the Guidance Department to help those students who are having difficulty adjusting to high school.

In addition, preventive measures are often used by the unit in screening kindergarten and first grade children to determine the existence of possible educational difficulties and potential learning handicaps. It should be the overall aim of the child study unit in educational planning to see that the school program is designed so that the individuality of each child will be given the fullest educational and social expression.

. . .Unit Report to Principal

To: J. BENSON, PRINCIPAL
From: CHILD STUDY UNIT
Re: REPORT ON ADAM BRADY (CONFIDENTIAL)

On February 17, 19XX, Adam Brady, a junior at your school, was referred to us by you for study and possible classification and placement.

Adam Brady was seen by the school psychologist and Dr. Harold Lacey of the Children's Center. Copies of both reports are enclosed for your information. A study was also made of Adam Brady's school records prior to his enrollment in the Rock Township School System and those since his enrollment. Interviews were also conducted with several of his teachers as well as his parents. Again, copies of the reports from these interviews are enclosed.

Our basic findings indicate that Adam Brady has had a history of violent incidents since the second grade. These outbreaks of violent behavior are becoming more frequent as well as more violent in nature. This is true at home as well as in school, and reports from outside agencies indicate a growing negative involvement with legal authorities.

On the basis of these interviews and the reports from the psychologists, we feel that Adam Brady may be classified as Emotionally Disturbed and placed in the E.D. class.

This is, however, our preliminary finding only. A full disposition will be made within two weeks. At that time we will inform you of all ramifications of the decision. In the meantime, we wanted to keep you abreast of the matter and thank you for bringing it to our attention.

V

VACATION (See Also: CLOSING OF SCHOOL; DISMISSAL PROCEDURES; JUNE; KEYS; YEAR-END REPORT)

. . .Principal's Message to Faculty

To: FACULTY
From: J. BENSON, PRINCIPAL
Re: VACATION

In a few days, we'll be "closing up shop" for the summer, and each will be headed for a time of rest and relaxation. It is a rest which, in my opinion, you richly deserve. You have worked hard and well this past year with a professionalism which is exemplary, and which has made my job all the more rewarding.

Have the most enjoyable of summers, and I look forward to the honor of working with you in the fall.

. . .Teacher's Checklist Prior to

____

(TEACHER'S NAME)

With the exception of Item #1, which is to be checked out first in the guidance office, the following items are to be checked out in the Main Office on Friday, June 22, 19XX prior to leaving for summer vacation.

( ) 1. Marks recorded on office copies of student records (entire year).

( ) 2. Student Attendance Cards (Homeroom Teachers Only).

( ) 3. List of names of students who have failed the named subject with an explanation of the reason. If no students have failed, write "NONE."

( ) 4. Suggestions for Improvement sheet.

( ) 5. Events or Activities sheet.

( ) 6. Keys–ALL KEYS–tagged and identified in an envelope identified with your name and room number.

( ) 7. Name, summer address, and telephone number on two 3X5 cards.

( ) 8. One self-addressed envelope provided by the office for every teacher returning in September. This envelope is to have your SUMMER address with zip code and will be used to send out your assignment sheet and information relative to opening school in September, 19XX. You will receive them in late August. Teachers taking special contracts for next school year are to return TWO envelopes.

( ) 9. Unfinished business sheet.

( ) 10. Building report sheet.

( ) 11. This sheet.

____

(CHECKED OUT BY)

DEPARTMENT CHAIRPERSONS ONLY

( ) 1. Percentage promotion sheet.

( ) 2. Textbook discard and storage sheet (in duplicate) for department.

( ) 3. Field trip requests by month.

( ) 4. Dates for student and parent events (for use in handbook).

VANDALISM (See Also: BEHAVIOR; DISCIPLINE; EMERGENCY; POLICE AND JUVENILE AUTHORITIES; SUSPENSION)

. . .Damage Report

To: DR. THOMAS SMITH, SUPERINTENDENT
From: J. BENSON, PRINCIPAL
Re: VANDALISM DAMAGE REPORT

On the morning of Wednesday, May 11, 19XX, it was reported that three windows on the west side of the building were broken. Examination indicated that rocks had been thrown through these windows, obviously sometime during the previous twelve hours. No apparent attempt to enter the school was indicated, nor were any items missing from the rooms involved. We feel that the breaking of these windows can be attributed to common vandalism.

A custodian's report is enclosed. I ordered the immediate replacement of the broken window panes for the safety of the students. A cost estimate is attached to the custodian's report.

. . .Principal's Message on

To: ALL STUDENTS
From: J. BENSON, PRINCIPAL
Re: VANDALISM

Lately, there have been a number of incidents of vandalism at our school. Windows have been broken, furniture and classroom fittings mutilated, and certain lavatory facilities seriously damaged.

I cannot help but think that whoever is responsible must have a very low opinion of you, the students of our school. After all, the broken windows mean an inconvenience for *you* in the classroom; the classroom fittings that have been wrecked mean that *you* cannot now use them; and certainly the lavatory facilities that have been damaged impose a hardship only on *you*, the students.

It disturbs me that some of our students would think so poorly of their fellow students that they would impose these hardships on them. It is my hope that if anyone knows someone who is guilty of these acts of cruelty against the student body, he or she will talk to these people and ask them to stop this assault on *your* safety, well-being, and comfort.

VENDORS (See Also: ACCEPTANCE; BIDS; CONTRACT; FINANCIAL; QUALITY; REJECTION; WASTE)

. . .Awarding Contract

Dear ____________________,

This is to advise you that at the meeting of the Rock Township Board of Education held on ________________, 19________, your bid of $ was accepted for the following item(s):

Quantity	Item #	Item	Place of Delivery	Date of Delivery

It is essential that the item(s) listed be delivered promptly. If you are unable to meet a delivery date, it is essential that the Board of Education be notified immediately.

Sincerely,

Mary P. Auster,
Business Administrator,
Rock Township Board of Education

. . .Canceling Contract

Dear ____________________________,

On ____________________, 19 __________, we awarded you a contract for various items and/or services. Conditions of that contract included the following:

____

____

To date, these specifications have not been met. In repeated letters we have advised you of this situation and sought correction and/or fulfillment of your obligation.

Conditions of the contract are still not being met, and no improvement has been noted.

Therefore, we have no alternative but to cancel the contract as of this date as provided in the bid solicitation. You will be paid for that part of the contract which you did supply as soon as such payment is approved by the Board of Education.

Under the terms of our agreement, cancellation for non-completion means that for a period of three years the Board will entertain no bids from your company.

Sincerely,

Mary P. Auster,
Business Administrator,
Rock Township Board of Education

. . .Letter of Complaint on

(A) quality

Dear________________________,

In the contract awarded you on ____________________, 19 _____
for ____,
the following conditions were made regarding the quality of the item(s):
____
____

We have found that the item(s) supplied by you do not meet these qualifications for the following reason(s): __________ . __________
____
____

Please contact us at once in order that we may correct this very serious problem.

Sincerely,

Mary P. Auster,
Business Administrator,
Rock Township Board of Education

(B) slowness of delivery

Dear ________________________

On ______________________, 19 __________ you were awarded a contract for ____.
A stipulation of that contract was that the initial shipment arrive at our Central Supply Office on or before ______________________________.

That date has come and gone, and we have still not received delivery. As a result of this delay, we are encountering difficulties in the operation of our program.

We sincerely request that you expedite shipment at once. You are further reminded that avoidable delay of delivery is a ground for cancellation of contract.

Sincerely,

Mary P. Auster,
Business Administrator,
Rock Township Board of Education

VOLUNTEERS

(See Also: ADULT EDUCATION; APPRECIATION; FIELD TRIPS; INTRODUCTION; KINDERGARTEN; LIBRARY; OBSERVATION; P.T.A.; PUBLIC RELATIONS; THANKS)

. . .Soliciting Volunteers

Dear Parents,

We know how busy you are and what a premium time must be for you. Sometimes it seems that there are just not enough moments in the day for all we have to do.

And yet–if you can spare some of that valuable time, we can use your services.

Volunteers are needed now in all areas of our school. We need volunteers for our library, cafeteria, classrooms, after-school activities, dances, special events and more. Be assured, if you volunteer, you will be used.

The pay is non-existent, and the work is hard. Your reward is the knowledge that you are doing a service for our students and the school and, of course, our thanks and gratitude for your help.

Please call me at 234-5678 if you would like to give us a hand. I shall be happy to hear from you.

Sincerely,

J. Benson, Principal

. . .Thanking for Services

Dear Volunteers,

I want you to know how much I appreciate the volunteer work you have been doing for our students and our school. Your contribution of time and energy have helped to make our school a vital, harmonious, and a happy place to be, and you must take a large share of the credit for this.

I have had many favorable comments about you from faculty and students, who appreciate your services as do I.

Again, my deepest gratitude for your services to our school.

Sincerely,

J. Benson, Principal

. . .Volunteer Program Appraisal Sheet

VOLUNTEER PROGRAM

SCHOOL: ______________________________

PRINCIPAL: ______________________________

FOR THE SCHOOL YEAR 19 ________-19 ____________

NUMBER OF VOLUNTEERS IN PROGRAM: ______________

NUMBER OF VOLUNTEERS NEW THIS YEAR: ______________

AREAS IN WHICH VOLUNTEERS HAVE SERVED: ______________

____

AREAS IN WHICH VOLUNTEERS ARE NEEDED: ______________

____

ANY PROBLEMS WITH PROGRAM: ______________

____

GENERAL APPRAISAL OF VOLUNTEER PROGRAM: ______________

____

____

VOTING (See Also: CITIZENSHIP; ISSUES; PETITIONS; PUBLIC RELATIONS; REPRESENTATION)

. . .Form for School-Wide Election

The following are candidates for the office indicated for the 19___-19___ school year. Please place a check in the box before the name of the candidate of your choice for each office. If voting for more than one office, please vote for only one candidate per office. Voting for more than one candidate for an office will invalidate your vote.

	CANDIDATE	OFFICE
( )	________________	________________
( )	________________	________________
( )	________________	________________
( )	________________	________________
( )	________________	________________
( )	________________	________________

DATE OF ELECTION: ____________________________

. . .Procedures for Use of School in Civic Elections

The following are guidelines for the use of the school in civic elections when school is in session:

1. Voting will take place in the library. The library will be closed to student use during that day.
2. Voting machines are the property of the Board of Elections and, as such, must be moved only by appointed representatives of the Board.
3. Voting personnel should generally restrict themselves to the library and its immediate vicinity. In no instance must they interfere with the educational processes of the school.
4. Voting personnel may use the men's and women's lounges located to the left of the library entrance. Personnel may also avail themselves of the services of the school cafeteria.
5. No smoking is allowed in the library

6. Pay telephones are located in the hall outside the Main Office. Permission must be obtained before making any phone calls from the Main Office.
7. All the rules established by the Board of Education for the use of public school buildings will be in effect.

. . .Memo on Association Elections

To: FACULTY
From: JANET BENTLY, R.T.E.A. REPRESENTATIVE
Re: ASSOCIATION ELECTION

Tomorrow, Tuesday, May 16, 19XX, you will be voting for officers of the Rock Township Education Association for the 19XX-19XX school year.

Ballots for the election will be found in teacher's mailboxes at the start of the school day. Please vote for the representatives of your choice and place your ballot in the ballot box marked "R.T.E.A. ELECTION." This box will be located in the Main Office on the counter near the sign-in sheets. Please deposit your ballot before leaving the building for the school day, but no later than 4:00 p.m., at which time the ballots will be taken to the R.T.E.A. Office for counting.

Results will be made known to teachers on Wednesday, May 17, 19XX.

W

WASTE (See Also: BUILDING; CAFETERIA; CLEANUP; CUSTODIAL SERVICES; LUNCH; SUPPLIES)

. . .Message to Faculty on

To: FACULTY
From: J. BENSON, PRINCIPAL
Re: WASTE

What a marvelous world this would be if we had unlimited resources for all our wants and endeavors. Unfortunately, as those of us who have to live within budgets know all too well, such is not the case, neither within our personal lives nor within the financial setup of our school. I am asking, therefore, that we all apply ourselves to the judicious and sparing use of supplies. Let us use what we have in such a way that none of us will face June lacking the materials to conduct our classes. Keeping waste to a minimum and enthusiasm at a maximum, we should have a fantastic year.

. . .Message to Students on

NOTICE TO ALL STUDENTS:

I want to ask for your help. We all know how important money is. Money buys the paper and books and pencils we use here in school. This money comes from the taxes your parents pay. The less we waste, therefore, the more money will be available for materials which will help our school and everyone who goes to it.

You can help by stopping waste. Don't use two sheets of paper if one will do; take good care of your books; take only the materials you need; if you see other students wasting materials, ask them to stop.

If we all cooperate, we will save money, help prevent waste, and help our school and all students.

I know you can do it.

J. Benson, Principal

WORKING PAPERS

(See Also: CAREER; EMPLOYMENT; JOB; MEDICAL· WORK-STUDY PROGRAM)

. . .Confirmation of Employment Form

This is to certify that it is my intent to employ the following student:

STUDENT'S NAME: ______________________________

TYPE OF BUSINESS: ______________________________

NATURE OF STUDENT'S JOB: ______________________________

DAYS AND HOURS PER DAY THAT STUDENT IS TO WORK: ______________

____

TOTAL WEEKLY HOURS: ______________________________

WAGES PER HOUR: ______________________________

TOTAL WEEKLY WAGES: ______________________________

NAME OF EMPLOYER: ______________________________

ADDRESS: ____________________ TELEPHONE: ______________

____________________ ZIP: ______________

SIGNATURE OF EMPLOYER: ______________________________

DATE OF THIS CERTIFICATION: ______________________________

. . .Physician's Certificate for

DATE: ______________________________

THIS IS TO CERTIFY THAT I HAVE EXAMINED THE FOLLOWING STUDENT:

NAME: ______________________________

ADDRESS: ____________________ TELEPHONE: ______________

____________________ ZIP: ______________

BASED ON THIS PHYSICAL EXAMINATION I FIND THAT THE STUDENT:

( ) IS PHYSICALLY FIT FOR EMPLOYMENT AS PERMITTED UNDER THE STATE CHILD LABOR LAW FOR MINORS UNDER 18.

( ) IS *NOT* PHYSICALLY FIT FOR SUCH EMPLOYMENT, BECAUSE: ________

____

( ) IS FIT FOR EMPLOYMENT WITH THE FOLLOWING LIMITATIONS: _____

____

PHYSICIAN'S SIGNATURE: ________________________________

PHYSICIAN'S ADDRESS: ________________ TELEPHONE: ____________

____ ZIP: ____________

. . .School Record Form

NAME OF STUDENT: ________________________________

ADDRESS: ________________________ TELEPHONE: ____________

________________________________ ZIP: ____________

SCHOOL: ____

STUDENT HAS COMPLETED THE WORK OF THE ______________ GRADE

To the best of our knowledge, the student can perform the work indicated and still retain his or her progress in school.

SIGNATURE OF PRINCIPAL: ________________________________

SIGNATURE OF GUIDANCE COUNSELOR: ________________________

DATE OF SIGNATURES: ________________________________

. . . Student's Directions for Application

In order to obtain Working Papers, you must:

1. Have the SCHOOL RECORD FORM completed by the school you are presently attending.
2. Have the PHYSICIAN'S CERTIFICATE filled out by a doctor.
3. Have the EMPLOYMENT CERTIFICATION filled out by your prospective employer. Be certain that the entire form is filled **out,** including hours to be worked and salary

4. Bring ALL FORMS along with your BIRTH CERTIFICATE or BAPTISMAL CERTIFICATE to your Guidance Office. Your forms will be processed by the State Department of Labor. Your Birth or Baptismal Certificate will be returned to you by mail along with your Working Papers.

WORK-STUDY PROGRAM

(See Also: CAREER; EMPLOYMENT; JOB; RECOMMENDATION; REFERENCES; WORKING PAPERS)

. . .Counselor's Evaluation Form

WORK-STUDY PLAN EVALUATION OF

STUDENT: ______________________________ DATE: __________

SCHOOL: ______________________________ GRADE: __________

DATE STUDENT ENTERED PROGRAM: ______________________

INITIAL RECOMMENDATION FOR PLACEMENT MADE BY: __________

PLACE OF EMPLOYMENT: ______________________________

NATURE OF EMPLOYMENT: ______________________________

GRADE AVERAGE PRIOR TO PLACEMENT: ______________________

GRADE AVERAGE SINCE PLACEMENT: ______________________

SUMMARY OF EMPLOYER'S COMMENTS: ______________________

____

SUMMARY OF TEACHER'S COMMENTS: ______________________

____

GENERAL EVALUATION: ______________________________

____

____

____

SIGNATURE OF COUNSELOR: ______________________

DATE OF EVALUATION: ______________________

. . .Employer's Evaluation Form

NAME OF STUDENT: ______________________________ DATE: ____________

SCHOOL: ____

- -

EMPLOYER: ____

NATURE OF BUSINESS: ____

NATURE OF STUDENT'S JOB: ____

DATE STUDENT FIRST EMPLOYED: _______________________________________

HAS STUDENT'S WORK BEEN SATISFACTORY: ______________________________

IF "NO," EXPLAIN: ____

____

HOW WOULD YOU EVALUATE THE STUDENT'S PROGRESS SINCE HE OR SHE HAS BEEN IN YOUR EMPLOY (INCLUDE ATTITUDE, WORK HABITS, PUNCTUALITY, ETC.):

____

____

____

SIGNATURE OF EMPLOYER: _____________________________

DATE OF EVALUATION: _____________________________

. . .Faculty Recommendation for Placement in

To: GUIDANCE DEPARTMENT

From: ____

Re: PLACEMENT IN WORK-STUDY PROGRAM

I recommend the following student for possible placement in this school's Work-Study Program:

NAME OF STUDENT: ______________________________ GRADE: ____________

HOMEROOM TEACHER: ___________________________ HOMEROOM: _______

BRIEFLY STATE THE REASON(S) FOR THIS REFERRAL: ____________________

____

____

HOW DO YOU FEEL THE STUDENT WILL BENEFIT FROM THE WORK-STUDY PROGRAM: ____

____

____

____

SIGNATURE OF TEACHER: ______________________

DEPARTMENT AND/OR SUBJECT: ______________________

DATE OF REFERRAL: ______________________

. . .Letter to Parents Concerning

Dear ______________________,

Your son/daughter, ______________________, a __________ grade student at Rock Township High School, has been recommended for placement in the Work-Study Program currently being conducted at our school.

In the Work-Study Program, a student spends approximately half the school day taking required subjects in school and the other half working at a salaried position with a cooperating employer here in Rock Township.

We have found in the past that this program can be enormously beneficial to some students, providing them with maturity and experience in real-life situations.

We are anxious to talk to you about this program and your son's/daughter's participation in it. If you will please call me at 234-5678, Ext. 4, we will be happy to arrange an interview and answer any questions you may have concerning the program itself or your child's part in this program

I look forward to meeting you

Sincerely,

______________________.

Guidance Counselor

X

X-RAYS (See Also: MEDICAL; PERMANENT RECORDS)

. . .Notice to Personnel of Possible X-Ray Test

To: ALL SCHOOL PERSONNEL
From: ANSON KITTENGER, ASST. SUPERINTENDENT
Re: SCHOOL TUBERCULIN TESTING

Under the rules and regulations of the State Department of Education, you are required to have an intradermal test for evidence of tuberculous infection. Board of Education Policy requires that this be a Mantoux test, as it has been determined that this test is more reliable.

1. All employees who are positive reactors (ten or more m.m. of induration) or who have been exempted from the Mantoux test shall be required to have an annual chest X-Ray unless documentation is provided that one year of Chemotherapy has been completed.
2. All employees who are tuberculin negative shall be retested with an intradermal test every three years.
3. Any employee shall be exempt from intradermal testing upon presentation of documentation of a prior positive reaction (i.e., ten m.m. or more of induration) following a Mantoux test with five Tuberculin Units of stabilized PPD tuberculin or by presentation of a medical contra-indication form signed by a physician which specifically states the reason(s) for the exemption.

All exempting documentation must be presented to the High School Health Office.

Sincerely,

Anson Kittenger,
Asst. Superintendent

. . .X-Ray Release Form

To Whom It May Concern:

I hereby freely grant permission for the release of the following X-Rays to the Rock Township Board of Education and/or their assignees:

Type of X-Ray: ______________________________

Date Taken: ______________________________

Place Taken: ______________________________

Physician or Technician: ______________________________

Signature: ______________________________

Date of Release: ______________________________

Y

YEARBOOK (See Also: APPRECIATION; CLUBS; EXTRA-CURRICULAR ACTIVITIES; PUBLIC RELATIONS)

. . .Dedication

Because she is always there when you need her, because she always has a smile and a kind word; because she listens and understands; because she can always be counted upon to do what is best; because she always stands ready to help; because she is more than a teacher and vice-principal; because we are proud to call her our friend, this Yearbook is gratefully dedicated to Mrs. Arlene Gibbons.

. . .Letter to Yearbook Advisor

Dear Harry,

It has just been my pleasure to review the copy of SIGNPOSTS which you were kind enough to present to me. It is an outstanding publication, and one which is highly reflective of the amount of work and dedication to excellence that went into its preparation. Not only does it serve as a record of the events of this past year, but it seems to capture the spirit, the very essence of our school. Years from now, it will continue to be a source of pleasant memory to faculty and students alike.

Your staff is to be congratulated on the fine job which they accomplished, and we are also mindful of the fact that a great deal of the excellence and professionalism they displayed is reflective of the leadership and guidance they received from you. I am certain you must find satisfaction and justifiable pride in your part in this undertaking.

Again, my heartiest congratulations on a most outstanding yearbook and my personal thanks for your concern and devotion.

Sincerely,
J. Benson, Principal

. .Principal's Message in

A MESSAGE TO STUDENTS . . .

It is already tomorrow. Time, which never stops on its journey, will pass before your eyes, and in only a few moments you will be members of the community looking back on the years you spent at Rock Township High School. When you do, the photos, facts and memories in this book will be your stepping stones to a happy reminiscence.

May your memories of Rock Township High School be pleasant ones, and may your futures be filled with happiness and success.

With every wish for a bright tomorrow,

J. Benson, Principal

YEAR-END REPORT

(See Also: ACCOUNTABILITY; DISMISSAL PROCEDURES; EVALUATION; JUNE; MONTHLY REPORTS; PERCENTAGE OF PROMOTION SHEETS; QUALITY; RETENTION; VACATION)

. . .Checklist for

PRINCIPAL:______________________________ SCHOOL:____________________

In the Year-End Report due in the Central Administration Offices by 4:00 p.m. on Friday, June, 22, 19XX, I have included the following:

( ) Percentage of Attendance List	( ) Percentage of Promotion Sheet (Grade)
( ) Average Daily Attendance	( ) Percentage of Promotion Sheet (School)
( ) All Accounting Ledgers	( ) Teacher's Suggestions
( ) Guidance Office Report	( ) Outstanding Activities List
( ) Monthly Building Report	( ) Teacher's Summer Address Envelopes
( ) Yearly Building Report	( ) All Bankbooks for All Funds
( ) All Attendance Cards	( ) Principal's Summary Sheet

YEAR-END REPORT

. . .Excerpt from a Report

". . . In all, it has been a year of changes, adjustments and progress. The changes we have taken in stride, thanks mainly to the cooperation and understanding of students and faculty who worked together for the good of our school. The adjustments have been well made by all of us, thanks again to the cooperation of all parties. The progress has been in all aspects of school life as we uniformly continue to grow, to expand and to work toward our ultimate goal of the finest possible education for every student in our school in relation to the individual child's needs and abilities. I sincerely feel that our school is as fine an institution of learning as you will find anywhere "

Z

ZONING (See Also: ADDRESS; INQUIRIES; PARENTS; STUDENT INFORMATION)

. . .Letter to Parents Regarding

Dear Parents,

The Board of Education has the responsibility to establish boundary lines for each elementary, junior high school and the senior high school. Because the Township population shifts occasionally, the board is called upon, periodically, to re-examine boundary lines and make appropriate adjustments to equalize student populations in all schools. The Board changes boundary lines only after careful study. Students must attend assigned schools as established.

The following diagram shows where the secondary schools receive their student populations:

Parke Elementary Johnson Elementary Towne Elementary	-- Lester Jr. High	-- Rock Township High
Castle Elementary Downey Elementary Ranch Elementary	-- Morton Jr. High	

You may rest assured that the general public will be notified and a public meeting held prior to any zoning changes.

Sincerely,
Rock Township Board of Education

ZONING

. . .Notice of Change in

To: ALL PARENTS IN THE LAKEVIEW, FARMOOR,
AND STONECREST DEVELOPMENTS
From: ROCK TOWNSHIP BOARD OF EDUCATION
Re: RE-ZONING

As you are aware, the opening of several housing developments within our Township has been instrumental in causing an increased enrollment in several elementary schools as well as the high school. While our schools are trying their best, the fact that the influx of students is not equally distributed throughout the Township has caused undue hardship in Parke Elementary School. Overcrowding in that particular school can only be detrimental to the education of the students attending, and no one wants that, least of all your Board of Education.

Consequently, the Board proposes to re-zone the sending districts in order to alleviate overcrowding. The proposed change would affect the students as follows: Elementary students in the Lakeview Development would continue to attend Parke Elementary School, while those in the Farmoor and Stonecrest Developments would attend Castle Elementary School.

There will be a public meeting on this topic prior to its adoption by the Board of Education. This meeting will take place on Tuesday, May 17, 19XX at 8:00 p.m. at the Board of Education Offices.

If you are interested, we would welcome your presence.

Sincerely,
Rock Township Board of Education